Data Science for Web3

A comprehensive guide to decoding blockchain data with data analysis basics and machine learning cases

Gabriela Castillo Areco

BIRMINGHAM—MUMBAI

Data Science for Web3

Group Product Manager: Niranjan Naikwadi
Publishing Product Managers: Dinesh Chaudhary and Sanjana Gupta
Book Project Manager: Hemangi Lotlikar
Content Development Editor: Shreya Moharir
Technical Editor: Rahul Limbachiya
Copy Editor: Safis Editing
Proofreader: Safis Editing
Indexer: Hemangini Bari
Production Designer: Prafulla Nikalje
DevRel Marketing Executive: Vinishka Kalra

First published: December 2023
Production reference: 1261223

Published by Packt Publishing Ltd.
Grosvenor House
11 St Paul's Square
Birmingham
B3 1RB, UK

ISBN 978-1-83763-754-6

www.packtpub.com

To my family, who gifted me the wings to soar.

And to my loving husband, my co-pilot in life – thank you for sharing this incredible flight.

Foreword

In the ever-evolving landscape of data science, Gabriela's *Data Science for Web3* stands as a formidable guide, navigating the intricate intersection of blockchain, data science, and new decentralized businesses.

This book, meticulously crafted, provides a practical roadmap for those versed in economics, programming, blockchain, and data science. Gabriela's clear and independent approach demystifies complex concepts, offering both a glossary for the initiated and a launching pad for those embarking on new projects.

As you delve into these pages, you will discover not only theoretical foundations but also tangible insights that can be applied to real-world scenarios. *Data Science for Web3* is not just an exploration of possibilities; it is a functional tool for individuals seeking to enhance their skills and contribute meaningfully to the evolving landscape of Web3 and fintech.

– José Dahlquist
Rootstock Engineer Director of IOVLabs

Contributors

About the author

Gabriela Castillo Areco holds an MSc in big data science from the TECNUM School of Engineering, University of Navarra. With extensive experience in both the business and data facets of blockchain technology, Gabriela has undertaken roles as a data scientist, machine learning analyst, and blockchain consultant in both large corporations and small ventures. She served as a professor of new crypto businesses at Torcuato di Tella University and is currently a member of the BizOps data team at IOVLabs.

Special thanks to the data leaders I had the chance to interview for Chapter 14, who generously shared their time and vision.

In addition, I extend my gratitude to Shreya Moharir and Hemangi Lotlikar for their invaluable help and support throughout the writing process.

My appreciation also goes to my colleagues, clients, and mentors who have provided me with the opportunity to learn and work alongside them.

About the reviewer

Mayukh Mukhopadhyay is a full-time technology consultant with more than 13 years of experience in designing business continuity solutions using complex digital transformation programs. He did his MEng at Jadavpur University and his MBA at IIT Kharagpur. He is currently pursuing a PhD (industry track) at IIM Indore. He has authored the book *Ethereum Smart Contract Development* for Packt Publishing and Scopus-indexed teaching cases on generative AI and blockchain for Sage Publications. He is an active professional member of Association for Computing Machinery (ACM), a Professional Scrum Master I, and an Azure Certified Solution Architect.

I am forever indebted to my spouse, Mrittika, and my daughter, Abriti, for their sacrifices in every walk of life to support my academic endeavors.

Table of Contents

3

Working with Off-Chain Data   51

4

Exploring the Digital Uniqueness of NFTs – Games, Art, and Identity   77

5

Exploring Analytics on DeFi   107

Part 2: Web3 Machine Learning Cases

6

Preparing and Exploring Our Data   135

7

A Primer on Machine Learning and Deep Learning   151

8

Sentiment Analysis – NLP and Crypto News   171

9

Generative Art for NFTs   191

10

A Primer on Security and Fraud Detection   217

11

Price Prediction with Time Series   231

12

Marketing Discovery with Graphs   251

Part 3: Appendix

13

Building Experience with Crypto Data – BUIDL   271

14

Interviews with Web3 Data Leaders   279

Preface

The advent of Web3 has ushered in a trove of data, characterized by its distinctive properties, giving rise to novel concepts and breathing new life into established ones. Within the expansive Web3 ecosystem, data assumes diverse forms, stored across multiple platforms and formats, ranging from on-chain transactional data to independent news aggregators, oracles, and social networks. In essence, Web3 is a continuous generator of data directly or indirectly related to its ecosystem.

Web3, with its inherent characteristics, has unlocked value on various fronts. **Decentralization** has demonstrated that businesses without central authorities are possible. **Trustless** interactions have driven coordination between entities, facilitating smooth exchanges of goods and services over the blockchain, even among strangers and without intermediaries. This has resulted in value transfers reaching remote corners of the world at minimal costs, fostering direct connections between artists and collectors and facilitating crowdfunding by directly supporting product developers, among a myriad of other applications.

However, one aspect of Web3 that remains relatively unexplored, yet holds immense value to unlock, is **transparency**. Transparency fosters reliance, a cornerstone for mass adoption. A significant milestone for the industry will be achieved when ordinary individuals seamlessly engage with it, grounded in trust due to accessible and verifiable information. To fully realize the potential of transparency, many Web3 data scientists and analysts, equipped with the requisite skills, conceptual knowledge, tools, and a profound understanding of the data and business landscape, are needed. This is what this book aims to do – empower you to evolve into Web3 data specialists capable of understanding and extracting value from data.

The book is structured into three parts. The first section covers foundational concepts necessary to execute data analysis tasks. You will gain insights into on-chain data, learn to access and extract insights, explore sources of relevant off-chain data, and navigate potential obstacles. Additionally, two domains that generate vast amounts of data, namely NFTs and DeFi, are examined in depth, each presenting its own set of business rules and technical concepts.

The second part of the book shifts focus to machine learning use cases utilizing Web3 data. We have curated practical cases that data scientists, whether freelancers or employed professionals, may encounter in their work.

The *Appendix* addresses the question, what should we do with the knowledge acquired? It provides guidance on navigating the decentralized work landscape, understanding industry expectations for prospective data employees, and identifying the soft and hard skills necessary for success. In order to offer a glimpse into the future of the industry, we have engaged with Web3 data leaders who share their experiences, perspectives, and visions. The intent of this part is to shorten the time required to find jobs or other ways to contribute in the industry.

The benefits of decentralization, trustless interactions, and transparency in trade cannot be ignored, and that is why the industry continues to grow year by year, unlocking new use cases and creating new jobs. The purpose of this book is to contribute to the understanding of the data that Web3 generates so that you can be prepared to shape *the next era of the internet*.

Who this book is for

The format of the book and the list of topics covered make it suitable for data professionals interested in the Web3 ecosystem. The explanations have been simplified, catering to professionals with no data science background but eager to leverage data tools for in-depth analysis of blockchain data. You are encouraged to engage with the shared repository and experiment with the provided solutions, fostering a hands-on learning experience. Although not mandatory, a basic understanding of statistics, machine learning, SQL, and Python would be advantageous.

What this book covers

Chapter 1, *Where Data and Web3 Meet*, introduces the fundamental concepts of Web3 and data science tools.

Chapter 2, *Working with On-Chain Data*, explores the structure of on-chain data.

Chapter 3, *Working with Off-Chain Data*, delves into relevant off-chain data for the industry and guidance on where to locate it.

Chapter 4, *Exploring the Digital Uniqueness of NFTs – Games, Art, and Identity*, examines NFT businesses and how to calculate pertinent metrics.

Chapter 5, *Exploring Analytics on DeFi*, introduces DeFi businesses and how to calculate essential metrics.

Chapter 6, *Preparing and Exploring Our Data*, showcases preprocessing steps that are useful when dealing with Web3 data.

Chapter 7, *A Primer on Machine Learning and Deep Learning*, delves into the core concepts necessary for advancing through the machine learning cases explored in *Part 2*.

Chapter 8, *Sentiment Analysis – NLP and Crypto News*, explores the application of natural language processing (NLP) in crypto sentiment analysis.

Chapter 9, *Generative Art for NFTs*, examines examples of art generation to support NFT initiatives.

Chapter 10, A Primer on Security and Fraud Detection, explores an application for fraud detection.

Chapter 11, Price Prediction with Time Series, delves into an application for predicting prices with time series.

Chapter 12, Marketing Discovery with Graphs, examines an application to identify influencers and communities with on-chain data.

Chapter 13, Building Experience with Crypto Data – BUIDL, covers various options for job searching or continuing studies in the Web3 domain.

Chapter 14, Interviews with Web3 Data Leaders, concludes the book by delving into the perspectives of Web3 data leaders regarding the industry and its future.

To get the most out of this book

A Jupyter or a Google Colab notebook is sufficient to cover all the examples. In some cases, to access data, we will need to sign up for an account and obtain API keys.

Software/hardware covered in the book	Operating system requirements
Python 3.7+	Windows, macOS, or Linux
Google Colaboratory or Jupyter notebook	

If you are using the digital version of this book, we advise you to type the code yourself or access the code from the book's GitHub repository (a link is available in the next section). Doing so will help you avoid any potential errors related to the copying and pasting of code.

> **Disclaimer**
>
> All opinions expressed in this book are just opinions and should not be considered an inducement to invest or follow a particular strategy. They are intended for informational purposes only and should not be relied upon for making investment decisions. Please consult with a qualified financial advisor before making any investment decisions.

Download the example code files

You can download the example code files for this book from GitHub at `https://github.com/PacktPublishing/Data-Science-for-Web3`. If there's an update to the code, it will be updated in the GitHub repository.

We also have other code bundles from our rich catalog of books and videos available at `https://github.com/PacktPublishing/`. Check them out!

Conventions used

There are a number of text conventions used throughout this book.

`Code in text`: Indicates code words in text, database table names, folder names, filenames, file extensions, pathnames, dummy URLs, user input, and Twitter handles. Here is an example: "The following information was taken from the CSV file, filtered by the `Betweenness centrality` column."

A block of code is set as follows:

```
{'domain': {'id': '131',
'name': 'Unified Twitter Taxonomy',
'description': 'A taxonomy of user interests. '},
'entity': {'id': '913142676819648512',
'name': 'Cryptocurrencies',
'description': 'Cryptocurrency'}},
```

When we wish to draw your attention to a particular part of a code block, the relevant lines or items are set in bold:

```
'annotations': 'annotations': [{'start': 10,
'end': 18,
'probability': 0.8568,
'type': 'Organization',
'normalized_text': 'Blackrock'},
```

Any command-line input or output is written as follows:

```
decompose = seasonal_decompose(df, model= 'additive').
plot(observed=True, seasonal=True, trend=True, resid=True,
weights=False)
```

Bold: Indicates a new term, an important word, or words that you see on screen. For instance, words in menus or dialog boxes appear in **bold**. Here is an example: "Once we have filled in the mandatory requirements on the API page, we can press the blue **Execute** button, which will return the URL we can use."

> **Tips or important notes**
> Appear like this.

Get in touch

Feedback from our readers is always welcome.

General feedback: If you have questions about any aspect of this book, email us at `customercare@packtpub.com` and mention the book title in the subject of your message.

Errata: Although we have taken every care to ensure the accuracy of our content, mistakes do happen. If you have found a mistake in this book, we would be grateful if you would report this to us. Please visit `www.packtpub.com/support/errata` and fill in the form.

Piracy: If you come across any illegal copies of our works in any form on the internet, we would be grateful if you would provide us with the location address or website name. Please contact us at `copyright@packt.com` with a link to the material.

If you are interested in becoming an author: If there is a topic that you have expertise in and you are interested in either writing or contributing to a book, please visit `authors.packtpub.com`.

Share Your Thoughts

Once you've read *Data Science for Web3*, we'd love to hear your thoughts! Scan the following QR code to go straight to the Amazon review page for this book and share your feedback.

`https://packt.link/r/1-837-63754-7`

Your review is important to us and the tech community and will help us make sure we're delivering excellent-quality content.

Download a free PDF copy of this book

Thanks for purchasing this book!

Do you like to read on the go but are unable to carry your print books everywhere? Is your e-book purchase not compatible with the device of your choice?

Don't worry, now with every Packt book you get a DRM-free PDF version of that book at no cost.

Read anywhere, on any device. Search, copy, and paste code from your favorite technical books directly into your application.

The perks don't stop there! You can get exclusive access to discounts, newsletters, and great free content in your inbox daily

Follow these simple steps to get the benefits:

1. Scan the following QR code or visit the link:

https://packt.link/free-ebook/9781837637546

2. Submit your proof of purchase.
3. That's it! We'll send your free PDF and other benefits to your email directly.

Part 1
Web3 Data Analysis Basics

In this part of the book, we will explore what Web3 data looks like and identify reliable sources for its extraction. Throughout the chapters, we will examine the business flow of the most important protocols and learn how to gain actionable insights from the data generated within their ecosystems.

This part includes the following chapters:

- *Chapter 1, Where Data and Web3 Meet*
- *Chapter 2, Working with On-Chain Data*
- *Chapter 3, Working with Off-Chain Data*
- *Chapter 4, Exploring the Digital Uniqueness of NFTs – Games, Art, and Identity*
- *Chapter 5, Exploring Analytics on DeFi*

1
Where Data and Web3 Meet

As we assume no prior knowledge of data or blockchain, this chapter introduces the basic concepts of both topics. A good understanding of these concepts is essential to tackle Web3 data science projects, as we will refer to them. A Web3 data science project tries to solve a business problem or unlock new value with data; it is an example of applied science. It has two main components, the data science ingredients and the blockchain ingredients, which we will cover in this chapter.

In the *Exploring the data ingredients* section, we will analyze the concept of data science, available data tools, and the general steps we will follow, and provide a gentle practical introduction to Python. In the *Understanding the blockchain ingredients* section, we will cover what blockchain is, its main characteristics, and why it is called the internet of value.

In the final part of this chapter, we will dive into some industry concepts and how to use them. We will also analyze challenges related to the quality and standardization of data and concepts, respectively. Lastly, we will briefly review the concept of APIs and describe the ones that we will be using throughout the book.

In this chapter, we will cover the following topics:

- What is a business data science project?
- What are data ingredients?
- Introducing the blockchain ingredients
- Approaching relevant industry metrics
- The challenges with data quality and standards
- Classifying the APIs

Technical requirements

We will utilize Web3.py, a library designed for interacting with EVM-based blockchains such as Ethereum. Originally a JavaScript library, it has since evolved *"towards the needs and creature comforts of Python developers,"* as stated in its documentation. Web3.py is a library that facilitates connection and interaction with the blockchain.

If you have not worked with Web3.py before, it can be installed with the following code:

```
pip install web3
```

The blockchain data is reached after connecting to a copy of the blockchain hosted on a node. **Infura** serves as a cloud-based infrastructure provider that streamlines our connection to the Ethereum network, eliminating the need to run our own nodes. Detailed steps for creating an account and obtaining an API key are provided in the *Appendix 1*.

Additionally, we will employ **Ganache**, a program that creates a local blockchain on our computer for testing and developing purposes. This tool allows us to simulate the behavior of a real blockchain without the necessity of spending real cryptocurrency for interactions. For a comprehensive guide on how to utilize Ganache, please refer to the *Appendix 1*.

You can find all the data and code files for this chapter in the book's GitHub repository at https://github.com/PacktPublishing/Data-Science-for-Web3/tree/main/Chapter01. We recommend that you read through the code files in the Chapter01 folder to follow along.

Exploring the data ingredients

> **Important note**
>
> If you have a background in data science, you may skip this section.
>
> However, if you do not, this basic introduction is essential to understand the concepts and tools discussed throughout the book.

Data science is an interdisciplinary field that combines mathematics, statistics, programming, and machine learning with specific subject matter knowledge to extract meaningful insights.

Imagine you work at a top-tier bank that is considering making its first investment in a blockchain protocol, and they have asked you to present a shortlist of protocols to invest in based on relevant metrics. You may have some ideas about what metrics to consider, but how do you know which metric and value is the most relevant to determine which protocol should make it on your list? And once you know the metric, how do you find the data and calculate it?

This is where data science comes in. By analyzing transaction data (on-chain data) and data that is not on-chain (off-chain data), we can identify patterns and insights that will help us make informed decisions. For example, we might find that certain protocols are more active during business hours in a time zone different from where the bank is located. In this case, the bank can decide whether they are ready to make an investment in a product serving clients in a different time zone. We may also check the value locked in the protocol to assess the general investors' trust in that smart contract, among many other metrics.

But data science is not just about analyzing past data. We can also use predictive modeling to forecast future trends and add those trends to our assessment. For instance, we could use machine learning algorithms to predict the price range of the token issued by the protocol based on its price history.

For this data analysis, we require the right tools, skills, and business knowledge. We'll need to know how to collect and clean our data, how to analyze it using statistical techniques, how to separate what is business-relevant from what is not, and how to visualize our findings so we can communicate them effectively. Making data-driven decisions is the most effective way to improve all the relevant metrics for a business, which is more valuable than ever in this competitive world.

Due to the fast pace of data creation and the shortage of data scientists on the market, data scientist has been referred to as "*the sexiest job of the 21st century*" by the Harvard Business Review. The data economy has opened the door to multiple roles, such as data analyst, data scientist, data engineer, data architect, Business Intelligence (BI) analyst, and machine learning engineer. Depending on the complexity of the problem and the size of the data, we can see them playing a role in a typical data science project.

A typical Web3 data science project involves the following steps:

1. **Problem definition**: At this stage, we try to answer the question of whether the problem can be solved with data, and if so, what data would be useful to answer it. Collaboration between data scientists and business users is crucial in defining the problem, as the latter are the specialists and those who will use what the data scientist produces. BI tools such as Tableau, Looker, and Power BI, or Python data visualization libraries such as Seaborn and Matplotlib, are useful in meetings with business stakeholders. It is worth noting that while many BI tools currently provide optimization packages for commonly used data sources, such as Facebook Ads or HubSpot, as of the time of writing, I have not seen any optimization for on-chain data. Therefore, it is preferable to choose highly flexible data visualization tools that can adapt to any visualization needs.

2. **Investigation and data ingestion**: At this stage, we try to answer the question: where can we find the necessary data to use for this project? Throughout this book, especially *Chapters 2* and *3*, we will list multiple data sources related to Web3 that will help answer this question. Once we find where the data is, we need to build an ingestion pipeline for consumption by the data scientist. This process is called **ETL**, which stands for **extract, transform, and load**. These steps are necessary to make clean and organized data available to the data analyst or data scientist.

Data collection or **extraction** is the first step of the ETL process and can include manual entry, web scraping, live streaming from devices, or a connection to an API. Data can be presented in a structured format, meaning that it is stored in a predefined way, or an unstructured format, meaning that it has no predefined storage format and is simply stored in its native way. **Transformation** consists of modifying the raw data to be stored or analyzed. Some of the activities that data transformation can involve include data normalization, data deduplication, and data cleaning. Finally, **loading** is the act of moving the transformed data into data storage and making it available. There are a few additional aspects to consider when referring to data availability, such as storing data in the correct format, including all related metadata, providing the correct access privileges to the right team members, and ensuring the data is up to date, accurate, or enough to fulfill the data scientist's needs. The ETL process is generally led by the data engineer, but the business owner and the data scientist will have a say when identifying the data source.

3. **Analysis/modeling**: In this stage, we analyze the data to extract conclusions and may need to model it to try to predict future outcomes. Once the data is available, we can perform the following:

    - **Descriptive analysis**: This uses data analysis and methods to describe what the data shows, gaining insights into trends, composition, distribution, and more. For example, a descriptive analysis of a **Decentralized Finance** (**DeFi**) protocol can reveal when its clients are most active and the **Total Value Locked** (**TVL**) and how the locked value has evolved over time.

    - **Diagnostic analysis**: This uses data analysis to explain the reasons behind the occurrence of certain matters. Techniques such as data composition, correlations, and drill-down are used in these types of analyses. For example, a blockchain analyst may try to understand the correlation between a peak in new addresses and the activity of certain addresses to identify the applications that these users give to the chain.

    - **Predictive analysis**: This uses historical data to make forecasts about trends or events in the future. Techniques can include machine learning, cluster analysis, and time series forecasting. For example, a trader may try to predict the evolution of a certain cryptocurrency based on its historical performance.

    - **Prescriptive analysis**: This uses the result of predictive analysis as an input to suggest the optimum response or best course of action. For example, a bot can suggest whether to sell or buy certain cryptocurrency.

    - **Generative AI**: This uses machine learning techniques and huge amounts of data to learn patterns and generates new and original outputs. Artificial intelligence can create images, videos, audio, text, and more. Applications of generative models include ChatGPT, Leonardo AI, and Midjourney.

4. **Evaluation**: In this stage, the result of our analysis or modeling is evaluated and tested to confirm it meets the project goals and provides value to the business. Any bias or weakness of our models is identified, and if necessary, the process starts again to address those errors.

5. **Presentation/deployment**: The final stage of the process depends on the problem. If it is an analysis from which the company will make a decision, our job will probably conclude with a presentation and explanation of our findings. Alternatively, if we are working as part of a larger software pipeline, our model will most likely be deployed or integrated into the data pipeline.

This is an iterative process, meaning that many times, especially in *step 4*, we will receive valuable feedback from the business team about our analysis, and we will change the initial conclusions accordingly. What is true for traditional data science is reinforced for the Web3 industry as this is one of the industries where data plays a key role in building trust, leading investments, and, in general, unlocking new value.

Although data science is not a programming career, it heavily relies on programming because of the large amount of data available. In this book, we will work with the **Python** language and some **SQL** to query databases. Python is a general-purpose programming language commonly used by the data science community, and it is easy to learn due to its simple syntax. An alternative to Python is R, which is a statistical programming language commonly used for data analysis, machine learning, scientific research, and data visualization. A simple way to access Python or R and their associated libraries and tools is to install the Anaconda distribution. It includes popular data science libraries (such as NumPy, pandas, and Matplotlib for Python) and simplifies the process of setting up an environment to start working on data analysis and machine learning projects.

The activities in this book will be carried out in three work environments:

- **Notebooks**: For example, Anaconda Jupyter notebooks or Google Colaboratory (also frequently referred to as Colab). These files are saved in `.ipynb` format and are very useful for data analysis or training models. We will use Colab notebooks in the machine learning chapters due to the access it provides to GPU resources in its free tier.

- **IDEs**: PyCharm, Visual Studio Code, or any other IDE that supports Python. Their files are saved in `.py` format and are very useful for building applications. Most IDEs allow the user to download extensions to work with notebook files.

- **Query platforms**: In *Chapter 2*, we will access on-chain data platforms that have built-in query systems. Examples of those platforms are Dune Analytics, Flipside, Footprint Analytics, and Increment.

Anaconda Jupyter notebooks and IDEs use our computer resources (e.g., RAM), while Google Colaboratory uses cloud services (more on resources can be found in the *Appendix 1*).

Please refer to the *Appendix 1* to install any of the environments mentioned previously.

Once we have a clean notebook, we will warm up our Python skills with the `Chapter01/Python_warm_up` notebook, which follows a tutorial by `https://learnxinyminutes.com/docs/python/`. For a more thorough study of Python, we encourage you to check out *Data Science with Python,* by Packt Publishing, or *Python Data Science Handbook*, both of which are listed in the *Further reading* section of this chapter.

Once we have completed the warm-up exercise, we will initiate the Web3 client using the Web3.py library. Let's learn about these concepts in the following section.

Understanding the blockchain ingredients

If you have a background in blockchain development, you may skip this section. Web3 represents a new generation of the World Wide Web that is based on decentralized databases, permissionless and trustless interactions, and native payments. This new concept of the internet opens up various business possibilities, some of which are still in their early stages.

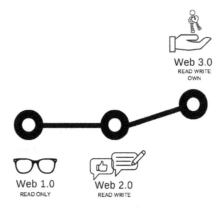

Figure 1.1 – Evolution of the web

Currently, we are in the Web2 stage, where centralized companies store significant amounts of data sourced from our interactions with apps. The promise of Web3 is that we will interact with **Decentralized Apps (dApps)** that store only the relevant information on the blockchain, accessible to everyone.

As of the time of writing, Web3 has some limitations recognized by the Ethereum organization:

- **Velocity**: The speed at which the blockchain is updated poses a scalability challenge. Multiple initiatives are being tested to try to solve this issue.

- **Intuition**: Interacting with Web3 is still difficult to understand. The logic and user experience are not as intuitive as in Web2 and a lot of education will be necessary before users can start utilizing it on a massive scale.

- **Cost**: Recording an entire business process on the chain is expensive. Having multiple smart contracts as part of a dApp costs a lot for the developer and the user.

Blockchain technology is a foundational technology that underpins Web3. It is based on **Distributed Ledger Technology (DLT)**, which stores information once it is cryptographically verified. Once reflected on the ledger, each transaction cannot be modified and multiple parties have a complete copy of it.

Two structural characteristics of the technology are the following:

- It is structured as a set of blocks, where each block contains information (cryptographically hashed – we will learn more about this in this chapter) about the previous block, making it impossible to alter it at a later stage. Each block is chained to the previous one by this cryptographic sharing mechanism.

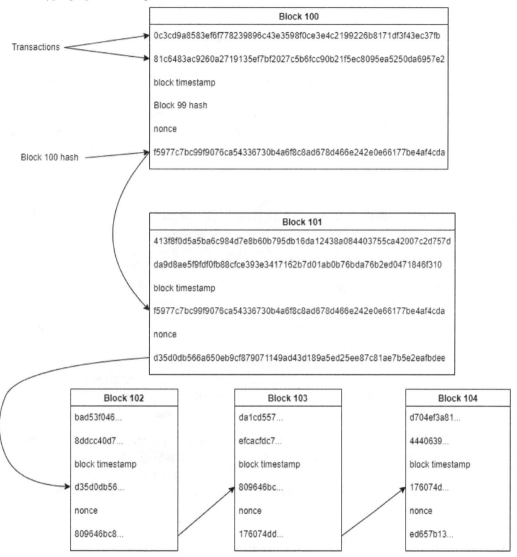

Figure 1.2 – Representation of a set of blocks

- It is decentralized. The copy of the entire ledger is distributed among several servers, which we will call nodes. Each node has a complete copy of the ledger and verifies consistency every time it adds a new block on top of the blockchain.

This structure provides the solution to double spending, enabling for the first time the decentralized transfer of value through the internet. This is why Web3 is known as the *internet of value*.

Since the complete version of the ledger is distributed among all the participants of the blockchain, any new transaction that contradicts previously stored information will not be successfully processed (there will be no consensus to add it). This characteristic facilitates transactions among parties that do not know each other without the need for an intermediary acting as a guarantor between them, which is why this technology is known as trustless.

The decentralized storage also takes control away from each server and, thus, there is no sole authority with sufficient power to change any data point once the transaction is added to the blockchain. Since taking down one node will not affect the network, if a hacker wants to attack the database, they would require such high computing power that the attempt would be economically unfeasible. This adds a security level that centralized servers do not have.

Three generations of blockchain

The first-generation blockchain is **Bitcoin**, which is based on Satoshi Nakamoto's paper *Bitcoin: A Peer-to-Peer Electronic Cash System*. The primary use case of this blockchain is financial. Although the technology was initially seen as a way to bypass intermediaries such as banks, currently, traditional financial systems and the crypto world are starting to work together, especially with regard to Bitcoin because it is now considered a digital store of value, a sort of digital gold. Notwithstanding the preceding, there are still many regulatory and practical barriers to the integration of the two systems.

The second-generation blockchain added the concept of smart contracts to the database structure described previously, and **Ethereum** was the first to introduce this. With Ethereum, users can agree on terms and conditions before a transaction is carried out. This chain started the smart contracts era, and as Nick Szabo describes it, the smart contract logic is that of a vending machine that can execute code autonomously, including the management of digital assets, which is a real revolution. To achieve this, the network has an **Ethereum Virtual Machine** (**EVM**) that can execute arbitrary code.

Lastly, the third-generation blockchain builds upon the previous generations and aims to solve scalability and interoperability problems. When referring to *on-chain* data in this book, we will be talking about data generated by the second- and third-generation blockchains that are EVM compatible, as this is where most development is being carried out at the time of writing (e.g., Ethereum, BSC, or Rootstock). Consequently, Bitcoin data and non-EVM structures are not covered.

Introducing the blockchain ingredients

Now, let's understand some important additional concepts regarding blockchain.

Gas

In order to make a car move forward, we use gas as fuel. This enables us to reach our desired destination, but it comes at a cost. The price of gas fluctuates based on various factors, such as oil prices and transportation costs. The same concept applies to the blockchain technology. To save a transaction on a chain, it is necessary to pay for gas. In short, gas is the instruction cost paid to the network to carry out our transactions. The purpose of establishing a cost is twofold: the proceeds of the gas payment go to the miners/validators as a payment for their services and as an incentive to continue being integrated into the blockchain; it also sets a price for users to be mindful of when using resources, encouraging the use of the blockchain to record only what is worth more than the gas value paid. This concept is universal to all networks we will study in this book.

Gas has several cost implications. As the price of gas is paid in the network's native coin, if the price increases, the cost of using the network can become excessively expensive, discouraging adoption. This is what happened with Ethereum, which led to multiple changes to its internal rules to solve this issue.

As mentioned earlier, each interaction with the blockchain incurs a cost. Therefore, not everything needs to be stored in it and the adoption of such a database as blockchain needs to be validated by business requirements.

Cryptocurrencies can be divided into smaller units of that cryptocurrency, just like how a dollar can be divided into cents. The smaller unit of a Bitcoin is a Satoshi and the smaller denomination of an Ether is Wei. The following is a chart with the denominations, which will be useful for tracking gas costs.

Unit name	Wei	Ether
Wei	1	10^{-18}
Kwei	1,000	10^{-15}
Mwei	1,000,000	10^{-12}
Gwei	1,000,000,000	10^{-9}
Microether	1,000,000,000,000	10^{-6}
Milliether	1,000,000,000,000,000	10^{-3}
Ether	1,000,000,000,000,000,000	1

Table 1.1 – Unit denominations and their values

Address

When we use a payment method other than cash, we transmit a sequence of letters or numbers, or a combination of both, to transfer our funds. This sequence of characters is essential for identifying the country, bank, and account of the recipient, for the entity that holds our funds. Similarly, an address performs a comparable function and serves as an identification number on the blockchain. It is a string of letters and numbers that can *send or receive* cryptocurrency. For example, Ethereum addresses consist of 42 hexadecimal characters. An address is the public key hash of an asymmetric key pair, which is all the information required by a third party to transfer cryptocurrency. This public key is derived from a private key, but the reverse process (deriving the private key from a public key) cannot be performed. The private key is required to authorize/sign transactions or access the funds stored in the account.

Addresses can be classified into two categories: **Externally Owned Addresses** (**EOAs**) and contract accounts. Both of them can receive, hold, and send funds and interact with smart contracts. EOAs are owned by users who hold the private key, and users can create as many as they need. Contract accounts are those where smart contracts are deployed and are controlled by their contract code. Another difference between them is the cost of creating them. Creating an EOA does not cost gas but creating a smart contract address has to pay for gas. Only EOA accounts can initiate transactions.

There is another product in the market known as smart accounts that leverage the account abstraction concept. The idea behind this development is to facilitate users to program more security and better user experiences into their accounts, such as setting rules on daily spending limits or selecting the token to pay for gas. These are programmable smart contracts.

Although the terms "wallet" and "address" are often used interchangeably, there is a technical distinction between them. As mentioned before, an address is the public key hash of an asymmetric key pair. On the other hand, a wallet is the abstract location where the public and private keys are stored together. It is a software interface or application that simplifies interacting with the network and facilitates querying our accounts, transaction signing, and more.

Consensus protocols

When multiple parties work together, especially if they do not know each other, it is necessary to agree on a set of rules to work sustainably. In the blockchain case, it is necessary to determine how to add transactions to a block and alter its state. This is where the consensus protocol comes into play. Consensus refers to the agreement reached by all nodes of the blockchain to change the state of the chain by adding a new block to it. The protocol comprises a set of rules for participation, rewards/penalties to align incentives, and more. The more nodes participate, the more decentralized the network becomes, making it more secure.

Consensus can be reached in several ways, but two main concepts exist in open networks.

Proof of Work (PoW)

This is the consensus protocol used by Bitcoin. It involves solving mathematical equations that vary in difficulty depending on how congested the network is.

Solving these puzzles consumes a lot of energy, resulting in a hardware-intensive competition. Parties trying to solve the puzzle are known as miners.

The winning party finds an integer that complies with the equation rules and informs the other nodes of the answer. The other parties verify that the answer is correct and add the block to their copy of the blockchain. The winning party gets the reward for solving the puzzle, which is a predefined amount of cryptocurrency. This is how the system issues Bitcoin that has never been spent and is known as a Coinbase transaction.

In Bitcoin protocol, the reward is halved every 21,000 blocks.

Proof of Stake (PoS)

This is the current protocol used by the Ethereum blockchain (up to September 15, 2022, the consensus protocol was PoW) and many others, such as Cardano.

The rationale behind PoS is that parties become validators in the blockchain by staking their own cryptocurrency in exchange for the chance to validate transactions, update the blockchain, and earn rewards. Generally, there is a minimum amount of cryptocurrency that must be staked to become a validator. It is "at stake" because the rules include potential penalizations or "slashing" of the deposited cryptocurrency if the validator (node that processes transactions and adds new blocks to the chain) goes offline or behaves poorly. Slashing means losing a percentage of the deposited cryptocurrency.

As we can see, there are rewards and penalties to align the incentives of all participants toward a single version of the blockchain.

The list of consensus protocols is continuously evolving, reflecting the ongoing search to solve some of the limitations identified in Web3, such as speed or cost. Some alternative consensus protocols include proof of authority – where a small number of nodes have the power to validate transactions and add blocks to the chain – and proof of space – which uses disk space to validate transactions.

Making the first transaction

With these concepts in mind, we will now carry out a transaction on our local environment with local Ethereum from Ganache.

To get started, let's open a local Jupyter notebook and a quick-start version of Ganache.

Here is the information we need:

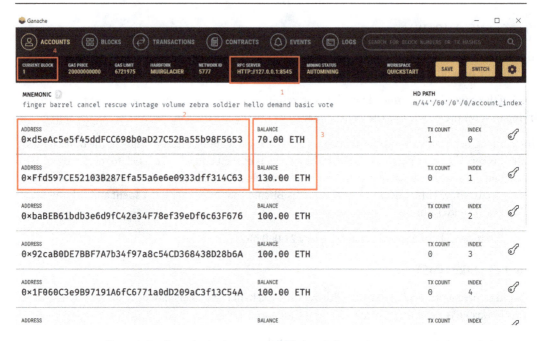

Figure 1.3 – Ganache main page and relevant information to connect

Let's look at the code:

1. Import the Web3.py library:

    ```
    from web3 import Web3
    ```

2. Connect to the blockchain running on the port described in our Ganache page (item 1):

    ```
    ganache_url= "http://127.0.0.1:8545"
    web3= Web3(Web3.HTTPProvider(ganache_url))
    ```

3. Define the receiving and sending addresses (item 2):

    ```
    from_account="0xd5eAc5e5f45ddFCC698b0aD27C52Ba55b98F5653"
    to_account= "0xFfd597CE52103B287Efa55a6e6e0933dff314C63"
    ```

4. Define the transaction. In this case, we are transferring 30 ether between the accounts defined previously:

    ```
    transaction= web3.eth.send_transaction({
       'to': to_account,
       'from': from_account,
       'value': web3.toWei(30, "ether")
    })
    ```

5. We can review the account balances before and after the transaction with the following code snippet:

```
web3.fromWei(web3.eth.getBalance(from_account),'ether'))
web3.fromWei (web3.eth.getBalance(to_account), 'ether'))
```

Congratulations! If you have never before transferred value on a blockchain, you have achieved your first milestone. The complete code can be found in `Chapter01/First_transaction`.

A word on CBDC

What is **CBDC**? The acronym stands for **Central Bank Digital Currency**. It is a new form of electronic money issued by the central banks of countries.

Many countries are at different stages in this roadmap. On January 20, 2022, the Federal Reserve Board issued discussion papers about CBDC, and prior to the COVID-19 pandemic, they also informed of ongoing research regarding the benefits that could be brought to their system. As of July 2022, there were 100 CBDCs in research and development. Countries are looking for the best infrastructure, studying the impact on their communities, and are mindful of a new range of risks that this new way of transferring value will pose to financial systems that may be reluctant to change.

Some of the concepts that we have covered in this chapter will be useful for the CBDC era, but depending on the project and its characteristics, not all of them will be present. It will be especially interesting to see how they solve centralization issues. A very informative tracker on the status of the projects is available at the following link: `https://cbdctracker.org/`.

In this section, we analyzed the fundamentals of blockchain technology, including key concepts such as gas, addresses, and consensus protocols, and explored the evolution of Web3. We also executed a transaction using Ganache and Web3.py.

With this basic understanding of the transaction flow, we will now shift our focus toward analyzing initial metrics and gaining a better understanding of the data challenges in this industry.

Approaching Web3 industry metrics

There are some metrics that are pretty standard on every Web3 dashboard that we review in this section. However, this is just a basic layer, and each player in the industry will add additional metrics relevant to them.

To extract information from the Ethereum blockchain, we need to establish a connection to the blockchain through a node that holds a copy of it. There are multiple ways to connect to the blockchain, which we will explore in more detail in *Chapter 2*. For the following metrics, we will make use of **Infura**. *For a step by step guide to connect to Infura, refer to the Appendix 1.*

Block height

This refers to the current block on the blockchain. The Genesis block is commonly referred to as block 0 and subsequent blocks are numbered accordingly. To check the block height, use the following code snippet:

```
web3.eth.blockNumber
```

The block number can be used as the ID of the block. Tracking it can be useful to determine the number of confirmations a transaction has, which is equivalent to the number of additional blocks that were mined or added after the block of interest. The deeper a transaction is in the chain, the safer and more irreversible it becomes.

Time

When discussing time in the context of blockchain, two concepts need to be taken into account. The first is the time between blocks, which varies depending on the blockchain. In Ethereum, after the recent protocol change, there are 12-second slots. Each validator is given a slot to propose a block during that time, and if all validators are online, there will be no empty slots, resulting in a new block being added every 12 seconds. The second concept is the timestamp for when a block was added to the blockchain, which is typically stored in Unix timestamp format. The Unix timestamp is a way of tracking the time elapsed as a running total of seconds from January 1, 1970, in UTC.

To extract the block timestamps, use the following code snippet:

```
web3.eth.get_block(latest).timestamp
```

Tokenomics

Tokenomics refers to the characteristics of the internal economy of token projects on the blockchain, including supply, demand, and inflation. This involves determining how many digital assets will be issued, whether there is a cap on the total offer, the use cases of the token, and the burning schema to control the number of assets in circulation.

The token white paper typically contains the official explanation for basic tokenomics questions.

> **Bitcoin tokenomics**
>
> The Bitcoin supply is capped at 21 million Bitcoins, and this amount cannot be exceeded. New Bitcoin enters circulation through mining, and miners are rewarded each time they successfully add a block to the chain.
>
> Each block is mined approximately every 10 minutes, so all 21 million Bitcoins will be in circulation by 2140.
>
> The number of Bitcoins rewarded is halved every time 210,000 blocks are mined, resulting in a halving approximately every four years. Once all 21 million Bitcoins have been mined, miners will no longer receive block rewards and will rely solely on transaction fees for revenue.

Tokens, and therefore their tokenomics, play a fundamental role in the functioning and sustainability of DeFi platforms. One of the industries most impacted by this technology is the financial industry, which has given birth to a new concept known as **Decentralized Finance**, or **DeFi**. DeFi consists of peer-to-peer financial solutions built on public blockchains. These initiatives offer services that are similar to those offered by banks and other financial institutions, such as earning interest on deposits, lending, and trading assets, without the intervention of banks or other centralized financial institutions. This is achieved through a set of smart contracts (or protocols) that are open to anyone with an address to participate.

One concrete example of DeFi is Aave, a lending and borrowing platform that allows users to lend and borrow various cryptocurrencies without intermediaries such as banks. For instance, if Jane wants to borrow 10 ETH, she can go to Aave, create a borrowing request, and wait for the smart contract to match her request with available lenders who are willing to lend ETH. The borrowed ETH is lent with an interest rate percentage that reflects supply and demand levels. The money lent comes from a liquidity pool where lenders deposit their cryptocurrencies to earn interest on them. With Aave's decentralized platform, borrowers and lenders can transact directly with each other without needing to go through a traditional financial institution.

We will dive deep into DeFi in *Chapter 5*.

Total Value Locked (TVL)

TVL refers to the total value of assets currently locked in a specific DeFi protocol. It measures the health of a certain protocol by the amount of money users secure in it. The TVL will increase when users deposit more assets in the protocol, and vice versa, it will decrease when the users withdraw it. It is calculated by summing the value of the assets locked in the protocol and multiplying them by the current price.

Different DeFi protocols may have specific ways of measuring their TVL, and accurately calculating it requires an understanding of how each protocol works. A website that specializes in measuring TVL is DefiLlama (available at `https://defillama.com/`).

TVL also helps traders determine whether a certain token is undervalued or not by dividing that number by the market cap (or total supply in circulation) of the token issued by said protocol.

This metric helps compare DeFi protocols with each other.

Total market cap

Market capitalization represents the size of the market for a certain token and is closely related to traditional financial concepts. It is calculated by multiplying the number of coins or tokens issued by their current market price. The **circulating supply** is the sum of tokens currently held by public holders. To get this number, we calculate the tokens in all addresses that are not the minting and burning addresses and subtract the value held by addresses that we know are controlled by the protocol or are allocated to the development team or some investors, and so on.

The **max supply** or **total supply** of tokens is the total number of tokens that will be issued by a certain smart contract. Multiplying the max supply by the current price will result in a fully diluted market cap. There are two ways to get the total supply, with state data and transactional data.

In *Chapter 2*, we will learn how to access state data as tokens as smart contracts have a function that can be queried with Web3.py. To do this, we will need the **Application Binary Interface** (ABI) of the smart contract and a connection to a node, such as Infura. Example code for this can be found in `Chapter01/Relevant metrics II.ipynb`.

Another way to access the transactions database and calculate the total supply is by summing all the minting events of a smart contract and subtracting the burning events with SQL. We will learn how to do this in *Chapter 5*.

The market cap value is dynamic, as it can change as the market price and the supply of tokens fluctuate. A token market cap is widely used in the cryptocurrency industry as a benchmark for the performance of different tokens.

In `Chapter01/Relevant metrics II.ipynb`, we analyze the **Wrapped BTC (WBTC)** token, which is one of those cases where the TVL and total market cap coincide, as the token is pegged 1:1 with the collateral.

One of the biggest challenges data scientists will face is agreeing on common definitions and finding trustworthy data sources. We may have a good grasp of mathematical formulas to calculate complex financial indicators, but without reliable data and community consensus on standards, our ability to communicate our findings will be constrained. In the next section, we will explore these challenges and discuss ways to overcome them.

Data quality challenges

In this section, we will discuss the challenges of data quality, which are not unique to Web3 but relevant to all professionals who make decisions based on data. Data quality challenges range from access to incomplete, inaccurate, or inconsistent data to matters of data security, privacy, or governance. However, one of the most important challenges that a Web3 data analyst will face is the reliability of sources.

For instance, the market cap is the result of a simple multiplication of two data sources: the blockchain data that informs the total supply of tokens in circulation and the market price. However, the result of such multiplication varies depending on the source. Let's take an example of the market cap for USDT. In one source, the following information appears:

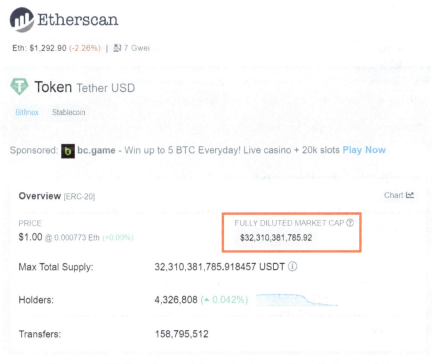

Figure 1.4 – USDT market cap information (source: https://etherscan.io/
token/0xdac17f958d2ee523a2206206994597c13d831ec7)

On the CoinMarketCap website, for the same token, the fully diluted market cap is $70,158,658,274 (https://coinmarketcap.com/currencies/tether/).

As we see from the example, the same concept is shown differently depending on the source we review. So, how do we choose when we have multiple sources of information?

The most trustworthy and comprehensive source of truth regarding blockchain activity is the *full copy of a node*. Accessing a node ensures that we will always have access to the latest version of the blockchain. Some services index the blockchain to facilitate access and querying, such as Google BigQuery, Covalent, or Dune, continuously updating their copies. These copies are controlled and centralized.

When it comes to prices, there are numerous sources. A common approach to sourcing prices is connecting to an online marketplace for cryptocurrencies, commonly known as exchanges, such as **Binance** or **Kraken**, to extract their market prices. However, commercialization in these markets can be halted for various reasons. For example, during the well-known **Terra USD** (**TUSD**) de-peg incident, when the stablecoin lost its 1:1 peg to the US dollar, many exchanges ceased commercialization, citing consumer protection concerns. If our workflow relies on such data, it can be disrupted or show inaccurate old prices. To solve this issue, it is advisable to source prices from sources that average the prices from multiple exchanges, providing more robust information.

At this stage, it is crucial to understand what constitutes quality for our company. Do we prioritize fast and readily available information updated by the second, or do we value highly precise information with relatively slower access? While it may not be necessary to consider this for every project, deciding on certain sources and standardizing processes will save us time in the future.

Once we have determined the quality of the information we will consume, we need to agree on the concepts we want to analyze.

Data standards challenges

As a young industry, there is still no complete consensus on the meaning of many concepts. Let's examine a few examples.

Retail

Within the cryptocurrency space, there is a complete aquatic ecosystem used to categorize addresses based on the amount of cryptocurrencies they hold. Larger addresses are often referred to as "whales," while smaller addresses have their own names. Please refer to the following illustration for reference:

	Humpback Whale	5000 BTC or more
	Whale	1000 - 5000 BTC
	Shark	500 - 1000 BTC
	Dolphin	100 - 500 BTC
	Fish	50 - 100 BTC
	Octopus	10 - 50 BTC
	Crab	1 - 10 BTC
	Shrimp	less than 1 BTC

Figure 1.5 – Sizes of crypto holdings and their aquatic equivalent

While there is a consensus on the aquatic equivalents used for categorization, there is no unified agreement on the specific number of Bitcoins that each category represents. A quick Google search will reveal varying criteria for what constitutes an address in one category or another.

Another classification, which is particularly valuable for analysts, distinguishes between retail addresses (small investors) and professional addresses. The challenge lies in determining the threshold that distinguishes one from the other. Various approaches are in use, and we can follow the aquatic equivalent definition as mentioned previously or opt for the definition proposed by a forensic company called Chainalysis, which states: "*Retail traders (…) deposit less than $10,000 USD worth of Bitcoin at a time on exchanges.*"

Confirmations

In a traditional bank or centralized organization, when a user sends a transaction, once received, it is confirmed and can be considered complete. In the blockchain space, the decentralized nature of the network introduces a different dynamic and, consequently, it is common to see the number of confirmations required for transactions of different amounts to be considered valid.

Within a decentralized network, it is entirely possible for two blocks to be mined simultaneously in different parts of the world. The protocol waits for the next block to be mined and, depending on where it attaches, determines which chain is the longest (the longest chain is deemed the valid one). A block in Bitcoin that doesn't become part of the longest chain is referred to as a **stale block**, while in Ethereum (prior to the merge), they were known as **uncle blocks**. Once a transaction is incorporated into a block, it is assigned one confirmation. If our transaction finds its way into a stale block, it will be reversed and return to the mempool in Bitcoin or be added to another block in Ethereum, resuming the count of confirmations.

Given the possibility of reversal, however slim, it has become customary for transaction counterparties to request a certain number of confirmations before accepting that their transactions are irreversible. The longer the chain grows after the block that included our transaction, the less likely it is to be reversed. Following the merge in Ethereum (which took place at block 15537394), uncle blocks ceased to be generated, but some of these practices persist among market participants.

There are no universal standards for the number of confirmations required. Recommendations can vary, with some suggesting six confirmations for Bitcoin and only two for small transfer amounts. For Ethereum, the range was typically between 20 and 40 confirmations. Notably, centralized exchanges such as Coinbase may still require two confirmations for Bitcoin and 35 for Ethereum.

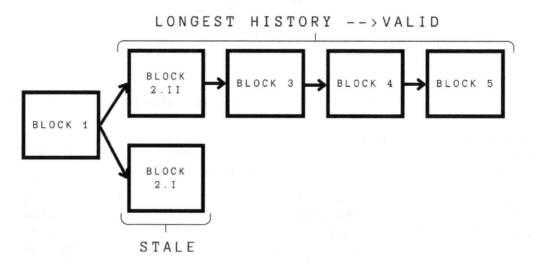

Figure 1.6– Stale and valid transactions

NFT Floor Price

The NFT Floor Price serves as a metric for determining the minimum price at which any NFT within a collection can be sold, providing market participants with valuable insights into a project's fair pricing.

There is no universally accepted method for its calculation. One basic approach involves finding the minimum price at which an NFT within a collection has previously been sold. However, due to the presence of multiple marketplaces, each with its unique pricing structure, an alternative approach is to consider prices from the most prominent art marketplaces or to aggregate prices from various sources, giving more weight to the significant marketplaces.

Furthermore, it is crucial to account for practices such as wash trading, which artificially inflates the metric under analysis. We will analyze more of this concept in *Chapter 4*.

The concept of "lost"

Suppose we need to calculate the circulating supply of Bitcoins for the next five years. For such a calculation, we must take into account not only how much will be mined but also how many Bitcoins can be considered "lost." How do we determine that a certain amount of crypto is lost?

To move assets on the blockchain, we need to sign the transfer with our private key. If that private key is lost, we cannot access those assets, and therefore, those assets have to be counted as lost. With this information in mind, it is safe to assume that some of the Bitcoin supplied as of today is already lost or will be. When reading the blockchain, we can see those funds in possession of a certain address, but it is entirely possible that such an address is unable to dispose of them. Since this is a pseudo-anonymous system, we cannot contact the Bitcoin holders and ask them to verify whether they have access to their funds; there is no centralized way to do it.

The forensics company named Chainalysis proposed the definition that *"Bitcoin that has not moved for five years now is considered lost."* The consequence of such a definition is that 20% of the mined bitcoins would be lost. This is a proposed concept, and it is yet to be seen whether it becomes a standard.

In conclusion, we can agree on three ideal ways of approaching data in Web3:

- Deep dive into the metrics that will be available in our dashboards or the data that will be consumed by our model. Read the concepts and documentation thoroughly.

- Be open to finding different approaches to the same market subject. Since the industry is growing, there is no established way of doing some things.

- Be prepared to witness concepts change as the industry matures and fine-tunes its best practices.

To understand the technical aspects of smart contracts, the OpenZeppelin documentation is a valuable reference. Similarly, for market-related concepts, as mentioned previously, Chainalysis defines many concepts and can help as a starting point.

A brief overview of APIs

APIs, or **application programming interfaces**, facilitate communication between two software services through a series of requests and responses. For instance, when we receive a notification about a token's price drop in our telephone app, it means that our app is communicating with a price provider such as CoinMarketCap via an API. To structure a request for the desired response, we must always refer to the relevant API documentation.

For a more comprehensive understanding of APIs, we can find additional information in the book *Python API Development Fundamentals* by Packt Publishing . Since we will frequently interact with APIs to extract information, it's beneficial to review the primary characteristics of different APIs. This will greatly assist us when we aim to programmatically access information.

For this purpose, we will focus on the following:

- **Remote Procedure Call (RPC) APIs**: In RPC APIs, the client initiates a function on the server, and the server sends back the output. In practice, we include the method (endpoints) of the function in the URL and the arguments in the query string. In this case, the client needs to possess all the information about the endpoints, and sometimes it involves constructing a workflow with information queried from other URLs. An example of an RPC API encoded in JSON format is the Infura suite, which we have utilized in previous sections.

- **Representational State Transfer (REST) API**: This API is stateless, meaning that it does not save the client's data between requests. This is one of the most popular methods on the market because it is lightweight and easy to maintain and scale.

  The client sends requests to the server in the form of a web URL, including methods such as GET, POST, PUT, or DELETE, and the server responds, typically in JSON format. A REST request typically comprises the HTTP method, endpoint, headers, and body. The endpoint identifies the resource online, headers provide server information, such as authentication, and the body contains the information the sender wishes to transmit to the server as a request.

An alternative approach was developed by Facebook as an open source query language named **GraphQL**. The key difference from the aforementioned APIs is that GraphQL is a query language, whereas REST is an architectural concept for software. GraphQL is a syntax for data retrieval that empowers the client to specify the required information, unlike the REST infrastructure, where queries return fixed datasets for each endpoint (sometimes including more information than necessary).

A noteworthy feature of GraphQL is its ability to construct requests that fetch data from multiple resources using a single API call. The **Graph** is an indexer and query protocol for the Ethereum network that is queried using GraphQL; we will delve into it further in *Chapter 2*.

Summary

In this chapter, we provided an overview of data science and Web3 concepts, covering fundamental aspects such as the typical steps involved in a data science project, the evolution of Web3, and essential concepts such as consensus, addresses, and gas. We also delved into prevalent metrics and challenges that exist in the rapidly evolving field of Web3.

In the forthcoming chapter, we will take a deeper dive into on-chain data, the primary dataset of Web3. Our exploration will encompass a detailed examination of blocks and transactions. We will also discuss various methods for accessing this invaluable data. By the end of that chapter, you will have acquired a robust understanding of on-chain data and how to effectively navigate and utilize it.

Further reading

To complement this chapter, the following links may help:

- The data ingredients:

  - Style guide for Python code: `https://peps.python.org/pep-0008/`

  - *Data Science with Python*: `https://www.packtpub.com/product/data-science-with-python/9781789346251`

  - *Python Data Science Handbook*: `https://jakevdp.github.io/PythonDataScienceHandbook/`

  - Web3.py documentation: `https://web3py.readthedocs.io/en/latest/#`

- The blockchain ingredients:

  - The EVM documentation: `https://ethereum.org/en/developers/docs/evm/`

  - Satoshi Nakamoto's paper: `https://bitcoin.org/bitcoin.pdf`

  - EVM explanation: `https://www.youtube.com/watch?v=GPoze5RmDVU`

  - The gas documentation: `https://ethereum.org/en/developers/docs/gas/`

  - Wackerow, P. et. al, 2022. Web2 vs Web3 | ethereum.org. [online] ethereum.org. Available at `https://ethereum.org/en/developers/docs/web2-vs-web3/`

  - Szabo, N., 2022. Smart Contracts: Building Blocks for Digital Markets. [online] Fon.hum.uva.nl. Available at `https://www.fon.hum.uva.nl/rob/Courses/InformationInSpeech/CDROM/Literature/LOTwinterschool2006/szabo.best.vwh.net/smart_contracts_2.html`

  - Stanley, A., 2022. THE ASCENT OF CBDCS. [online]. Available at `<https://www.imf.org/en/Publications/fandd/issues/2022/09/Picture-this-The-ascent-of-CBDCs>`

  - Covalent. 2022. Covalent Blockchain Data API Reference – Covalent [online]. Available at `https://www.covalenthq.com/docs/api/#/0/0/USD/1`.

  - Ethereum-etl.readthedocs.io. 2022. Google BigQuery – Ethereum ETL [online]. Available at `https://ethereum-etl.readthedocs.io/en/latest/google-bigquery/`

- Relevant industry metrics:

  - More on gas calculation: `https://growingdata.com.au/how-to-calculate-gas-fees-on-ethereum/`

  - Ethereum yellow paper: `https://ethereum.github.io/yellowpaper/paper.pdf`

  - *Smart Corpus: An Organized Repository of Ethereum Smart Contracts Source Code and Metrics*: `https://arxiv.org/pdf/2011.01723.pdf`

  - Evolution of NFT floor price: `https://chain.link/education-hub/what-is-an-nft-floor-price`

  - Team, Chainalysis., 2022. *60% of Bitcoin is Held Long Term as Digital Gold. What About the Rest?* Available at <`https://blog.chainalysis.com/reports/bitcoin-market-data-exchanges-trading/`> [accessed 12 October 2022]

  - Liiv, Innar (2021) *Data Science Techniques for Cryptocurrency Blockchains*. Springer's Collection on Behaviormetrics: Quantitative Approaches to Human Behavior

2
Working with On-Chain Data

In *Chapter 1*, we learned about the fundamental concepts of a blockchain. We discovered that a blockchain is a distributed ledger composed of a chain of blocks, where each block is cryptographically linked to the previous one. Each block contains transaction information and the hash of the preceding block. Additionally, transactions can modify state data in **Ethereum Virtual Machine** (**EVM**)-based chains.

On-chain data represents the trace left by each transaction within the blockchain. It is stored as byte data, which requires parsing in order to become human-readable. To illustrate this follows a fragment of the Bitcoin genesis block in its raw format, sourced from `https://wiki.bitcoinsv.io/index.php/Genesis_block` (license: CC BY 3.0):

```
00000000   01 00 00 00 00 00 00 00   00 00 00 00 00 00 00 00
...
00000080   01 04 45 54 68 65 20 54   69 6D 65 73 20 30 33 2F
..Ethe Times 03/
00000090   4A 61 6E 2F 32 30 30 39   20 43 68 61 6E 63 65 6C
Jan/2009 Chancel
000000A0   6C 6F 72 20 6F 6E 20 62   72 69 6E 6B 20 6F 66 20
lor on brink of
000000B0   73 65 63 6F 6E 64 20 62   61 69 6C 6F 75 74 20 66
second bailout f
000000C0   s6F 72 20 62 61 6E 6B 73   FF FF FF FF 01 00 F2 05
or banksÿÿÿÿ..ò.
...
00000110   8A 4C 70 2B 6B F1 1D 5F   AC 00 00 00 00
ŠLp+kñ._¬
```

This data can be parsed and enriched by providing additional information:

```
{"hash":
"000000000019d6689c085ae165831e934ff763ae46a2a6c172b3f1b60a8ce26f"
, …, "minerInfo": { "name": "\u0004��\u0000\u001d\u0001\u0004Ethe
Times 03/
Jan/2009 Chancellor on brink of second
bailout for banks\n"}}],...blockhash":
"000000000019d6689c085ae165831e934ff763ae46a2a6c172b3f1b60a8ce26f",
"confirmations": 765769, "time": 1231006505, … }}
```

Nodes store copies of this data, typically as `.dat` files containing the raw concatenated block data.

Data stored *on-chain* is serialized, so in order to extract valuable insights, we must understand its structure, decode its content, and make it readable. With that in mind, in this chapter, we will delve into blockchain transactions and dissect the anatomy of a transaction. We will examine its essential components, such as sender and recipient addresses, transaction amounts, gas fees, and more. Furthermore, we will focus on the building blocks of a blockchain – the blocks. We will explore the block structure, including the block header, timestamp, difficulty, and nonce.

Additionally, we will delve into blockchain state data, learning how to connect with smart contracts and retrieve contract variables' values for any block.

Toward the end of the chapter, we will explore popular on-chain data providers and APIs, understanding how to access the exact source that suits our needs, while considering their advantages and disadvantages.

In summary, this chapter will cover the following topics:

- Dissecting a transaction
- Dissecting a block
- Exploring state data
- Reviewing data sources

Technical requirements

In this chapter, we will extensively utilize the `requests` library. This popular and user-friendly Python library simplifies the process of sending HTTP requests and handling responses. HTTP requests form the foundation of client-server communication in web applications and APIs, enabling clients to request specific resources or perform actions on the server, such as data retrieval, creation, modification, and deletion.

If you haven't installed `requests` yet, you can do so by executing the following command:

```
pip install requests
```

The documentation for `requests` is available at the following link: `https://requests.readthedocs.io/en/latest/`.

You can find all the data and code files for this chapter in the book's GitHub repository, accessible here: `https://github.com/PacktPublishing/Data-Science-for-Web3/tree/main/Chapter02`.

We recommend that you read through the code files in the `Chapter02` folder to follow along with the chapter.

A note on differences between blockchains and databases

Blockchains and databases have architectural differences. We have observed that a blockchain leverages distributed ledger technology while databases operate on a client-server relationship. This fundamental difference has an impact on two aspects: authority and performance. There is no sole server in charge of a blockchain; therefore, to modify anything on it, the nodes will need to reach a consensus, which takes time and results in slower performance. In contrast, databases are highly time-efficient and continue to improve their speed every day.

Another consequence of this relates to the manipulation of stored information. In the case of a blockchain, it is not possible to update a data point that has been added to a block. On the other hand, databases offer **Create, Read, Update, Delete (CRUD)** operations, with their only limitation being dependent on admin privileges.

It is worth noting that these characteristics primarily apply to public blockchains. Hybrid blockchains, commonly used for corporate purposes, blur the distinction between traditional databases and blockchains.

Let's visualize each transaction as a row in the blockchain ledger, and imagine that these rows fill up the pages of a book. Each completed page represents a block containing a collection of transactions. We will start our analysis by studying the data each row contains.

Dissecting a transaction

As data analysts, it's crucial for us to grasp the unique structure of each blockchain we analyze, as it influences how we search for and interpret information.

For instance, Bitcoin follows a structure based on spent and unspent transactions, while Ethereum operates on an account-based protocol. The underlying structure changes our approach to the data we want to fetch.

In the case of Ethereum, a transaction is a message initiated by an **Externally Owned Account** (**EOA**) that gets recorded on the network. A transaction is the kick-off moment that triggers the Ethereum machinery and leads to a change in its state.

To exemplify the concepts described in the subsequent sections, we will dissect a transaction associated with the `0x1aD91ee08f21bE3dE0BA2ba6918E714dA6B45836` Address. This address belongs to the mining pool named *Hiveon*.

The transaction's hash is `0x032ed60363beb809a2b9c9790bb7dadd83b743040945a087aeecbe9e6b2dc2af`. By pasting this hash into Etherscan, we can gather more information about the transaction:

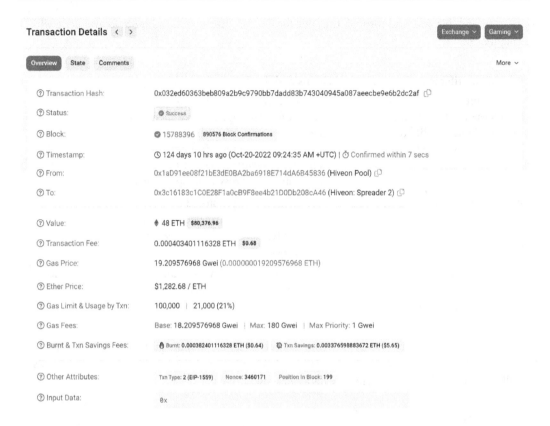

Figure 2.1 – Transaction details on Etherscan

Etherscan provides valuable metadata that offers context about when the transaction was executed, helping us understand it with its user-friendly interface.

We will begin by examining the basic transaction data, which consists of the following fields, as extracted in `Chapter01/Transaction.ipynb`:

Nonce	3460171
Gas Price	0.000000019209576968 Ether (19.209576968 Gwei)
Gas Limit	100000
Recipient	0x3c16183c1C0E28F1a0cB9F8ee4b21D0Db208cA46

Value	48000000000000000000
Data	0x
V,R,S	(1, '0x2c1561644259bffe2872ea57690d103b c57b611c8882ed7f2b5e0bfe40e4c807', '0x4bc9255e7b24d321edd9af354589140 acc7347e35d91fcffde07fb81c27741d8')

Table 2.1 – Transaction information stored on-chain

Let's delve into the details of each of these fields.

Nonce

A nonce is a cumulative number that keeps track of the total transactions sent by the executing address. Smart contracts also have a nonce that keeps track of the number of contract creations.

The *Ethereum Yellow Paper* defines it as follows: "*nonce: A scalar value equal to the number of transactions sent from this address or, in the case of accounts with associated code, the number of contract-creations made by this account.*"

As per the definition, the nonce provides information about the sending address. It serves two purposes:

- It establishes the order of transaction processing for each address. A transaction with a higher nonce number will not be processed until all transactions with smaller nonces have been validated.

- It identifies a transaction. Multiple transactions with the same nonce can be sent to mempool, but once a transaction with a particular nonce is added to the blockchain, subsequent transactions with the same nonce will not be processed.

We can extract the next nonce of an address with the following code:

```
web3.eth.getTransactionCount(address)
```

The nonce of a specific transaction can be extracted with the following code:

```
web3.eth.get_transaction(transaction).nonce
```

The nonce counting starts at zero, so the result of the transaction count always reflects the next available transaction for that specific address. We can refer to the First transaction notebook from Chapter01/First_transaction.ipynb, specifically the last cell, as a reference:

```
[8]: web3.eth.get_transaction(transaction)

[8]: AttributeDict({'hash': HexBytes('0x50d01c103ff4c421b8125afc1b97e8dab2cfee0c7e150b410231c896f163636b'),
     'nonce': 0,
     'blockHash': HexBytes('0x36fb6214283bc9ed5a203877f4a68e41c2a2742b3c9161fc25eda53081dc2b12'),
     'blockNumber': 1,
     'transactionIndex': 0,
     'from': '0xd5eAc5e5f45ddFCC698b0aD27C52Ba55b98F5653',
     'to': '0xFfd597CE52103B287Efa55a6e6e0933dff314C63',
     'value': 30000000000000000000,
     'gas': 121000,
     'gasPrice': 20000000000,
     'input': '0x',
     'v': 37,
     'r': HexBytes('0xdbd216095b185a8813767da571c9cbaa0812d61266c9e63fc579f12bebdbef3d'),
     's': HexBytes('0x081c6712849e0fb875aab6977928b71d77312e40dd683845cdbd0f349735559d')})
```

Figure 2.2 – Screenshot displaying the first nonce of an address

Gas price

Gas price (`gasPrice`, as seen in *Figure 2.2*) is determined by the sender of the transaction and represents the price they are willing to pay for each unit of gas. Transactions with higher gas prices are prioritized for confirmation. The gas price is denoted in *Wei per unit of gas*.

To extract the gas price of a transaction, we can use the following code:

```
web3.eth.get_transaction(transaction).gasPrice
```

Gas limit

Gas limit (or `gas`) represents the maximum number of gas units (money invested) that the sender is willing to spend on the transaction. It is the upper limit of gas consumption for a transaction.

To extract the gas limit of a transaction, you can use the following code:

```
web3.eth.get_transaction(transaction).gas
```

Recipient

The recipient of a transaction is specified in the `to` parameter, which contains the public address of the recipient. In the case of Ethereum, addresses are 42 characters long (40 hexadecimal characters beginning with `0x`) and can be either an EOA or a smart contract. At the public address level, there is no distinction between the two. On other blockchains, additional information may be required to identify the recipient (for example, a tag ID/memo for EOS transfers).

It is important to note that any combination of characters that meets the technical requirements mentioned in the preceding paragraph will generate a valid transaction. If we send tokens to an address that has no private key, we cannot access those tokens, resulting in them being effectively *burned*. Burning tokens can be a deliberate part of a token's economy or may occur as a result of a mistake. To address the latter, protocols such as **Ethereum Name Service** (**ENS**) or **RIF Name Service** (**RNS**) have been created, following the idea of traditional DNS. These protocols enable the leasing of human-readable names on the blockchain, which can replace long string addresses.

To extract the `to` field of a transaction, we can use the following code:

```
web3.eth.get_transaction(transaction).to
```

Depending on what information this field has, we can classify transactions into these categories:

- **Regular**: A transaction from one address to another address.
- **Contract deployment**: A transaction where the `to` field is `null` and where the `data` field is used for the contract code. In this case, the sender is creating a smart contract.
- **Execution of a contract**: The `to` field is a smart contract address, and therefore the transaction represents the interaction with a deployed smart contract.

Sender

This is the address that signs the transaction and will be found in the `from` parameter. The address will be an externally-owned account given that contract accounts cannot send transactions.

To extract the `from` field of a transaction, we can use the following code:

```
web3.eth.get_transaction(transaction).from
```

The sender address is derived from the signature (the V,R,S letters shown in *Table 2.1*).

Value

The `value` field denotes the quantity of the native currency transferred in the transaction, expressed with the number of decimal places particular to the specific blockchain. In this instance, the value represents Ether and it is expressed with 18 decimal places. In other blockchains, the native currency will vary; for instance, Rootstock Platform (RSK) employs RBTC, while Cardano uses ADA, and so on.

To extract the value and transform it into decimal values, we can use the following code:

```
value= web3.eth.get_transaction(transaction).value
value*10**-18
```

The transfer of tokens is not stored in the `value` field; for that information, we need access to the transaction logs.

Input data

The input data field contains "*Any extra information required by the transaction,*" as defined by the Ethereum documentation. This field is mostly used when interacting with or deploying a smart contract.

When a transaction interacts with a smart contract, the input data comprises the function and parameters necessary for interacting with the contract. This input data adheres to the type format outlined in the smart contract's **Application Binary Interface (ABI)**. To decode the data field for our analysis, we will require the ABI.

In the case of a transaction that deploys a contract, the input data field contains the contract bytecode.

To extract the input data of a transaction, we can use the following code:

```
web3.eth.get_transaction(transaction).input
```

As you may have noticed, in the transaction we have been analyzing, there is no input data. However, let's change that for example purposes. Let's consider a transaction that mints a Bored Ape Yacht Club NFT ("Bored Ape" for future reference). For example, let's take Bored Ape ID 6633 (as of the day of this writing, held by Neymar Jr.).

We can observe that the minting transaction is hashed as
0xb3827bb3cca1a693ec69edb744755f64d8ff8c90f89f69cbfbfafd17b0083159.

In this transaction, the 0x9909017A0F637380af916257D05c3e7dD2F6c68a
address interacts with the smart contract at this address:
0xBC4CA0EdA7647A8aB7C2061c2E118A18a936f13D.
This transaction has the following input data: 'input':
'0xa723533e0000000000000000000000000000000000000000000000000000000000000001'.

This input data holds a meaning in the context of the Bored Ape ABI. An ABI documents the smart contract's functions, state data, and events. Smart contracts are compiled at the machine code level, and ABIs serve as translators to decode them, as they include each function's input and return parameters. ABIs enable the readability of all the functions of a smart contract.

In summary, to translate the input data, we need to access the ABI document. One way to do this is by following these steps:

1. Navigate to https://etherscan.io/address/[smart_contract_address]; in this case, this is https://etherscan.io/address/0xBC4CA0EdA7647A8aB7C2061c2E118A18a936f13D.

2. Scroll down to the middle of the page and find the horizontal menu. Click on **Contract**:

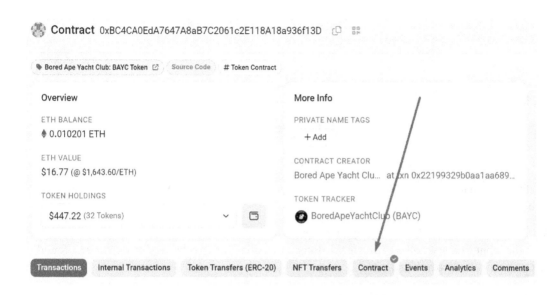

Figure 2.3 – Contract tab on Etherscan

3. Scroll down and you will find the **Contract ABI** Section:

Figure 2.4 – Export ABI option selection

Now, you can copy and paste the ABI in a text or JSON format. Be cautious and delete the initial parts of the text where some metadata from Etherscan's API is also written, as detailed in the following note. An alternative is to programmatically obtain it by creating a free account with an API key.

Note that, Etherscan adds extra text to the ABI JSON when its official API isn't used. This text should be removed when incorporating it into our code in Jupyter Notebook.

Delete the text at the beginning of the JSON:

{"status":"1","message":"OK-Missing/Invalid API Key, rate limit of 1/5sec applied","result":"[
ENS\",\"name\":\"_ens\",\"type\":\"address\"},

And at the end:

{\"internalType\":\"bytes\",\"name\":\"data\",\"type\":\"bytes\"}],\"name\":\"upgradeToAndCal:
{\"stateMutability\":\"payable\",\"type\":\"receive\"}]"}

Figure 2.5 – Text to be deleted from the JSON data

For simplicity purposes, we have also uploaded the Bored Ape ABI to the book's GitHub repository.

There are alternative tools to retrieve the ABI when the code is not verified. These tools, although still in beta, are listed in the *Further reading* section.

With the `decode_function_input` method, we can combine the information from the ABI with the input data text and we will see the decoded version. The step-by-step process can be found in `Chapter02/Transaction`:

```
function, parameters = baContract.decode_function_input(bored_ape["input"])
print (function, 'parameters: ',parameters )
```

```
<Function mintApe(uint256)> parameters:  {'numberOfTokens': 1}
```

Figure 2.6 – The decode_function_input method

As we can see, the `mintApe` function was triggered by this transaction, and Ape 6633 was born. This is a simple function with one parameter, but we need to be prepared for more complex functions, such as swapping contracts, lending, bids, and more.

V,R,S

These are the components of the signature by the `from` address. The digital signature gives validity that the message sent was executed by the originating address. For more on this matter, you can read the *Mastering Ethereum* book. Depending on where we obtain our transaction data, we may not encounter this field (for example, Covalent does not provide it when querying for a specific transaction).

Transaction receipt

Once the transaction is executed, we gain access to a valuable source of information, called a transaction receipt. This receipt stores information that results from executing the transaction.

Of particular interest to us are the following fields: `status`, `gasUsed`, `cumulativeGasUsed`, and `logs`.

Status

The status field can have a value of either 1 or 0. A value of 1 indicates a successful transaction, while a value of 0 indicates an unsuccessful transaction, leading to the transaction being reverted.

Gas used and Cumulative gas used

The Gas used field represents the amount of gas that was actually consumed by the transaction. This value will be below the gas limit. We can retrieve it with the following code:

```
web3.eth.getTransactionReceipt (transaction).gasUsed
```

Additionally, we have the Cumulative gas used field, which provides the total amount of gas consumed by all previous transactions within the same block, including the transaction under analysis.

Gas prices are crucial data points that analysts often consider. These fields represent the actual cost of using the blockchain for a specific transaction. Analyzing gas costs can help answer questions such as: What is the best time of the day to execute a set of transactions? When should we deploy a set of smart contracts to minimize gas expenses?.... and so on.

Logs

Any change on the blockchain can be stored in state data or event logs. The latter is less expensive and provides a very rich source of information. We will analyze state data in the following section.

In the context of smart contract operations, logs are short pieces of information that record specific events at a given point in time.

An event log, or log record, can be created by providing specific instructions to the EVM. These instructions are known as **opcodes**, and there are five opcodes that emit event logs. The *Ethereum Yellow Paper* provides more information about opcodes under the title *Logging operations*.

Log events consist of two components: topics and data. When examining the source code, we will find that log events are preceded by the `event` or `emit` keyword.

Topics describe the nature of an event and can include up to a maximum of four topics per log. Typically, topics consist of the event's signature or name, along with the type of parameters passed.

Topics are searchable but limited in terms of the number of bytes they can include. As a result, the information contained within topics is usually referential. In the context of a Python dictionary, topics can be considered as keys.

Data, the other component, has no such limit in terms of number of bytes and is less expensive to store on the blockchain. This allows for more flexibility in the information that can be included, such as larger strings. If we were to compare this with a Python dictionary, data would correspond to the values.

Let's continue the examination of the minting of Bored Ape 6633. Depending on the data provider we use to query the blockchain, we may receive the logs already decoded or we might need to decode them ourselves. To be able to decode them, we will need the ABI, as extracted in the previously analyzed *Input data* section. The code essentially compares events from the ABI with events from the log. If there is a match, the code translates the log. In Chapter02/Transaction.ipynb, we will see the entire process, which is summarized in the following steps:

1. Creates a list of events from the contract.

2. Generates a hexadecimal value for each event extracted from the ABI.

3. Extracts the receipt for the transaction.

4. Iterates through each log and compares the hexadecimal value of the first parameter of the log (the topic) with the list created in *step 2*. If there is a match, the code uses the name within the processReceipt function, and it will return a tuple with the decoded logs.

In the Bored Ape transaction under analysis, the log contains some interesting information. It provides details about the minting of the NFT, the original holder, and the corresponding ID. We can use the ID to view the information in the gallery using the **BY ID** search filter (https://boredapeyachtclub.com/#/gallery).

We have reviewed the main components of a transaction and the information they provide; we now shift our focus to the next vital element of the blockchain ecosystem: the block. As transactions are the purpose of a blockchain, blocks serve as the foundational units that bring together multiple transactions, creating a comprehensive ledger of activity.

Dissecting a block

A block is formed by combining a list of transactions with a header. As depicted in the flow diagram in *Figure 2.7*, when transactions are added to a block, they alter the state of the blockchain:

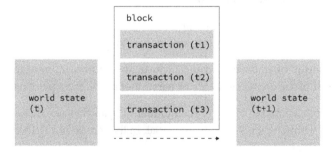

Figure 2.7 – How a blockchain evolves (adapted from https://ethereum.org/en/developers/docs/blocks)

The preceding diagram illustrates the progressive evolution of blockchain state data, one block at a time. Blocks are strictly ordered, allowing us to trace the history of each state variation.

In the *Ethereum Yellow Paper*, a block is defined as *"the collection of relevant pieces of information (known as block header) [...], together with information corresponding to the comprised transactions, [...] and a set of other block headers [...] that are known to have a parent equal to the present's block's parent (such blocks are known as ommers)."*

Therefore, a block consists of three main components:

- A block header
- A list of transactions
- An uncle block header

Uncle blocks refer to blocks that were mined simultaneously. Since the Merge on September 15, 2022, when the Ethereum network transitioned from **Proof-of-Work (PoW)** to **Proof-of-Stake (PoS)** consensus, the uncle block header is now empty as uncle blocks no longer occur.

Let's begin by understanding the information provided by the block header. For explanatory purposes, let's consider block `15813288`. If we want to review the Etherscan version, we can access it through the following URL: `https://etherscan.io/block/15813288`.

In `Chapter02/Block.ipynb`, we programmatically access it, and we can observe the following fields:

parentHash	0x9b930569ef6794eb018d54d6a0768f4445f757d62ddffa79698cd5c1fea04b31
beneficiary	0x690B9A9E9aa1C9dB991C7721a92d351Db4FaC990
stateRoot	0x91c1b2292997a9aa87aa7bf75b387df4bc5a6869fa83b3ce9d4c6793d3acaaa1
transactionsRoot	0x7896f544f241e7aa3bae8e3f70b45d9db34794ddb60187c1d46dd80958ea3e41
receiptsRoot	0x6698a263fd7b24a301e1060c624e7aa7510db8d4d215779ee43ebe8f5c18889a
difficulty	0
totalDifficulty	58750003716598352816469
number	15813288
size	63648
gasLimit	30000000
gasUsed	13247169
baseFeePerGas	15649778689
timestamp	1666557983
extraData	0x406275696c64657230783639
nonce	0x0000000000000000
transactions	List of 112 transactions

Table 2.2 – 15813288 block information

Let's understand what information each field comprises:

- `parentHash`: This is the hash of the previous block, establishing a link between blocks in the blockchain and providing historical order to the network.

- `beneficiary`: This field indicates the address of the miner or validator who successfully added the block to the chain and received rewards and fees.

- `stateRoot/transactionRoot/receiptsRoot`: These fields provide the hash of the trie structure containing information related to the modified state, transactions, and transaction receipts. A Merkle Patricia Trie is an internal structure utilized by Ethereum to expedite data retrieval.

- `difficulty` and `totalDifficulty`: `difficulty` represents the level of mining difficulty required for this block. `totalDifficulty` denotes the cumulative difficulty of the entire blockchain up to the specific block. These features changed after the Merge as they were associated with the previous PoW consensus. `totalDifficulty` has remained unchanged since the transition, and `difficulty` was set to zero. Refer to block 15537393 to have a look at the last block mined using PoW.

- `number`: This indicates the block height, as discussed in *Chapter 1*, following a sequential order of blocks. The genesis block, mined in July 2015, holds the block number 0.

- `size`: This denotes the data storage capacity of a block in bytes, with the limit imposed by the required gas for validation.

- `gasLimit/gasUsed`: `gasLimit` represents the maximum amount of gas allowed to be expended in the block, while `gasUsed` indicates the total gas consumed by all transactions within the analyzed block. If `gasUsed` if below `gasLimit`, we can observe that blocks are not fully utilized, leaving idle space.

- `baseFeePerGas`: This field represents the reserve price or minimum price required for a transaction to ensure its inclusion in a block. The calculation is based on previous blocks, aiming to provide more predictability for gas costs to end users.

- `timestamp`: This denotes the Unix timestamp at the time the block was mined, representing the cumulative number of seconds elapsed since January 1, 1970.

- `extraData`: This arbitrary array contains data relevant to the specific block. It was previously written by miners and is now populated by validators.

- nonce: Short for "number used only once," this field is a number added to the block that must generate a hash meeting the difficulty criteria. It is still used in Bitcoin to regulate difficulty. After the merge in Ethereum, this number was set to 0.

- transactions: This field returns a list of transactions added to the block; in the example under analysis, this is 112 transactions. The following code snippet provides a list of each transaction, along with the information reviewed in the previous section:

```
web3.eth.getBlock(block_identifier=15813288).transactions
```

Analyzing block data is very useful when trying to grasp a general overview of the chain under analysis. Aggregating the data from the fields detailed previously, we are able to answer questions about how a chain is used, the average transaction per block, the time between blocks, how expensive the base fee is, and so on.

Having examined the structure and components of a transaction and a block in detail, we now shift our focus to the state data within the Ethereum blockchain. State data encompasses the current state of all accounts, contracts, and smart contracts on the network, reflecting the outcome of executed transactions and operations. It serves as a fundamental building block for the blockchain's functionality and provides a comprehensive snapshot of the system at any given point in time.

Exploring state data

In the *Ethereum Yellow Paper*, the state, also known as the world state, is defined as "*a mapping between addresses and account states.*" Up to this point, we have been discussing transactional data that is permanent, meaning that once incorporated into the blockchain, it cannot be changed. Unlike transactional data, the state is dynamic and evolves with each new block.

To ensure accessibility for users interacting with accounts and contracts, Ethereum employs **trie** data structures. Specifically, the state trie contains key-value pairs for every existing account that has engaged in a valid transaction. The key represents the Ethereum account's address, while the value comprises hashed information encompassing the account balance, nonce, code, and storage root.

The concept of roots leads us to an explanation of tries and the special implementation of the **Merkle Patricia Trie** on Ethereum (that exceeds the scope of this work). We will briefly mention that the trie structure or search tree is used for storing and searching a key in a set. It facilitates the searching, adding, and deleting complexities for sequences of characters. The trie starts with a root and connects characters in its branches. We have seen roots in our previous analysis: the state, transaction, and receipt's roots hashes are part of the block information. The state root, together with additional information, is stored as the value of the address.

For a more in-depth understanding, please refer to the cited documentation in the *Further reading* section.

Why is this useful for data analysis?

The storage of state data in this manner enables us to easily retrieve the blockchain's status at specific points in time—a capability leveraged by smart contracts.

To illustrate this, let's consider the Bored Ape smart contract we examined earlier.

On the Jupyter notebook on `Chapter02/State.ipynb`, do the following:

1. Upload the ABI following the instructions outlined in the *Dissecting a transaction* section.

2. With the following code, we will gain access to all the contract's functions:

```
baContract.all_functions()
```

We can see that each function tells us which parameter it needs to be able to execute the query. For example, `<Function ownerOf(uint256)>` tells us that it needs an integer, which in the context of this example is the Bored Ape ID under analysis: 6633.

The code will be as follows:

```
baContract.functions.ownerOf(6633).call()
```

After executing this cell, we will see that the current owner of the Bored Ape ID is `0xC4505dB8CC490767fA6f4b6f0F2bDd668B357A5D`. If no `block_identifier` parameter is specified, the call retrieves the current state data, assuming `latest` as the default value.

Let's imagine that we want to know who was the previous owner of the Bored Ape 6633 ID. In that case, we would need to provide in the `block_identifier` parameter the number of the block previous to the transfer to the current owner occurring. In the case of Bored Ape 6633, the transfer took place in block `14044022`, so we query the state of the blockchain at block `14044021` with the following code:

```
baContract.functions.ownerOf(6633).call(block_identifier=14044021)
```

The result is that the previous owner was `0xDE2b87d1539904f4b37E98C0d5CE383E890006eF`. An alternative is using Etherscan's **Read Contract** function, which will only respond with the current state data.

The steps are the following:

1. Paste and search the smart contract address on Etherscan:

Figure 2.8 – Etherscan search bar

2. Navigate to the **Contract** tab, shown in *Figure 2.3*.

3. Click on the **Read Contract** tab:

Figure 2.9 – Read Contract tab

4. Locate the relevant function; in this case, the `ownerOf` function:

Figure 2.10 – ownerOf function

5.   Add 6633 to it and click on **Query**. The response provides the current owner of Bored Ape ID 6633:

Figure 2.11 – Response to function execution

This approach is useful for extracting state data really fast.

After studying state data and understanding its significance, the next step is to gain access to on-chain data for practical use. In the following section, we will explore multiple data sources and learn to connect with them.

Reviewing data sources

Alice: Would you tell me, please, which way I ought to go from here?

The Cheshire Cat: That depends a good deal on where you want to get to.
- Lewis Carroll, Alice in Wonderland

We will encounter a similar dilemma to Alice's when trying to access *on-chain* data without context or a clear vision of the needs and resources that are at our disposal.

The choice of a data source relies on various factors, primarily driven by our needs and available resources. As discussed in *Chapter 1*, our approach to blockchain data will be shaped by the problems we aim to solve and the questions we seek to answer. If we need to add to a dashboard aggregated metrics that involve comprehensive scanning of the entire blockchain, we will need access to SQL-based solutions. On the other hand, integrating specific data points, such as balances or token prices, into our platform may lead us toward extracting information from a node with web3.py.

Additionally, each data source carries its own set of costs and levels of flexibility. The expertise of the data scientists responsible for managing these resources also influences our decision-making process. Options ranging from traditional SQL-based datasets to MongoDB and GraphQL are at our disposal.

Importantly, our decision must consider whether integration of on-chain data with off-chain data is necessary, and the ease with which it can be achieved. Seamlessly merging these two worlds should be taken into account. A website that gives us continuous updates is `primodata.org/blockchain_data`, which is maintained by the X account, `twitter.org/primodata`.

Let us now present some available options, bearing in mind that this list requires periodic updates to keep pace with the ever-evolving landscape. We test each of the alternatives in `Chapter02/Data Sources.ipynb`.

Block explorers

A block explorer is a user-friendly tool that provides detailed analytics about a blockchain network. For Ethereum, we have been interacting with Etherscan (`https://etherscan.io/`), and for RSK, Rootstock (`https://rootstock.blockscout.com/`) among many other examples. A block explorer acts as a search engine and browser where users can find information about individual blocks, public addresses, and transactions associated with a specific cryptocurrency. Each chain has its own block explorer. Of all the sources described here, this is the only one that is widely used by blockchain enthusiasts and everyday users to explore and monitor the activities happening on a blockchain network.

Infura

Infura is one of the providers that we have utilized throughout the book's exercises and examples. It offers API access over HTTPS and WebSockets to a node, making it accessible for querying through clients such as `web3.py` or `web3.js`.

For more detailed information, please visit `https://blog.infura.io/post/getting-started-with-infura-28e41844cc89`.

Additionally, a comprehensive step-by-step guide on how to start interacting with this source can be found in *Appendix 1*. It's important to note that the node provided by Infura is situated within a developer suite specifically designed for dApp development. Consequently, the most effective approach to accessing this dataset is through programming languages such as Python or Java. The API's response is in the widely used JSON format.

Moralis

Similar to Infura, Moralis is considered part of a developer suite for blockchain developers. It indexes EVM-based chains and Solana, but what sets it apart is its advanced features, including pre-built queries that enable cross-analysis. Accessing Moralis requires an API key, and the response data is in JSON format.

For more detailed information, please visit `https://docs.moralis.io/docs/quickstart`.

GetBlock

GetBlock is another **node as-a-service (NaaS)** provider, similar to Infura. However, Getblock offers access to a broader range of chains compared to Infura and Moralis. To use GetBlock, you'll need to set up an account, and the response from the API will be in JSON format.

For more detailed information, please visit `https://getblock.io/`.

Dune

Dune is an excellent web-based data analysis tool for creating interactive dashboards and charts. It offers both free and premium versions, with the latter allowing the creation of private dashboards. The data is indexed at various stages of decoding, ranging from raw Ethereum data to tables enriched with extensive metadata contributed by the community. One notable aspect is the platform's commitment to knowledge sharing, as queries and dashboards are openly accessible to everyone.

If we want to see how a query was built, we have to click on the title of the metric, as shown in *Figure 2.12*, and it will open the query space with the relevant query. Dune Analytics uses the DuneSQL query engine, based on Trino:

Figure 2.12 – Dune Analytics access to query

Additionally, Dune Analytics provides valuable resources such as tutorials, documentation, and a forum to support users on their analytical journey.

For more detailed information, please visit `https://dune.com/docs`.

Covalent

Covalent is another API that necessitates users to create an account and acquire API keys. The company has indexed over 40 chains and consistently updates the data with minimal delay compared to the node. Similar to Infura, interaction with Covalent's API follows a programmatic approach, and the response is in JSON format. Covalent provides a range of pre-defined basic endpoints that are valuable for data scientists. Furthermore, certain on-chain data endpoints offer enriched information, such as prices or 24-hour aggregations of specific metrics. For more detailed information, please visit `https://www.covalenthq.com/platform/#/auth/register/`.

Notably, Covalent is currently developing a new **business intelligence** (**BI**) product called **Increment**, which offers greater flexibility. Increment is a comprehensive database encompassing all the indexed chains (EVM compatible), enabling users to query the data using SQL or a simple no-code drag-and-drop system. The database contains all the data generated by all chains collectively, recognizing the growing number of blockchains and the necessity for companies to monitor users and value across multiple chains. Increment's unified database provides a convenient solution for this purpose. It's important to note that certain information stored in this database is encoded in hexadecimal format, including addresses, transaction input data, and transaction value. To access Increment, please visit `https://www.covalenthq.com/platform/#/increment/` and create an account.

Once we have access, we will notice that there are dashboards built by the community. If we come across a metric of interest and wish to understand how a query was constructed, click on the dots of the metric, select **Go to SQL**, and it will open the SQL builder on a separate page with the logic:

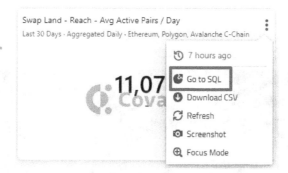

Figure 2.13 – Increment access to query

Flipside

Flipside is another excellent provider that allows us to query on-chain tables using SQL for multiple chains, including some external tables maintained by market authorities such as DefiLlama for **Total Value Locked** (**TVL**).

Flipside offers two main products. The first one is Flipside Data Studio (`https://www.flipsidecrypto.xyz/`), which enables dashboard visualizations in a social network environment with an impressive community. All the queries are open, and analysts compete to create useful dashboards for the community.

The other product is the Flipside API (`http://flipsidecrypto.xyz`), which allows us to submit queries directly from our developer environment. This service, included in the free tier, enables us to query the database and retrieve results that we can ingest in our systems, internal dashboards, and so on.

To use Flipside, we need to create an account and obtain the necessary API keys. For more detailed information, please visit `https://docs.flipsidecrypto.com/`.

The Graph

The Graph is based on GraphQL and is primarily focused on smart contracts. Currently, subgraphs are limited to the Ethereum blockchain. Subgraphs allow access to the ecosystem created by a specific protocol rather than the entire blockchain. It operates in a decentralized and collaborative manner to index blockchain information, with various roles such as **Developer**, **Indexer**, **Curator**, and **Delegator**, each incentivized to participate.

Queries can be accessed through a URL, making integration into our apps possible. It is particularly interesting that each subgraph comes with its own documentation and a playground where we can test our queries.

Numerous projects are actively developing subgraphs to facilitate decentralized access to their data. At present, I have come across ENS, Sablier, and Superfluid are examples of projects maintaining subgraphs on this service.

To test our queries, we can use the online playground, which requires creating an account and connecting our wallet to obtain the necessary API keys:

Figure 2.14 – Screenshot of The Graph's playground

For more detailed information, please visit `https://thegraph.com/explorer`.

Google BigQuery

Google BigQuery maintains a table indexing for both the Ethereum and Bitcoin chains. You can access the data using Google Cloud. A limited tier is accessible through the Kaggle website. To access the data, please visit `https://bigquery.cloud.google.com/dataset/bigquery-public-data:crypto_ethereum`.

Lastly, it's important to note that each product uses its own terminology to refer to the same information. This brings us back to the first part of the chapter, which focuses on how data is presented. The data we observe from the aforementioned providers is subject to translation, and each indexer applies its own criteria. It will be our responsibility to determine the specific information we require.

A note on decentralization

These are information providers. With the exception of The Graph, whose product is a decentralized information protocol, the remaining companies primarily focus on keeping updated their indexes or node points, rather than prioritizing decentralization.

It is important to emphasize this point because, in a decentralized ecosystem, these providers serve as centralized points. Consequently, they can be influenced by regulations, leading to potential exposure of information or censorship, among other possibilities. A recent example involves Infura, which, while attempting to comply with international sanctions in the Ukraine-Russia conflict, also blocked MetaMask access to Venezuela. MetaMask relies on Infura's suite, and this decision affected all IPs, even those located in countries geographically distant from the sanctioned areas.

It may or may not be relevant for the data area of our company but, as mentioned in *Chapter 1*, our job is typically aligned with a business that may have, as a product feature, respect for decentralization and all its benefits.

Summary

In conclusion, this chapter delved into the world of on-chain data, which serves as the primary data source in Web3. We started the chapter by dissecting individual transactions and gaining insights into their structure and components. This understanding was further expanded as we explored the anatomy of blocks.

Moving forward, we delved into an analysis of state data. By examining state variables and their significance, we gained a deeper understanding of how data is stored and accessed within a blockchain.

To further enhance our ability to work with on-chain data, we explored a range of data providers. From widely used block explorers such as Etherscan to powerful APIs such as Infura, Moralis, and Covalent, and SQL-accessible tables such us Dune and Flipside, we built a comprehensive list of resources that grant us access to on-chain data. Each provider offers unique features, data formats, and querying capabilities, allowing us to tailor our approach based on the specific needs of our projects.

Throughout this chapter, we have acquired the foundational knowledge necessary to navigate and interact with on-chain data effectively. In the next chapter, we will study how off-chain data can play a key role in Web3.

Further reading

To complement this chapter, the following links may help:

- Dissecting a transaction:

  - *Antonopoulos, Andreas. Mastering Ethereum* book, Chapter 6: Transactions · GitBook, 2018, `cypherpunks-core.github.io/ethereumbook/06transactions.html`.

  - *Piper Merriam* and *Jason Carver. Ethereum Name Service — Web3.py documentation*, 2018, `https://web3py.readthedocs.io/en/stable/ens_overview.html`.

  - *KLmoney. Bitcoin: Dissecting Transactions | CryptoTokens, May 26, 2017,* `https://klmoney.wordpress.com/bitcoin-dissecting-transactions`.

  - A very detailed analysis of the Bitcoin transaction can be found in Nick Furneaux's book *Investigating Cryptocurrencies*.

  - `https://abi-parser-nvk.vercel.app/` and `https://github.com/shazow/whatsabi`.

- Dissecting a block:

  - *Buterin, Vitalik. Merkling in Ethereum | Ethereum Foundation Blog, 2015,* `https://blog.ethereum.org/2015/11/15/merkling-in-ethereum`.

  - *Furneaux, Nick. Investigating Cryptocurrencies, Chapter 3: Understanding, Extracting, and Analyzing Blockchain Evidence, Wiley, 2018.*

- State data:

  - *Ethereum.org. Merkle Patricia Trie, ,* `https://ethereum.org/en/developers/docs/data-structures-and-encoding/patricia-merkle-trie/`.

  - *Day, Allen* and *Evgeny Medvedev. GitHub - Blockchain-etl/Awesome-bigquery-views: Useful SQL Queries for Blockchain ETL Datasets in BigQuery, GitHub, October 27, 2022,* `https://github.com/blockchain-etl/awesome-bigquery-views`.

3

Working with Off-Chain Data

In the previous chapter, we learned that on-chain data serves as the primary source of Web3 data analysis. It is open, distributed, and trustworthy. While on-chain data will be key to answering most business data science questions, it is essential to complement it with relevant information from off-chain data sources, which is the focus of this chapter.

Consider a scenario where we receive a request to assess the economic relevance of a smart contract. We can query the number of tokens locked in it, but to finalize the analysis, we need to determine the monetary value of those tokens. To accomplish this, we must integrate on-chain data with prices, often derived from off-chain sources.

Prices, news, and opinions are not stored on-chain and must be retrieved from external sources. In this chapter, we will delve into those sources and acquire data from selected APIs. Specifically, we will discuss alternatives for fetching prices, analyze a crypto news aggregator, and explore the significance of social media, particularly X (formerly Twitter).

Off-chain data differs in nature from on-chain data, and it is crucial to exercise caution regarding reliability when dealing with these sources. The sources discussed in this chapter are typically centralized, meaning the entities have complete control over their data. This directly affects the datasets we will utilize, as data points may be subject to deletion, missing entries, or manipulation. In contrast, on-chain data transactions, as a rule, cannot be modified.

This chapter specifically covers the following topics:

- Integrating prices into our dataset
- Incorporating news into our dataset
- Adding social network data to our dataset

Technical requirements

We will be using **Tweepy**, a Python library that allows us to easily interact with X. With Tweepy, we can fetch, post, and retrieve information about tweets, users, and much more. To start using Tweepy, we first need to register for a developer account on the Twitter developer website and obtain a set of API keys, as explained in *Appendix 2*. The documentation for Tweepy is available at `https://docs.tweepy.org/en/stable/`.

If you have not worked with Tweepy before, it can be installed with the following code:

```
pip install tweepy
```

Additionally, we'll be utilizing Plotly **graph objects** and Plotly **Express**, two visualization libraries that empower us to create interactive visualizations with Python. Plotly Express is a high-level library that allows us to plot common types of graphs—such as scatter plots, line charts, maps, pie charts, and more—with minimal lines of code. The documentation for Plotly Express can be found at `https://plotly.com/python/plotly-express/`.

Plotly graph objects offer more flexibility and control over visualizations, allowing the creation of complex plots with a high degree of customization. The documentation for Plotly graph objects is available at `https://plotly.com/python/graph-objects/`.

To use both libraries, we need to have the Plotly library installed. If you have not worked with Plotly before, it can be installed with the following code snippet:

```
pip install plotly
```

You can find Jupyter notebooks containing examples discussed in this chapter in the book's GitHub repository at `https://github.com/PacktPublishing/Data-Science-for-Web3/tree/main/Chapter03`. We recommend reading through the code files in the `Chapter03` folder to follow along.

Introductory example – listing data sources

Let's examine this headline:

Dogecoin gains 25% after Elon Musk confirms Tesla will accept DOGE for merchandise

(Source – Cointelegraph: `https://cointelegraph.com/news/dogecoin-gains-25-after-elon-musk-confirms-tesla-will-accept-doge-for-merchandise.`)

This headline references three data sources:

- **Headline (news)**: An online newspaper specializing in the Web3 industry generates this headline. Blockchain news is gradually entering mainstream platforms, and similar information can also be found in traditional financial news indexes such as Reuters.

- **Prices**: The headline refers to the price variation of a particular cryptocurrency. Price data is not typically fetched from the on-chain sources; rather, it is a piece of information data scientists find useful to integrate from a third-party data source.

- **X (formerly Twitter)/social networks**: Numerous market-impact events unfold on social networks, where key figures in the Web3 ecosystem have established significant online reputations. A single tweet from these influential individuals can alter prices or bring attention to a scam or failed negotiation. Most Web3 companies maintain a presence on X, often before creating a LinkedIn page. In this case, the impact on Dogecoin, as mentioned in the headline, originated from Elon Musk's tweet: *"Tesla will make some merch buyable with Doge and see how it goes"* (source: `https://twitter.com/elonmusk/status/1470703708677840896`).

We described three off-chain data sources that will be relevant for our business data science projects and that we must learn how to consume in a data scientist-friendly format to integrate them effectively. We will discuss each of them in the subsequent sections.

Adding prices to our dataset

Price information is typically stored off-chain, and various sources provide access to this data. Some of the most popular APIs include the following:

- CoinGecko
- CoinMarketCap
- Binance
- Chainlink
- OHLC data: Kraken

Each API comes with its own limitations, which we need to consider when deciding whether to integrate them into our projects. Specific details can be found in their respective documentation.

Regarding price data, it is important to understand how it is calculated, as in these examples:

- CoinMarketCap calculates an asset's price by considering the volume-weighted average of all markets where the asset is traded. This approach is based on the notion that more liquid markets are less susceptible to price fluctuations or manipulation and, therefore, more reliable.

- Binance reports prices based on transactions conducted on their platform. Depending on the pair, it provides the price of the last trade executed in their market.

Let's briefly analyze each of them.

CoinGecko

The **CoinGecko** (`https://www.coingecko.com/`) documentation is straightforward and easy to understand, and they offer a free tier that does not require any registration. With their URL engine, which can build the endpoint URL based on what the user needs, making the requests more efficient.

We can find their documentation at `https://www.coingecko.com/api/documentation`. Let's test the `simple/price` endpoint, which is accessible through this link, too.

Figure 3.1 – CoinGecko API view

As shown in *Figure 3.2*, the *required* parameters for this endpoint are `ids` and `vs_currencies`:

Figure 3.2 – Partial view of the simple/price query parameters

There are also several optional parameters, such as the following:

- `include_market_cap`
- `include_24hr_vol`
- `include_24hr_change`
- `include_last_updated_at`
- `precision`

To obtain the *ID* for a specific asset, we go to CoinGecko's main page and search for the asset by name. If, for example, we want to fetch the current price of Bitcoin, we would need to add Bitcoin's ID in our query. To look for it, we go to CoinGecko's main page and type `Bitcoin` in the search bar, as shown in *Figure 3.3*:

Figure 3.3 – CoinGecko search bar

This will lead us to the Bitcoin information page on CoinGecko (`https://www.coingecko.com/en/coins/bitcoin`) where, as shown in *Figure 3.4*, we can find the API ID that we will source as a parameter in the query:

Figure 3.4 – CoinGecko Bitcoin (BTC) page view

For our `simple/price` request, we also need to input the `vs_currencies` parameter, which determines the currency of the price. In this case, we will use `usd`.

Once we have filled in the mandatory requirements on the API page, we can press the blue **Execute** button, which will return the URL we can use:

```
https://api.coingecko.com/api/v3/simple/price?ids=bitcoin&vs_
currencies=usd
```

Let's see how this works in `prices.ipynb`.

CoinMarketCap

CoinMarketCap (`https://coinmarketcap.com/`) provides extensive documentation, available at the following link: `https://coinmarketcap.com/api/documentation/v1/`. Although this documentation may seem overwhelming, for our purposes, locate the **CRYPTOCURRENCY** category on the left-hand side of the page, accessible through a drop-down menu containing several endpoints related to prices:

Figure 3.5 – CoinMarketCap left bar view

For our purposes, we will utilize the endpoint documented at this link: `https://coinmarketcap.com/api/documentation/v1/#operation/getV2CryptocurrencyQuotesLatest`.

CoinMarketCap offers multiple tiers of services with varying API limits and endpoints. For this introductory explanation, we will rely on the free tier.

We extract the latest Bitcoin price using CoinMarketCap's API in the `prices.ipynb` notebook. To identify the ID of a specific coin, we can execute the map ID endpoint, which shows all cryptocurrencies listed on the CoinMarketCap website with their unique ID. Additional details about this endpoint can be accessed in the documentation: `https://coinmarketcap.com/api/documentation/v1/#operation/getV1CryptocurrencyMap`. The ID for Bitcoin is **1**. Alternatively, we can use the `slug` parameter, which consists of the string name of the cryptocurrency – in our case, simply `bitcoin`.

> **A note on links and scams**
>
> Highly sophisticated scams can deceive victims through search engines. Accessing a project, especially smaller or less-known ones that we have not visited before, by clicking from a search engine where scammers can manipulate web pages into top suggestions elevates the risks. CoinGecko and CoinMarketCap have proven to be reliable for having authentic links to official websites. A more in-depth exploration of security will be provided in *Chapter 10*.

Binance

This is one of the most important centralized exchanges currently active. The exchange offers a basic data plan that does not require registration. The documentation is organized based on the products available on the exchange.

Figure 3.6 – Binance main menu

To extract the spot price of Bitcoin, navigate to the **Spot/Margin/Savings/Mining** tab, as illustrated in *Figure 3.6*. The documentation and available endpoints are listed in a drop-down menu on the left-hand side of the page.

The URL for the endpoint is composed of two parts – a general base endpoint and the query part:

- The base endpoint is located in the **General Info** section, accessible at this link: `https://binance-docs.github.io/apidocs/spot/en/#general-info`

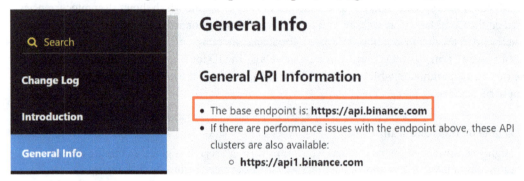

Figure 3.7 – Binance General Info view

- The query part we will use is as follows:

```
/api/v3/ticker/price
```

The documentation for this code is in the *Market Data Endpoints* section available at this link: `https://binance-docs.github.io/apidocs/spot/en/#symbol-price-ticker`.

In `prices.ipynb`, we extract the latest Bitcoin price from this source. The endpoint requires a `symbol` parameter, expressed in a trading pair format, and we use `BTCUSDT`.

To obtain the list of available trading pairs, there are two options. The first is on the Binance platform, and the second is on TradingView, where an account can be created at `https://es.tradingview.com/`.

On TradingView's main page, go to **Symbol Search**, as shown in *Figure 3.8*:

Figure 3.8 – TradingView Symbol Search bar

This opens a dropdown displaying the complete list of trading pairs. To filter by exchange, modify the **All sources** parameter, as shown in *Figure 3.9*:

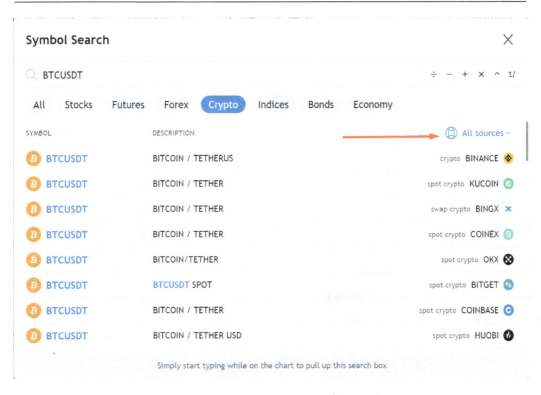

Figure 3.9 – TradingView sources

When the search box opens on **Sources**, we type `Binance` and press *Enter*:

Figure 3.10 – TradingView source selection

This will display all the trading pairs for the specific exchange under the **SYMBOL** column. This symbol is the string we will pass as a parameter to our query.

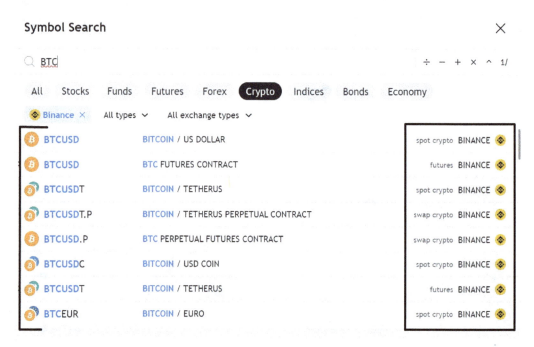

Figure 3.11 – Binance pairs/symbols as shown on TradingView

Binance's API provides comprehensive data beyond price information, making it a valuable resource for exploration.

Oracles – Chainlink

Oracles serve as bridges connecting a smart contract to real-world data. Consider an insurance smart contract designed to provide coverage against specific climate-related events, such as rain. In the closed environment of its blockchain, how can the smart contract ascertain whether it is currently raining or not? The solution lies in oracles, which establish the link between the smart contract and external information, ensuring that the necessary data is reflected within the blockchain.

Chainlink stands out as one of the most widely used sets of oracles. This chapter focuses on price feeds for smart contracts, though there are others such as proof of reserve feeds or NFT price feeds (explored in *Chapter 4*). Documentation for the steps discussed is available at `https://docs.chain.link/data-feeds/api-reference`.

Most price consensus occurs off-chain, and when it is necessary to update the blockchain, the agreed-upon price is recorded on-chain by price feed oracles.

For example, the Bitcoin price is continuously updated and can be seen at `https://data.chain.link/ethereum/mainnet/crypto-usd/btc-usd`. Prices are updated on-chain based on *trigger parameters*, as shown in *Figure 3.13*:

- **Deviation threshold**: Triggered when off-chain data deviates by more than 0.5% from the last updated price.

- **Heartbeat**: Activated after a specified time since the last update has elapsed. Each price feed has its specific time heartbeat. For the Bitcoin price feed, this interval is set to one hour. Consequently, the feed will be refreshed once an hour has passed, provided the previous trigger has not occurred before that.

If we want to source data from these smart contracts, we need to be aware of the heartbeat and check its timestamp to ensure that the latest answer is recent enough for our dataset to add it.

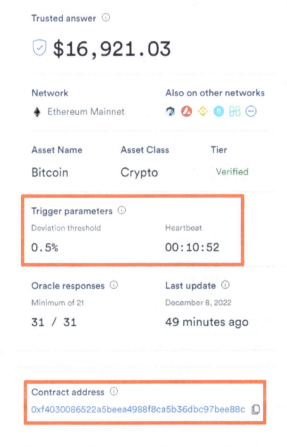

Figure 3.12 – Chainlink price feed information view

To extract the latest price or the **latest round** price, we will need the contract address, as indicated in the second red square of the preceding figure.

The contract **application binary interface** (**ABI**) is available in the documentation or on Etherscan. For simplicity, the ABI of the price feed smart contract has been added to `prices.ipynb`.

Available `read` functions for the price feed smart contract include the following:

- `decimals()`: Returns the number of decimals in the response. In the `prices.ipynb` example, this value is 8, retrieved with the following code snippet:

  ```
  contract.functions.decimals().call()
  ```

- `description()`: Returns the description of the data feed. In the `prices.ipynb` example, this result is `BTC / USD`, and it is retrieved with the following code snippet:

  ```
  contract.functions.description().call()
  ```

- `getRoundData(uint80)`: Returns the data in a specific round.

- `latestRoundData()`: Returns the latest round data.

- `version()`: Returns the contract version.

To get the price, we need to execute the `latestRoundData` function, as follows:

```
contract.functions.latestRoundData().call()
```

The result is a list composed of the following elements:

`roundId`	Each time the oracle is updated, it is known as a round and it has an identifier. That identifier is the `roundId` value. To retrieve the answer of a historical round, we need to call the `getRoundData(uint80)` function and provide this number as a parameter.
`answer`	This returns the price of the asset, the desired data point.
`startedAt`	This is the timestamp when the round started.
`updatedAt`	This is the timestamp when the round was updated.

Table 3.1 – Oracle response

There is one last element in the response (`answeredInRound`), which is a legacy variable and is no longer used.

Once the `answer` is retrieved, translate it to traditional decimal format by moving the comma as many places as indicated by the `decimals()` function:

```
latestData = contract.functions.latestRoundData().call()[1]
latestData*10**-decimal
```

28175.260000000002

Figure 3.13 – Bitcoin price as fed by Chainlink

OHLC – Kraken

Open, High, Low, Close (OHLC) data is a specific dataset where each row includes a timestamp and four columns:

- **Open price (O)**: This is the asset's price at the beginning of the analyzed period
- **High price (H)**: This is the highest price of the asset during the analyzed period
- **Low price (L)**: This is the lowest price of the asset during the analyzed period
- **Closing price (C)**: This is the last asset's price at the end of the analyzed period

An example can be seen in *Table 3.2*:

Timestamp	Open	High	Low	Close
2 0 2 2 - 1 2 - 0 6 00:00:00	16965.7	17089.1	16965.7	17011.0

Table 3.2 – An example of OHLC data

The OHLC columns provide information about the price variations of an asset over a specific period of time. *Figure 3.14* shows an example of a candlestick chart that can be created using OHLC data.

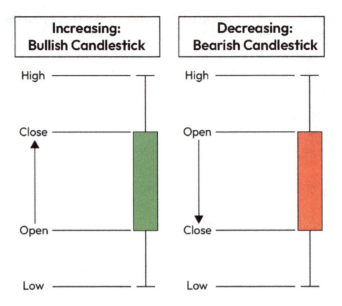

Figure 3.14 – Candlestick design

Each row of the dataset can be used to plot one candlestick. The *Close* and *Open* prices inform us whether, during a given period of time, the asset's price decreased (*Close* is lower than *Open*) or increased (*Close* is higher than *Open*). This information is used to color the body of the bar.

The OHLC data can include additional columns such as traded volume or the number of trades. See the example in `prices.ipynb`.

Technical indicators such as moving averages or Bollinger bands, which are popular in trading, can also be plotted using OHLC data.

The **Kraken** centralized exchange provides OHLC data in its open API, which is very well documented. As we learned with Binance, when using exchanges, every price search has to be expressed as a trading pair.

The documentation can be found at `https://docs.kraken.com/rest/#section/General-Usage`. The endpoint we will use is explained at `https://docs.kraken.com/rest/#tag/Market-Data/operation/getOHLCData`.

When working with OHLC data, it is important to consider the time intervals or granularity of the data. Prices that may appear high or low in a short time frame may be insignificant when analyzed over a longer period. Time granularity will depend on the API. Usually, it is possible to extract seconds, minutes, hours, and days and a combination of those. In Kraken, it is possible to extract with the following parameters:

QUERY PARAMETERS

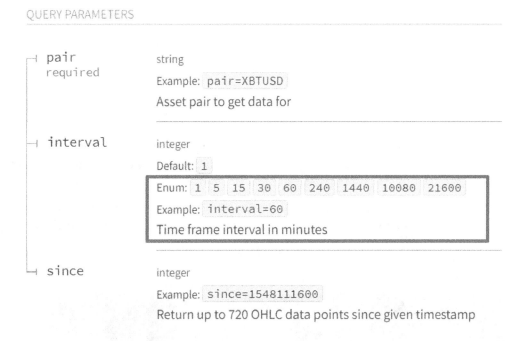

Figure 3.15 – Interval parameter expressed in seconds

To plot a candlestick chart, we can use the `plotly.graph_objects` library. In `prices.ipynb`, we fetch the OHLC dataset of the Bitcoin price with a four-hour period from April 01 to April 05, 2023, and use the library to plot the corresponding candlesticks.

Final thoughts on prices

After our thorough discussion on prices, here are a few key points to remember:

- Not all fiat currencies are supported by these APIs. For currencies that are not the US dollar or Euro, the API may reflect the central bank's official exchange rate with the US dollar, which can differ significantly from the real market price. This is especially true for countries with regulated economies or high inflation. It is necessary to understand where the APIs are sourcing their data from before adding those prices to our dataset.

- Prices of tokens or coins are not the sole products that we may have to track. We could also receive a request to track floor prices of an NFT collection.

- At the time of this writing, Web3 assets still exhibit significant price variations in short periods of time. When calculating averages, we have to be mindful of outliers that may affect them. Data sourced from low liquidity markets, such as small exchanges are more prone to outliers. Read the description of how those prices are calculated and compare them regularly with other sources or create a volume-weighted average as CoinMarketCap does.

News often triggers price fluctuations, so let's now explore a dedicated news aggregator that keeps track of relevant information in the Web3 world.

Adding news to our dataset

A professor once mentioned that in the crypto world, news takes only five minutes to impact the price of an asset.

News is not only important for its effect on prices but marketing teams may also request analysis of the social impact of a brand, a campaign, or a product, or it may be necessary to source an algorithm, among other applications. For that purpose, data scientists need news formatted for analysis.

As of today, there is a dedicated source named **CryptoPanic**, a data aggregator that specifically indexes news relevant to the Web3 ecosystem. The link to the website is `https://cryptopanic.com/`.

Its data can be consumed through an API and the API key is available upon registration.

On the main page, go to the **Sign In** tab on the left menu:

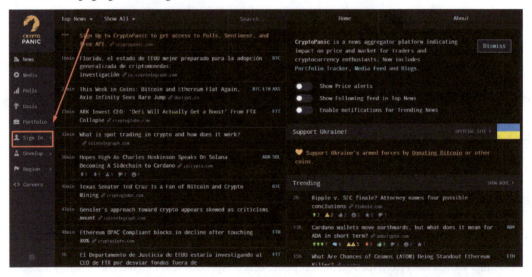

Figure 3.16 – An overview of the CryptoPanic main view

If it is your first time signing up, you will need to confirm your email. After that, you are registered. Click on the **Develop** tab located on the home page:

Figure 3.17 – The Develop tab

Click on either of the **API** tabs on the new page:

Figure 3.18 – API documentation

Click on **API Keys** and it will open a new page with the credentials:

Figure 3.19 – API keys

The documentation is available at this link: `https://cryptopanic.com/developers/api/`.

We will query with the traditional `requests` library, adding our API key to the endpoints listed in the documentation. A step-by-step guide to fetching a list of news can be seen on `news.ipynb`.

There are filters that can be applied to our requests to limit the amount of information received. The filters include the following:

- Currency: The asset referred to in the indexed news
- Region: The language
- UI: This included the following categories – rising, hot, bullish, bearish, important, saved, and lol
- Kind: This is either media or news

The filters can be combined, and each can accept multiple parameters. For example, it is possible to fetch news in English and Spanish by adding the following string to the URL:

```
regions=en,es
```

In `news.ipynb`, we apply two filters, currency and kind:

```
url= 'https://cryptopanic.com/api/v1/posts/?auth_token=[YOUR API
KEY]&currencies=BTC&kind=news'
response = requests.get(url)
```

The API also offers professional paid options (named "pro" on their website) that enable access to extra metadata or to get links to the original sources.

What is also very interesting about this API is that the request returns the following:

- The community's opinion on the sentiment of the headline. This can be particularly useful for sourcing a sentiment analysis algorithm, such as the one we will build in *Chapter 8*.

- The timestamp of the published news. This enables us to join the headlines with prices, allowing us to compare the historical impact of the news on prices.

As seen in the introductory example at the beginning of the chapter, what happens on social networks can heavily impact prices even before any journalist writes about it. Therefore, it is important to add their input to our dataset.

Adding social networks to our dataset

Web3 is an online industry so everything that happens online, from opinions to interactions, holds significant influence.

Sentiment analysis, gauging reactions to products or tokens, plays a crucial role for marketing teams, analysts, and traders alike. A noteworthy example illustrating the importance of such metrics is the CoinStats Fear and Greed indicator. This index, available at `https://coinstats.app/fear-and-greed/`, incorporates social media posts, among other factors, to measure market sentiment.

Figure 3.20 – Crypto Fear and Greed Indicator

According to CoinStats' explanation, the index combines data from various sources. To capture psychological momentum, they also draw insights from social media interactions on X, focusing on specific hashtags that carry both fear and greed components, which contribute to the overall calculation. The social media component holds a 15% weight in the final index, as per the documentation.

X (formerly Twitter)

X is probably the most important social media platform regarding Web3 conversations as of the day of this writing, and the service needs no presentation.

> **Note**
>
> We will use *X* and *Twitter* interchangeably. Although the platform's user interface now bears the name X, on the developer tools side and in all URLs, it retains its former name, Twitter.

A paradigmatic example of how what happens on X impacts the industry is the majority opinion that the FTX exchange speedily crashed after Binance announced on their official X page, "*As a result of corporate due diligence, as well as the latest news reports regarding mishandled customer funds and alleged US agency investigations, we have decided that we will not pursue the potential acquisition of FTX.com*" (source: `https://twitter.com/binance/status/1590449161069268992`).

Access to X data became a paid service in February 2023, with subscription details available through the developer portal at `https://developer.twitter.com/`. The exercises in this section leverage the Basic subscription and API v2.

To obtain API keys with reading privileges, we need to create a project and connect an app, as detailed in *Appendix 2*.

Most user tweets are public, and a tailored query allows us to fetch tweets based on diverse criteria such as user, topic, language, or location. In `social.ipynb`, we extract the latest 100 tweets containing the words *Bitcoin* and *BTC*, excluding retweets and limited to the English language, using the following query:

```
query = 'bitcoin btc -is:retweet lang:en'
```

Additional instructions for constructing effective queries can be found at `https://developer.twitter.com/en/docs/twitter-api/tweets/search/integrate/build-a-query`.

> **Checkpoint**
>
> A step-by-step version of the tweet extraction pipeline is detailed in `social.ipynb`. Alternatively, the resulting CSV file has been uploaded to the book's GitHub and is accessible at `tweets_100.csv`.

With v2 endpoints, it is possible to request `annotations`, adding contextual information to tweets. This feature is valuable for data analysis as it normalizes content within a limited taxonomy. For instance, consider the tweet shown in *Figure 3.21*:

JUST IN 📩

Blackrock files an amended S-1 form with the SEC for its Spot #Bitcoin ₿ ETF.

Another bullish news! 🐂

11:42 PM · Dec 4, 2023 · **16.2K** Views

Figure 3.21 – Example tweet (ID: 1731806102101033329)

X offers entity recognition and context annotations for this tweet. **Entity recognition** identifies locations and entities mentioned in the tweet text. Twitter identifies the following categories of entities: Person, Place, Product, Organization, and Other.

There are three entities recognized in the body of the tweet. Two are organizations –Blackrock and SEC – and the third is of the Other category, when referring to Bitcoin:

```
'annotations': 'annotations': [{'start': 10,
    'end': 18,
    'probability': 0.8568,
    'type': 'Organization',
    'normalized_text': 'Blackrock'},
    {'start': 55,
    'end': 57,
    'probability': 0.7281,
    'type': 'Organization',
    'normalized_text': 'SEC'},
    {'start': 73,
    'end': 79,
    'probability': 0.9581,
    'type': 'Other',
    'normalized_text': 'Bitcoin'}]
```

The complete dictionary of entities for this tweet can be seen in social.ipynb.

X further enriches tweet information through **context annotations,** which are inferred from the semantics of the text, keywords, and hashtags. A comprehensive list of keywords, hashtags, and handles has been developed, and tagged to specific contexts. If any of these elements appear in a tweet, they are appropriately tagged. As of June 2022, there are more than 80 context domains. The link to the relevant documentation can be found in the *Further reading* section.

One example follows:

```
{'domain': {'id': '131',
    'name': 'Unified Twitter Taxonomy',
    'description': 'A taxonomy of user interests. '},
    'entity': {'id': '913142676819648512',
    'name': 'Cryptocurrencies',
    'description': 'Cryptocurrency'}},
```

This information is valuable for categorization and NLP machine learning algorithms.

The complete list of context annotations for this tweet is available in `social.ipynb`.

A commonly employed method by marketing and product teams seeking insights into words associated with products or brands involves analyzing customer reviews, feedback, or social media comments. This approach provides a deeper understanding of the audience and their perceptions. One graphical way to achieve this is by creating word clouds, which highlight the most frequently mentioned words. This aids in identifying customer sentiments, preferences, and pain points at a glance.

To reproduce a word cloud, we utilize tweets as the data source, specifically extracting 1,000 tweets targeting a protocol in the NFT space introduced in *Chapter 4* – namely, OpenSea. To perform this extraction, we used the following query:

```
new_query = 'opensea -is:retweet lang:en'
```

> **Checkpoint**
>
> A step-by-step version of the tweet extraction pipeline is detailed in `social.ipynb`. Alternatively, the resulting CSV file has been uploaded to the book's GitHub and is accessible at `tweets_df.csv`.

In the notebook, we will find libraries and methods to clean the tweets to normalize them before counting the frequency of appearance of the words. These are traditional NLP steps that we will describe in more detail in *Chapter 8*. The resulting word cloud for OpenSea is shown in *Figure 3.22*:

Figure 3.22 – OpenSea word cloud

Once we learn to extract social off-chain data, we can combine it with on-chain data to expand our analysis. Tweets, Discord conversations, Telegram interactions, and other community forums have timestamps and geo-location tags that can be used to merge off-chain activity with transactions occurring on-chain. This helps analysts infer the active hours of a chain or a protocol, deduce the geographic location of customers, and more. These types of analyses are typically requested by marketing teams to improve the direction of their campaigns.

An example of a company leveraging this connection between the two worlds is Spindl, which is working on merging Web2 marketing data sources with on-chain data to build the first marketing funnel tool for the Web3 space.

> **A note on Twitter profiles to follow**
>
> Here are some interesting profiles to follow for Web3 data analysis/content, among many others:
>
> @0xGembus: `https://twitter.com/0xGembus`
>
> @0xAtomist: `https://twitter.com/0xAtomist`
>
> @hildobby_: `https://twitter.com/hildobby_`

Other social media data sources to explore are as follows:

- **Reddit**: This platform hosts numerous Web3-related conversations in the form of Subreddits. The posts and comments within these Subreddits offer valuable information.

- **BitcoinTalk.org forum**: The public posts on this forum also serve as an interesting source of information.

Summary

In this chapter, we examined various off-chain sources of data relevant to the Web3 economy, categorizing the analysis into three main areas. For prices, we explored multiple APIs from traditional sources to exchanges, as well as an oracle. With news, we learned how to extract real-time headlines from the best dedicated news indexer as of the time of writing – namely, CryptoPanic. For X (formerly Twitter), we utilized its API to gauge the sentiment around an NFT protocol. This list of resources is not exhaustive, and we have only scratched the surface of the uses we can give to all this data.

In the next chapter, we will delve into NFTs and their applications in the gaming, art, and name service industries.

Further reading

To complement this chapter, the following links may help:

- Prices:

  - Support CoinMarketCap. (2020). Security check. How are prices calculated on CoinMarketCap? `https://support.coinmarketcap.com/hc/en-us/articles/360015968632-How-are-prices-calculated-on-CoinMarketCap-`

  - Crypto API documentation. (n.d.). CoinGecko. `https://www.coingecko.com/api/documentation`

  - Account. (n.d.). Cryptocurrency Prices, Charts And Market Capitalizations | CoinMarketCap. `https://coinmarketcap.com/api/documentation/v1/`

  - CoinMarketCap. (n.d.). Most trusted cryptocurrency market data API | CoinMarketCap. coinmarketcap.com. `https://coinmarketcap.com/api/faq`

  - Useful Chainlink tutorials. Chainlink. (2022). Learning resources. Chainlink documentation: `https://docs.chain.link/getting-started/other-tutorials/`

  - To further expand on oracles. Chainlink, *What is an Oracle in blockchain? » explained*. Blockchain Oracles for Hybrid Smart Contracts | Chainlink: `https://chain.link/education/blockchain-oracles`

  - Data feeds API reference. (n.d.). Chainlink documentation. `https://docs.chain.link/data-feeds/api-reference`

  - Price feed contract addresses. (n.d.). Chainlink Documentation. `https://docs.chain.link/data-feeds/price-feeds/addresses/`

- News:

  - For a step-by-step process to download a website. Furneaux, Nick. "Investigating Cryptocurrencies. Understanding, Extracting, and Analyzing Blockchain Evidence" Wiley, 2018. Chapter 8.- Pages 125 to 130.

- Social networks:

  - Installation — Tweepy 4.13.0 documentation. (n.d.). Tweepy Documentation — tweepy 4.13.0 documentation. `https://docs.tweepy.org/en/stable/install.html`

  - Getting-started-with-the-twitter-api-v2-for-academic-research/5-how-to-write-search-queries. md at main · twitterdev/getting-started-with-the-twitter-api-v2-for-academic-research. (n.d.). GitHub. `https://github.com/twitterdev/getting-started-with-the-twitter-api-v2-for-academic-research/blob/main/modules/5-how-to-write-search-queries.md`

  - Overview. (n.d.). Use Cases, Tutorials, and Documentation | Twitter Developer Platform. `https://developer.twitter.com/en/docs/twitter-api/annotations/overview` and `https://developer.twitter.com/en/docs/twitter-api/annotations/faq`

4

Exploring the Digital Uniqueness of NFTs – Games, Art, and Identity

In this chapter, we will explore **non-fungible tokens** (**NFTs**) and their various economic use cases. We will begin by understanding what an NFT is, how the relevant information is logged in transaction data, and the alternatives to obtaining it. Additionally, we will analyze how this technology is being leveraged by the gaming, art, and identity industries and explore some of the metrics that hold relevance for each business.

Business initiatives are carried out by a set of smart contracts that we will refer to as "protocols." We will delve into the fundamental protocol metrics, offering quick insights into each protocol's structure and user composition. To do that, we can choose to use a data framework, which is a highly valuable tool for business analysts as it helps organize our analyses and craft a compelling narrative when presenting our findings. An example of such a structure is the *Reach, Retention, and Revenue* framework.

Reach metrics help us understand the origins of growth, customer acquisition costs, target markets, and more. Retention metrics provide a gauge for assessing the effectiveness of our product, encompassing factors such as the frequency of customer usage, churn rates, and cohort analysis. Revenue metrics offer insights into the profitability of a product. It's worth noting that the Covalent team has designed a data analyst training program, which we will cover in more detail in *Chapter 13*, that structures the on-chain analytics learning with this framework.

Throughout this chapter, we will explore concrete examples of metrics for each of these categories.

In this chapter, we will delve into the following topics:

- Introduction to NFT data
- Protocols and database exploration for the gaming, art, and identity industries
- Relevant metrics for the gaming, art, and identity businesses

Technical requirements

We will be using indexed data available in platforms like **Dune Analytics, Increment, Footprint Analytics,** and **Flipside**. To follow along, please open an account on these platforms while following the links provided in *Chapter 2*. Transactional data is queried with **SQL** services and the syntax varies depending on the query engines.

We will also utilize the web3.py **Ethereum Name Service** (**ENS**) library, which is a Python library that provides tools and functionalities for interacting with the ENS – a decentralized naming system on the Ethereum blockchain. This library allows developers to easily resolve Ethereum addresses from human-readable domain names registered on the ENS, manage ENS domain registrations, and perform various operations related to Ethereum's naming infrastructure. The ens module is included with web3.py, which we installed in *Chapter 1*. To work with it, simply import it using the following code snippet:

```
from ens import ENS
```

You can find Jupyter notebooks containing the examples discussed in this chapter in this book's GitHub repository at https://github.com/PacktPublishing/Data-Science-for-Web3/tree/main/Chapter04.

Additionally, there is a live dashboard on Dune displaying many of the queries explained in the chapter at https://dune.com/gabriela/chapter-4-nft. For all Dune dashboards, the query is available by clicking the title of the relevant chart. Here's an example:

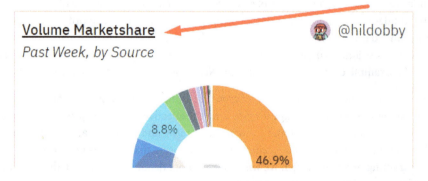

Figure 4.1 – Where to click to open the query. Dune dashboard by @ hildobby (https://dune.com/hildobby/NFTs)

We recommend exploring both resources for a comprehensive understanding.

Enabling unique asset tracking on the blockchain using NFT

This section comprises two main sections: *The business requests*, which will unravel the specific demands that were at the origin of this solution, and *The technical solution*, which will provide a structural overview of the standard smart contract, its methods, and events.

The business requests

An asset is considered **fungible** when it shares the same quality and value as another asset of the same nature, making them interchangeable. For example, one dollar is interchangeable with another dollar, and the same applies to native cryptocurrencies and tokens, such as DAI or USDT.

Conversely, if an asset is **non-fungible**, it means that it is unique and cannot be replaced by another because there is no equivalent. Consider Sorolla's "Walk on the Beach" painting. It is unique and while we can copy it from Google because we admire it, we do not truly own it and cannot prove ownership:

Figure 4.2 – Sorolla's painting, "Walk on the Beach"

A similar, even more acute dilemma arises with digital art. Once a piece of art is on the internet, it can be copied an infinite number of times without proper recognition of authorship or ownership, let alone the payment of royalties for that work.

The ownership of unique assets that can be tracked on the blockchain using blockchain technology offers a solution to this problem and has revolutionized industries where uniqueness is their trading value, such as art, games, or identity.

The technical solution

The **Ethereum Request for Comment 721**, or **ERC 721** standard, comprises a set of contracts that allow Ethereum to implement an API, providing an immutable identity to certain assets on the blockchain. Once that identity is given, those assets can be tracked, valued, sold, and more. The identity of an NFT consists of a pair of two data points:

Contract address + Token ID

Figure 4.3 – Identity of an NFT

The contract address may have different names depending on the industry under consideration. For instance, it may be referred to as the **registrar** contract when dealing with ENS or the **collection** contract when studying art.

It's important to note that with this standard, Ethereum enables connecting an external source, and the smart contract references a third-party server with information about the NFT. This means that if the URI pointed to by the smart contract changes, the information of the NFT may no longer be accessible or may change. Ethereum developers considered storing all the metadata of the assets on the blockchain, but this is prohibitively expensive due to the gas costs associated with registering on the blockchain, which would hinder usability.

The basic contract methods and events for this solution are detailed in ERC 721, as proposed by William Entriken, Dieter Shirley, Jacob Evans, and Nastassia Sachs in 2018. Another valuable source for more information is the Open Zeppelin implementation, which describes each function and method in detail.

The `read` methods we will encounter are as follows:

- `balanceOf(address _owner)`: This method tells us how many NFTs are owned by a specific address
- `ownerOf(uint256 _tokenId)`: This method informs us of the address that owns a particular NFT

Optionally, we will see the metadata extension:

- `name()`: The name of the collection
- `symbol()`
- `tokenURI(uint256 _tokenId)`

The enumeration extension is optional and enables a comprehensive view of the collections with the following methods:

- `totalSupply()`

- `tokenByIndex(uint256 _index)`

- `tokenOfOwnerByIndex(_owner, uint256 _index)`

Here are some important events:

- `Transfer(address indexed _from, address indexed _to, uint256 indexed _tokenId)`: This event is emitted when ownership of the NFT changes. The hashing of this event signature is 0xddf252ad1be2c89b69c2b068fc378daa952ba7f163c4a11628f55a4df523b3ef; we will see it in many queries.

- `Approval(address indexed _owner, address indexed _approved, uint256 indexed _tokenId)`.

- `ApprovalForAll(address indexed _owner, address indexed _operator, bool _approved)`.

The application of NFTs, particularly in games, highlighted the high cost of NFTs as initially proposed. Subsequently, another group of authors proposed the ERC 1155 Multi Token standard, also in 2018. ERC-1155 is used for a combination of both fungible tokens and NFTs within the same contract, saving time and gas costs while reducing redundant code on Ethereum.

We will encounter the following relevant read function method:

`balanceOfBatch(address[] calldata _owners, uint256[] calldata _ids)`: This allows you to query the ownership of multiple addresses regarding certain token IDs

The events are as follows:

- `TransferSingle`

- `TransferBatch`

- `ApprovalForAll`

- `URI`

So far, we have listed the events and functions we will encounter when analyzing NFT data. We learned how to interact with them in *Chapter 2*, so let's proceed directly to understand the use cases that have generated more data using NFTs and build metrics for them.

Blockchain gaming – the GameFi proposal

For each industry, we will briefly review the businesses that are currently active, the players, and the relevant metrics.

These metrics can be expanded depending on the business case. The *Further reading* section contains additional resources.

Introduction to the business landscape

The gaming industry has its own chapter in the blockchain saga and has been remarkably successful in driving the adoption of this technology while reshaping the landscape of rewards and ownership.

The gaming industry has undergone a significant transformation, shifting from a "pay-to-play" model where players were required to purchase physical cartridges, CDs, or subscriptions to access game content, to a "free-to-play" online format. The advent of blockchain technology has further pushed the boundaries by introducing the **Play-to-Earn (P2E)** model. P2E grants property rights to gamers, allowing them to truly own in-game assets. In the past, players might have acquired in-game perks or items, but they had no real ownership, making it impossible to sell or exchange such assets. The integration of NFTs into the gaming ecosystem has brought about real change, providing players with a genuine sense of ownership and paving the way for the convergence of gaming and finance through blockchain technology. This transformation has extended beyond the realm of the games themselves, impacting players' lives outside of the virtual world. Consequently, a new business structure has emerged, known as **gaming guilds**, which are designed to lease relevant in-game assets to players while also offering training and community support to their members.

The rise of blockchain-backed games began in 2018 with Cryptokitties, a game where digital cats could be bred and traded. This game introduced the concept of tradable digital collectibles. A significant milestone followed with Axie Infinity, which onboarded a massive number of non-crypto users into the ecosystem, achieving unprecedented numbers in the industry. Axie Infinity brought mainstream adoption to blockchain gaming. At the time of writing this book, numerous games are being launched, continually pushing the boundaries of innovation.

These blockchain games have created an evolving ecosystem with an economy that extends beyond players. This economy reached non-players, giving them a role, and has even popularized cross-border scholarships as a way to organize players with the support of investors through gaming guilds. This convergence of gaming and finance in a market segment is known as GameFi and is made possible by blockchain technology. Financial concepts and incentives have been integrated into the gaming industry such as yield farming, staking, or governance tokens within games.

GameFi has also democratized access to gaming data, which was previously under the total control of major gaming corporations. Now, with the right knowledge, we can track assets, players, and the entire in-game economy by querying the blockchain.

Analytics

Now, let's analyze a game that claims to have its entire dataset on the Ethereum network, known as the **Wolf Game**. In this game, sheep and wolves compete in games to earn $Wool, the ecosystem's currency.

To participate in the game, players must own a sheep or a wolf. These characters can be acquired in NFT marketplaces such as OpenSea, which we will define further in the *Redefining the art business with blockchain* section later in this chapter. Here is the link to the Wolf Game collection: https:// opensea.io/collection/wolf-game. We can start our analysis by identifying the smart contract of the Wolf Game collection, which is 0x7f36182dee28c45de6072a34d29855bae76dbe2f.

A note on methodology

When working on a project for the first time, especially one that is unfamiliar, we can follow these steps:

1. Define the specific question we want to answer using data.

2. Find one transaction that exemplifies the information required to answer the question.

3. Dissect the transaction, as we learned in *Chapter 2*, to understand how the smart contract logs the data.

Let's apply this methodology:

1. Let's say we want to determine the number of minted sheep and wolves in the Wolf Game. The number of minted NFTs serves as a valuable indicator of an NFT's scarcity.

2. To understand how the smart contract logs the minting data, we will search for a minting transaction. For example, let's consider the minting of **wolf 4618** under the 0xc7fa87b19a6cc7735c49753442fc034fd6ed5d5c1b5250c56eebed428376272e transaction hash.

On Etherscan, the transaction appears as follows:

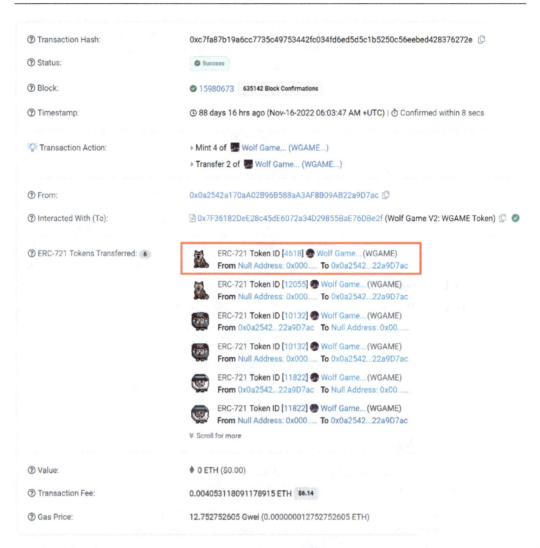

Figure 4.4 – An overview of the Etherscan view of the transaction hash under analysis

The transaction receipt log is displayed as follows:

Transaction Receipt Event Logs

Address 0x7f36182dee28c45de6072a34d29855bae76dbe2f 🔍 ⌄

Name Transfer (index_topic_1 address from, index_topic_2 address to, index_topic_3 uint256 tokenId) View Source

Topics 0 0xddf252ad1be2c89b69c2b068fc378daa952ba7f163c4a11628f55a4df523b3ef

1: from   Dec ⌄ → 0x0000000000000000000000000000000000000000

2: to   Dec ⌄ → 0x0a2542a170aA02B96B588aA3AF8B09AB22a9D7ac

3: tokenId   Dec ⌄ → 4618

Data 0x

Figure 4.5 – Etherscan view of the transaction log under analysis

We can also explore the logs in `Chapter4/Games.ipynb` while following the methodology described in *Chapter 2*, where we retrieve the transaction receipt and decode the logs. The decoded logs reveal the following data structure:

Event name or Topic [0]	**Transfer**
From - Topic [1]	0x0000000000000000000000000000000000000000
To - Topic [2]	0x0a2542a170aA02B96B588aA3AF8B09AB22a9D7ac (the EOA that initiated the transaction)
tokenID - Topic [3]	4618

Table 4.1 – Data structure of the decoded logs

From these results, we can deduce the following:

1. The data we are seeking is within the Ethereum **logs** associated with the smart contract address of the Wolf Game: 0x7f36182dee28c45de6072a34d29855bae76dbe2f.

2. Within these logs, we need to look for "Transfer" events where the "from" address is 0x0000 0000000000000000000000000000000000000000.

3. Finally, we have to count the unique `tokenID` values.

If we translate these steps into a SQL query, we can determine that 13,737 NFTs were minted. The SQL query is as follows:

```
SELECT count (distinct ("topic3")) as total_nfts
FROM ethereum.logs
WHERE "contract_address" = 0x7f36182dee28c45de6072a34d29855bae76dbe2f
AND "topic0" =
0xddf252ad1be2c89b69c2b068fc378daa952ba7f163c4a11628f55a4df523b3ef
AND "topic1" = 0x0000000000000000000000000000000000000000000000000000
000000000000
```

It is worth noting that if a transfer originates "from" an address, `0x0000`, we can interpret this as a minting event. If this address or `0x000dEad` is found in the "to" part of the transaction, it can be considered a burning transfer. In the same sense as with cryptocurrencies, *minting* an NFT signifies their creation, while *burning* means they are sent to an unrecoverable address, effectively removing them from circulation. This can be used to control supply or retire in-game assets that are no longer part of the market.

Another common metric to consider is identifying the **top holders** of a collection. This metric informs us about which addresses hold the most tokens and the quantity they possess. Based on the data structure we examined earlier, we can calculate this metric using the following SQL query:

```
WITH cte as (
select address, nftid, sum (indicator) as indicator
from
      (select "topic1" as address, "topic3" as nftid, -1 as indicator
        from ethereum.logs
        where "contract_address" =
0x7f36182dee28c45de6072a34d29855bae76dbe2f
        AND "topic0" =
0xddf252ad1be2c89b69c2b068fc378daa952ba7f163c4a11628f55a4df523b3ef
        union all
        select "topic2" as address, "topic3" as nftid, 1 as indicator
        from ethereum.logs
        where "contract_address" =
0x7f36182dee28c45de6072a34d29855bae76dbe2f
        AND "topic0" =
0xddf252ad1be2c89b69c2b068fc378daa952ba7f163c4a11628f55a4df523b3ef)
    GROUP BY address, nftid
    HAVING SUM(indicator) > 0)
select address, sum (indicator) as total_holdings
from cte
group by address
order by total_holdings DESC
limit 10
```

This query generates a table with two columns – one listing the hexadecimal addresses of the top holders and another indicating the number of NFTs they hold:

Query results   Wolf game holders

address	total_holdings
0x000000000000000000000000000000000000000000000000000000000000dead	925
0x0000000000000000000000000d3a316d5fa3811553f67d9974e457c37d1c098b8	817
0x0000000000000000000000000d24d79751236cbb715185aab4ea401f2287f9ca	342
0x0000000000000000000000000e10100b574fe551629d336a3b87747d5d5c80a9b	180

Figure 4.6 – Top holders of NFTs

We can verify this information on OpenSea analytics (`https://opensea.io/collection/wolf-game/analytics?tab=items`) to ensure the accuracy of the retrieved data matches the addresses and holdings:

Owners

Top 100

	NAME	WALLET	OWNED	% OWNED
1	BurnAddress	0x0000...dead	925	6.73%
2	D3A316	0xd3a3...98b8	817	5.95%
3	swapshoppro.eth	0x0d24...f9ca	342	2.49%
4	E10100	0xe101...0a9b	180	1.31%

Figure 4.7 – OpenSea analytics top owners

This result can also be validated with state data by selecting the following function:

```
contract.functions.balanceOf(address).call()
```

In `Chapter4/Games.ipynb`, we apply this function to the listed addresses; the results are the same as the transaction data we queried.

To access state data, we must follow these steps:

1. Search for the relevant ABI on Etherscan. For the Wolf Game, we already have the ABI in this book's GitHub repository.

2. Connect to the Ethereum network using Infura.

3. Use the `web3.eth.contract()` method to connect the smart contract address and the ABI.

4. Query the smart contract by executing the `balanceOf()` reading function. In this case, we pass a list of addresses to check the holdings. The result is the same as what we obtained by querying transaction data:

```
top_4_addresses = ['0x00000000000000000000000000000000000000dEaD',
                   '0xD3a316d5fA3811553f67D9974E457C37D1C098B8',
                   '0x0D24d79751236cBb715185aAb4eA401f2287f9CA',
                   '0xe10100B574fE551629d336A3B87747d5d5C80a9B']

for address in top_4_addresses:
    print ("Address {fname}, holds: ".format (fname=address) , wolfContract.functions.balanceOf(address).call())

Address 0x00000000000000000000000000000000000000dEaD, holds:  925
Address 0xD3a316d5fA3811553f67D9974E457C37D1C098B8, holds:  817
Address 0x0D24d79751236cBb715185aAb4eA401f2287f9CA, holds:  342
Address 0xe10100B574fE551629d336A3B87747d5d5C80a9B, holds:  180
```

Figure 4.8 – State data on holdings per address

For additional metrics and insights, consider exploring the Wolf Game dashboard, which is built on Dune: `https://dune.com/gabriela/chapter-4`.

Notably, Axie Infinity, operating on its dedicated chain named Ronin, has made a significant impact on the NFT space, until the hack that occurred in March 2022 for an amount of $600 million in ETH. Ronin has its own block explorer and its transactional data is indexed by all the data providers that we analyzed in *Chapter 2*. One of them, Flipside, maintains an interesting dashboard at `https://flipsidecrypto.xyz/dumplings/axie-infinity-axie-infinity-r5iPOK`.

The Ronin community is also robust and many developers have joined this ecosystem. The official Axie Infinity Discord server (`https://discord.gg/axie`) features a "tools-api-etc" channel offering assistance and information. Builders have created specific endpoints to access in-game data. For example, we can explore the REST API (`https://documenter.getpostman.com/view/23367645/2s7YfPfEGh#intro`) and also the following GraphQL endpoint: `https://axie-graphql.web.app/`.

Sky Mavis has also provided an official API for retrieving game data. To access this API, we must register so that we can obtain an API key. The documentation is available at `https://docs.skymavis.com/reference/general`. We can use this API to extract data about the items the game leader owns in the `Chapter4/Games.ipynb` notebook. This is very valuable information for competing players.

Having analyzed the games vertical, let's delve into another industry where NFTs are being utilized for identity-related purposes.

Identity in the blockchain

As we did in the previous section, we will briefly review some of the initiatives active in the identity business and understand the players and the relevant metrics.

Introduction to the business landscape

Identity has long been a focus area for Web3 initiatives. The online domain faces various challenges related to identity, such as solving identity theft, international credit score transfer, and preventing Sybil attacks, among others.

One noteworthy project is "Proof of Humanity," which aims to create a Sybil-proof list of individuals launched on the Ethereum network. To join the project, an already registered individual must vouch for your profile, thereby expanding the network of trust. The registration span is limited to 2 years to ensure that the registry is continuously updated so that deceased individuals or bots that previously made it into the list are taken out. Identity owners can de-register or update their information. The project's main page highlights various use cases where verified identity can offer significant benefits, including credit scoring, antispam tools, and self-sovereign identity.

A compelling incentive to encourage more individuals to join this network of trust is the concept of **Universal Basic Income** (**UBI**). UBI, in the off-chain world, is a welfare policy by which countries provide every citizen with a fixed, unconditional income. "Proof of Humanity" emulates this policy by distributing a token called $UBI to all successfully registered identities in the protocol. We can find relevant addresses on this web page: `https://kleros.gitbook.io/docs/developer/deployment-addresses`. An interesting $UBI dashboard can be found at `https://dune.com/jeremyarbid/Proof-of-Humanity-Universal-Basic-Income-(UBI)`.

> **Note on Sybil attacks**
>
> A Sybil attack constitutes a security threat to online systems in which one entity seeks to gain control over the network by creating multiple accounts, nodes, or computers. A simple example involves one person creating multiple social media accounts to manipulate a poll's outcome.

The main product that leverages NFTs in this field is the **Blockchain Name Service**. In *Chapter 2*, we introduced the protocol names of **ENS** for **Ethereum Name Service** and **RNS** for **RIF Name Service**. These projects follow the concept of the traditional **Domain Name Service** (**DNS**), which replaced IP addresses with human-readable names for accessing websites. In the same fashion, these protocols lease or sell human-readable names on the blockchain, which help replace the long hex strings that identify an address, making it easier to interact with brands and individuals on the blockchain. An added advantage is that these name services are decentralized and thus impervious to censorship by central authorities.

Several projects are active in addressing this use case, each presenting distinguishable value propositions. Some protocols offer name services for sale, while others provide leasing options, including variations such as subdomains. Most of these projects are built on the common foundation of the ERC-721 standard.

To extract data from these projects, start by locating the documentation and the list of smart contracts that constitute the entire project. Well-established projects typically provide a transparent list of contract addresses, as illustrated here:

Network	Contract address
Ethereum mainnet	0x...
Ethereum testnet (Goerli)	0x...
Polygon mainnet	0x...
Rootstock mainnet	0x...

Table 4.2 – Typical reference table of a project's addresses

This transparency simplifies access and verification. For ENS, the deployed smart contracts can be found at `https://docs.ens.domains/ens-deployments`.

Analytics

The ENS library streamlines interactions with the protocol and some of its applications can be found in `Chapter04/Identity.ipynb`. The following code snippet gets us the owner address of a specific ENS:

```
from ens import ENS
ns = ENS.fromWeb3(web3)
ns.owner("COMPLETE WITH THE ENS OF CHOICE")
```

The protocol comprises two types of smart contracts:

- *Registry*, which manages the minted names
- *Registrar*, which handles the procurement of new domains

The registrar addresses for each domain are as follows:

Domain	Contract address
.eth	0x57f1887a8BF19b14fC0dF6Fd9B2acc9Af147eA85
.art	0x828D6e836e586B53f1da3403FEda923AEd431019
.xyz	0x58774Bb8acD458A640aF0B88238369A167546ef2

Table 4.3 – Registrars' addresses. Source: https://docs.ens.domains/ens-deployments

In this book's GitHub repository, we have added the permanent registrar ABI from Etherscan, which aids in obtaining state data about specific token holders or a particular ENS. The following code snippet provides information about how many NFTs are held by an address:

```
ethregContract.functions.balanceOf(owner_address).call()
```

`Chapter04/Identity.ipynb` shows how to extract additional token information, such as the token ID and expiration date. The token ID corresponds to the hash of the normalized name or label that constitutes the domain. With this information, it is possible to retrieve the token's metadata, such as the associated image (if it exists) from the ENS API available at `https://metadata.ens.domains/docs`.

It is worth noting that the ENS documentation includes a special "ENS Data Guide" with a list of resources. The protocol has enabled a subgraph on **The Graph** service, and there are numerous tables available on Dune's SQL service. Please consider exploring `https://dune.com/makoto/ens`, which provides an overview of the ENS landscape metrics, including total ENS names created, participating addresses, and monthly variations in these metrics.

I invite you to explore these metrics listed for other projects or networks. Here is a list of some of them:

- **Unstoppable domains**: `https://unstoppabledomains.com/`
- **RIF name service**: `https://dev.rootstock.io/rif/rns/mainnet/`
- **Bitcoin name service**: `https://btc.us/`

With that, we have explained what the blockchain name service is and analyzed the sources of data and the main metrics of ENS, which is one of the products that leverages digital uniqueness associated with identity. Currently, only 2% of the addresses that were active in the last year hold an ENS, indicating that there is still much work to be done in the context of identity within the Web3 space.

In the next section, we will examine the impact of digital uniqueness in the world of art.

Redefining the art business with blockchain

In this section, we will briefly review the Web3 landscape, who the active participants are, and some relevant metrics.

Introduction to the business landscape

One of the most significant applications of ERC-721-backed protocols, in terms of transaction volume, is in the field of art. Blockchain technology has had a profound impact on the art business by enabling the trade of unique pieces and tracking authenticity, which is something that investors and galleries invest a lot of time and effort to guarantee. Traditional art players are already active in this field in multiple ways, from venturing into the world of digital art, as exemplified by the Belvedere Museum, which offers 10,000 digital pieces of the Klimt masterpiece "The Kiss," to offering traditional art on Web3 native platforms, expanding their services to a new audience.

Furthermore, companies originally not related to art are exploring the landscape. Covalent recently analyzed the revenues derived from Nike's entry into this technology, with the issuance of NFTs for its iconic sneakers. This move generated nearly $200 million from primary and secondary sales, which represent 0.4% of the revenue of this billion-dollar company in its initial foray into Web3.

New **decentralized applications (dApps)** have emerged, creating a direct connection between artists and consumers, often eliminating intermediaries. One example is **anotherblock.io**, which enables the tokenization of music rights and the distribution of royalties to NFT holders. For instance, a Rihanna song has been tokenized as an NFT with the `0xCB8399D84e17fD5B4e955C716647c7BB2C35Ab63` contract, offering royalties to the holders based on the artist's earnings.

The ecosystem is vast, dynamic, and continuously expanding, offering plenty of questions for data investigators to answer.

The participants in this industry can be categorized as follows:

- Artist
- Marketplace (may or may not be present)
- Client/collector

An **artist** can be an individual or a company that creates a rare and unique piece of artwork, whether it's a painting, a musical composition, or any file that can be uploaded online and registered. The artist may choose to sell it and, in some instances, establish a royalty structure to receive a percentage of each sale after the initial one (secondary sales).

A **marketplace** is a platform, typically a dApp, where art owners looking to sell and clients interested in buying can connect. It facilitates the creation of collections and is visually organized to showcase art pieces, providing all the necessary information and facilitating fund transfers. These marketplaces have evolved into beautifully organized online galleries with thousands of artworks on display. Their revenue is derived from a percentage of the proceeds from each sale conducted on their platform, and they may also charge fees for creating collections or displaying them. Relevant marketplaces include Open Sea, Rarible, Blur, and X2Y2.

Clients, whether they're collectors or art traders, are individuals willing to purchase artwork for personal enjoyment or speculation. If they own an artwork, they may sell it, and if the smart contract allows, a portion of the secondary sale price is transferred to the artist as royalties.

In this structure, the marketplace is optional. An artist can mint their collection and offer it for sale directly, although this approach requires a substantial amount of professional work to attract potential buyers. Marketplaces serve this role.

The art market is constantly evolving, and new players may emerge in the future.

Data extraction

Let's discuss the data extraction process by considering two cases.

Bored Ape collection case

One of the most famous digital art pieces that has been traded is the **Bored Ape Yacht Club** (**BAYC**) NFT. At the time of writing, it has generated 1,307,484 in traded ETH. The use case of the NFT is to serve as the Yacht Club membership card, which grants access to members-only benefits. The company that created this collection is called Yugga Labs and has issued a coin named Ape Coin. Based on this collection's importance in the digital art market, we will use it to learn about data in the NFT artistic world.

According to the Bored Ape collection web page (`https://boredapeyachtclub.com/#/provenance`), the collection address is `0xBC4CA0EdA7647A8aB7C2061c2E118A18a936f13D`:

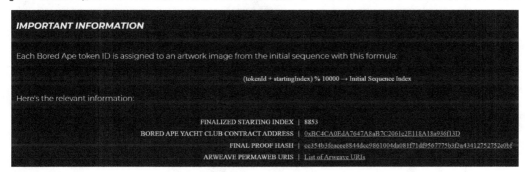

Figure 4.10 – BAYC's address web page

Each Bored Ape will be identified by its token ID. Let's take token ID 6633 as a study sample to analyze further – this can be found in `Chapter04/Art.ipynb`.

With the following script, we can find the owner's address:

```
baContract.functions.ownerOf(6633).call()
```

We can use any API that enables us to query a specific address to search the transfer history of Bored Ape 6633 up to the current owner. In the notebook, we have reviewed a quick search of the response that's retrieved from the Covalent API.

A note on blockchain investigations

Nick Furneaux, when providing hints for blockchain investigations, suggests "*Use the first five or six characters of an address when taking notes. The lengthy addresses of Bitcoin, Ethereum, or any cryptocurrency that uses private keys as its addressing system make it complex for the human eye to process. Using just the first five or six characters makes the string easier for your mind to process and recognize if you see it again.*"

Please also refer to a schematic representation showing the last three transfers of Bored Ape 6633 to the current owner (Neymar Jr.). Note that we use all the characters of the addresses and hashes for editorial purposes, but Nick Furneaux's suggestion has proven to be very useful:

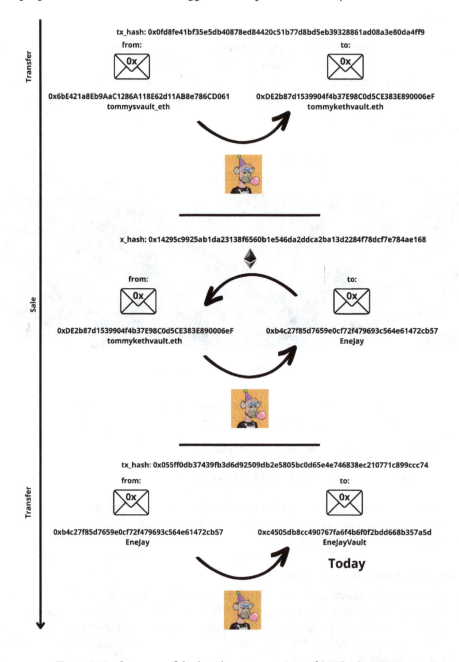

Figure 4.11 – Summary of the last three transactions of BAYC token 6633

If we search the last transfer of the token, we will get the following transaction hash and the details (as seen on Etherscan):

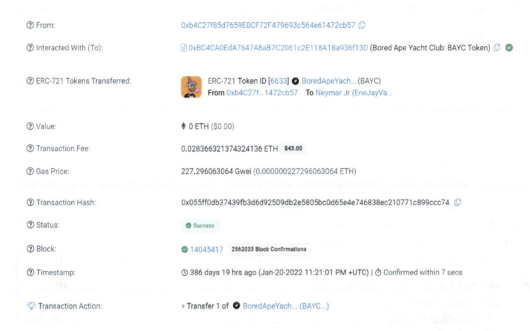

⑦ From:	0xb4C27f85d7659E0CF72F479693c564e61472cb57 📋
⑦ Interacted With (To):	📄 0xBC4CA0EdA7647A8aB7C2061c2E118A18a936f13D (Bored Ape Yacht Club: BAYC Token) 📋 ✅
⑦ ERC-721 Tokens Transferred:	ERC-721 **Token ID** [6633] ● BoredApeYach... (BAYC) From 0xb4C27f...1472cb57 **To** Neymar Jr (EneJayVa...
⑦ Value:	◈ 0 ETH ($0.00)
⑦ Transaction Fee:	0.028366321374324136 ETH **$43.00**
⑦ Gas Price:	227.296063064 Gwei (0.000000227296063064 ETH)
⑦ Transaction Hash:	0x055ff0db37439fb3d6d92509db2e5805bc0d65e4e746838ec210771c899ccc74 📋
⑦ Status:	✅ Success
⑦ Block:	✅ 14045417 **2562033 Block Confirmations**
⑦ Timestamp:	⏱ 386 days 19 hrs ago (Jan-20-2022 11:21:01 PM +UTC)	⏱ Confirmed within 7 secs
⑦ Transaction Action:	▸ Transfer 1 of ● BoredApeYach... (BAYC...)

Figure 4.12 – Etherscan view of the transaction under analysis

A very user-friendly token profile can be found in the marketplaces. For example, for this token, we can follow the link to OpenSea's website: `https://opensea.io/assets/ethereum/0xbc4ca0eda7647a8ab7c2061c2e118a18a936f13d/6633`.

Relevant information such as the price paid, the number of transactions of the token, and more can be extracted from the transaction's **logs**, in the same fashion as we analyzed in the *Blockchain gaming – the GameFi proposal* section.

In the next section, we will explore the marketplaces that have a very relevant role in this new industry.

Marketplaces

As anticipated, marketplaces currently play a significant role in the digital art ecosystem, leading to a high demand for data analysis related to them. To meet this demand, data services are gradually incorporating additional data points and preprocessing raw log tables, enhancing simplicity to facilitate analysts' access to information more easily and quickly.

In Dune, there is a specific table named **nft.trades** that indexes trades from the main marketplaces. According to their documentation (`https://dune.com/docs/data-tables/spellbook/top-tables/nft.trades/`), the trades for the following marketplaces can be found:

- OpenSea
- Rarible
- SuperRare
- CryptoPunks
- Foundation
- LooksRare

Also, in Increment, there is a specific table named `reports.nft_sales_all_chains` with 46 marketplaces in the 20 distinct chains they have indexed. NFT activity is not limited to Ethereum. Depending on the benefits of each chain, users will move their assets from one chain to the other and companies will build products that leverage the best of each of them. As analysts, we have to be ready to conduct or interpret multi-chain analysis, where this Increment tool is particularly useful.

An additional feature made possible thanks to blockchain is the direct distribution of **royalties** on secondary sales. Since the artist's address is known and will always be linked to that piece of art, marketplaces such as OpenSea or Rarible set the possibility to send the author a percentage of secondary sales of the art piece in their smart contracts. This has been solved in the physical world by placing an intermediary that usually takes a significant percentage of the artist's revenue. In Web3, this is done by design with a smart contract.

Each marketplace has its own rules, and they may also vary depending on the market climate. Some marketplaces have the royalty distribution feature marked as optional, so there are collections that may not be generating revenue for the author on secondary sales. What will always be generated is revenue for the platform.

The relevant percentages can be found in the documentation for each marketplace, so it is necessary to go through it to make the right query:

- OpenSea: `https://docs.opensea.io/docs/10-setting-fees-on-secondary-sales`
- Rarible: `https://docs.rarible.org/overview/tokens-fees-royalties/#royalties`

Dune has a `fees` table that we can query with the following SQL snippet:

```
select count (distinct (tx_hash)) as transactions,
       sum (platform_fee_amount_usd) as platform_fee,
       sum (royalty_fee_amount_usd) as authors_royalty,
```

```
        sum(royalty_fee_amount) as total_royalties
from nft.fees
where blockchain='ethereum'
and nft_contract_address= '0xbc4ca0eda7647a8ab7c2061c2e118a18a936f13d'
and project = 'opensea'
```

Another approach is querying the `trades` table and calculating the `fees` percentage out of the price of the sale:

```
select count (distinct ("tx_hash")) as transactions,
       sum ("original_amount")*0.025 as platform_fee
from nft.trades
where nft_contract_address= 0xbc4ca0eda7647a8ab7c2061c2e118a18a936f13d
and platform = 'OpenSea'
```

The result of these queries, among many other metrics, can be found on the Dune dashboard at `https://dune.com/gabriela/chapter-4-nft`.

Floor price and wash trading

Let's look at additional metrics that are relevant for NFTs in the art business.

Floor price: As anticipated in *Chapter 1*, the floor price of a collection can be defined as the minimum price of any NFT at a given time. This price answers the question of how much money is necessary to enter into the collection as a buyer while taking away any additional considerations that may add to the price, such as rarity, the identity of the seller, and so on.

This value may be heavily impacted by outliers and manipulated in the case of collections with centralized ownership, meaning that a small group of people have a large number of the NFTs of that collection, and it is not very liquid. A liquid asset can be rapidly converted into cash while retaining its market value. One way to avoid getting a floor price number that is impacted by outliers is to compare the value in multiple marketplaces or to calculate the median over a certain period.

A query to obtain the median prices for the BAYC collection could look like the following SQL snippet:

```
with cte1 as (select min ("amount_original") as min_price,
         "project" as platform, ----platform
         "block_time"
from nft.trades
where nft_contract_address= 0xbc4ca0eda7647a8ab7c2061c2e118a18a936f13d
and block_time > timestamp '2022-01-31 00:00:00'
and block_time < timestamp '2023-01-31 00:00:00'
and blockchain= 'ethereum'
and project in ('looksrare','opensea')
group by project, block_time)
```

```
select approx_percentile(min_price, 0.5) as floor_price ,
platform   ------   avg (min_price)
from cte1
group by platform
```

The result of the query can be seen in the following graph. The live version of this graph can be found on the Dune dashboard for this chapter at `https://dune.com/gabriela/chapter-4-nft`:

Figure 4.13 – Floor price for 2022

Another source of information for this metric is from specialized websites such as NFT Bank (`https://nftbank.ai/`) and oracles that aggregate data from various sources, both on-chain and off-chain. Although we do not have control over how these sources calculate the price, they can serve as useful points of comparison for our calculations. For Chainlink's response regarding floor price, you can refer to `Chapter4/Art.ipynb`.

Wash trading: Wash trading is the act of artificially creating transactions around a certain asset to inflate its price. This is a form of market manipulation that, in many jurisdictions, is considered illegal in non-crypto financial markets. If we apply the same criteria, we may consider wash trading as a form of fraud as prices do not reflect real demand but rather result from manipulation by the project owners. One of the objectives of project owners is to generate a **fear of missing out** (**FOMO**) around a certain collection. For example, increasing the floor price of a collection and having it appear in marketplace rankings can create a sense of urgency among potential buyers. Another objective may be to profit from the incentive programs launched by marketplaces to attract users.

A great set of two articles written by @hildobby highlights that wash trading is widespread in the NFT world and can significantly impact our metrics during analysis. The author proposes some basic checks to identify wash trading:

- When the buyer and seller addresses are same:

Figure 4.14 – Premise 1 of wash trading

- When the owner of two addresses transfers the same NFT between those addresses repeatedly:

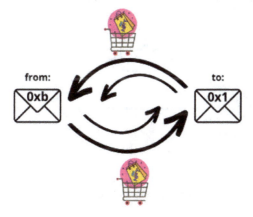

Figure 4.15 – Premise 2 of wash trading

- If the same addresses purchased or sold the same NFT more than three times:

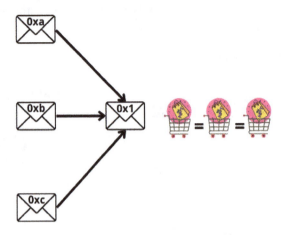

Figure 4.16 – Premise 3 of wash trading

- If the buyer and seller were funded by the same "mother" address:

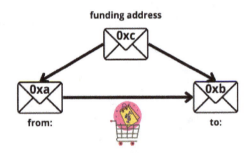

Figure 4.17 – Premise 4 of wash trading

The articles can be found in the Dune community blogs. You can get the queries by clicking on the dashboard's titles: `https://dune.com/hildobby/nfts-wash-trading`.

Dune also has a table named `nft.wash_trades` that specifically breaks down each transaction according to the wash trading criteria just described. A brief explanation of the columns of the table can be seen here:

	Criteria	Column Name
1	When the buyer and seller addresses are the same	`filter_1_same_buyer_seller`
2	When the owner of two addresses transfers the same NFT between those two addresses repeatedly	`Filter_2_back_and_forth_trade`
3	If the same addresses purchased or sold the same NFT more than three times	`Filter_3_bought_or_sold_3x`
4	If the buyer and seller were funded by the same "mother" address	`filter_4_first_funded_by_same_wallet`

Table 4.4 – Relevant columns of nft.wash_trades

The final column contains a flag for `is_wash_trade`, which can be either `true` or `false`. With a simple query, we can check whether there are wash trading transactions on any project, or calculate the percentage of wash trading for a project. For example, let's query the percentage of wash trading transactions for the BAYC project:

```
with is_wash as (select count (distinct tx_hash) as wash_trades, nft_
contract_address
from nft.wash_trades
where is_wash_trade = true
and nft_contract_address= 0xBC4CA0EdA7647A8aB7C2061c2E118A18a936f13D
group by nft_contract_address),
total_tx as (
select count (distinct tx_hash) as wash_trades_total, nft_contract_
address
from nft.wash_trades
where nft_contract_address=0xBC4CA0EdA7647A8aB7C2061c2E118A18a936f13D
group by nft_contract_address)
select wash_trades, wash_trades_total, (CAST(wash_trades AS double) /
CAST(wash_trades_total AS double))*100 as wash_trading_percentage
from total_tx t
left join is_wash i
on t.nft_contract_address=i.nft_contract_address
```

The result is that 13% of the transactions comply with one or more of the wash trading conditions listed here:

Query results Wash trading percentage on BAYC		
Wash trades	Total trades	WT Percentage (%)
5451	41935	13.00

Figure 4.18 – Wash trades of the BAYC project

This database offered by Dune is an excellent source to study projects before investing.

A complete list of additional motifs and patterns, along with a categorization of the level of complexity involved in the wash trading schema, is presented in the paper *Market Microstructure of Non-Fungible Tokens*, by Mayukh Mukhopadhyay and Kaushik Ghosh, and is referenced in the *Further reading* section.

A word on anti-money laundering (AML) practices

Money laundering and terror financing may seem unrelated to our work, but identifying abnormal money flows heavily relies on data analysis, and government attention is increasingly turning to the world of Web3.

Pieces of art have been used as a venue for money laundering in the past. In the traditional art market, various entities such as galleries, auction houses, dealers, and more interact and have knowledge that supports pricing in a relatively controlled environment. However, the Web3 market is intentionally more open, with anyone able to create and sell a collection without intermediaries. The price is determined by the interaction of supply and demand, and value can fluctuate subjectively. AML practitioners see a risk of money laundering occurring in this environment.

The sorts of crimes that AML provisions try to avoid are serious, and analysts be aware when some abnormal patterns appear. Examples of suspicious patterns may include constant outliers in the floor price of some NFTs or instances of wash trading. A recent paper issued by the US Government named *Study of the Facilitation of Money Laundering and Terror Finance through the Trade in Works of Art* mentioned wash trading as a way to self-launder flows of money in the following terms: "*Furthermore, NFTs can be used to conduct self-laundering, where criminals may purchase an NFT with illicit funds and proceed to transact with themselves to create records of sales on the blockchain. The NFT could then be sold to an unwitting individual who would compensate the criminal with clean funds not tied to a prior crime.*"

Summary

In this chapter, we delved into the world of NFTs, exploring their structure and gaining insights into acquiring data for three crucial use cases. We took a deep dive into the game use case, with the analysis of the Wolf Game. Additionally, we examined ENS, shedding light on its role in online identity. Finally, we ventured into the expansive and ever-evolving art ecosystem, where we covered the activities of artists and marketplaces and generated metrics related to floor price and wash trading. In all these cases, we combined metrics derived from transactional data duly showcased on a Dune dashboard (`https://dune.com/gabriela/chapter-4-nft`) and state data in this book's Jupyter notebooks.

It is important to note that the applications we've explored here are just the tip of the iceberg. The NFT landscape is incredibly diverse, and we might encounter requests to analyze NFTs in various other domains, such as fashion, proof-of-attendance protocols (POAPs) for specific events, government registries undergoing migration, or even non-nominative airplane tickets, as exemplified by TravelX.

Having the ability to comprehend these diverse NFT products poses intriguing questions that open new avenues for exploration. If we join on-chain data with Web2 data like some initiatives are doing (for example, `https://www.spindl.xyz/`), we can enhance the user base profiling of the participants of a certain NFT collection and improve the community's engagement, develop more targeted features, and improve our product based on data-driven decisions.

In the upcoming chapter, we'll shift our focus to the **decentralized finance (DeFi)** industry, where we'll explore its products and their impact.

Further reading

To complement this chapter, the following links may help:

- Technical introduction

  - More on the EIP 1155 proposal: `https://ethereum.org/en/developers/docs/standards/tokens/erc-1155/`

  - More on the EIP 721 proposal: `https://eips.ethereum.org/EIPS/eip-721`

  - Implementation by Open Zeppelin: `https://docs.openzeppelin.com/contracts/3.x/api/token/erc721#ERC721`

- How to build, deploy, and mint an NFT with Web3.py in Google Colab. Please have a look at these four videos:

  i. *Build a Solidity 0.8.12 NFT Smart Contract 2022*: `https://www.youtube.com/watch?v=SQ-chPSNgGw&list=PLw-9a9yL-pt0tD7ZBci5ybHy-T2XuHBtV&index=41`

  ii. *Compile an NFT Smart Contract with Python*: `https://www.youtube.com/watch?v=HOJ-Xl9_FYg&list=PLw-9a9yL-pt0tD7ZBci5ybHy-T2XuHBtV&index=42`

  iii. *Deploy an NFT Smart Contract with Python*: `https://www.youtube.com/watch?v=1L5s9FDYo64&list=PLw-9a9yL-pt0tD7ZBci5ybHy-T2XuHBtV&index=44`

  iv. *Interact with an NFT Smart Contract in Python*: `https://www.youtube.com/watch?v=DjMoJEnnvXs&list=PLw-9a9yL-pt0tD7ZBci5ybHy-T2XuHBtV&index=45`

- Games:

  - A very interesting analysis of the Game Fi landscape by Covalent: `https://www.covalenthq.com/blog/gamefi-ebook/`

  - Interesting analysis on a game NFT: `https://dune.com/sunflower_land/analytics`

- Identity

  - More on proof of humanity: `https://kleros.gitbook.io/docs/products/proof-of-humanity/proof-of-humanity-tutorial`

  - How the hashing occurs: `https://docs.ens.domains/contract-api-reference/name-processing`

  - ENS data guide: `https://docs.ens.domains/dapp-developer-guide/ens-data-guide`

  - ENS as NFTs: `https://docs.ens.domains/dapp-developer-guide/ens-as-nft`

- Art:

  - How Nike won with NFTs. (n.d.). *Blockchain Data for the New Economy* | Covalent: `https://www.covalenthq.com/blog/how-nike-won-with-nfts/`

  - *NIKE, Inc. Reports fiscal 2022 fourth quarter and full year results.* (2022, June 27). NIKE, Inc. - Investor Relations: `https://investors.nike.com/investors/news-events-and-reports/investor-news/investor-news-details/2022/`

NIKE-Inc.-Reports-Fiscal-2022-Fourth-Quarter-and-Full-Year-Results/default.aspx

- The traditional Belvedere Museum and the Klimt's NFTs: A digital declaration of love. (n.d.). Belvedere Museum Wien | Startseite: `https://www.belvedere.at/en/digital-declaration-love`

- Rihanna's song: `https://cdn.anotherblock.io/payouts/2.0/bbhmm.pdf`

- The Etherscan page of Rihanna's song: `https://etherscan.io/address/0xCB8399D84e17fD5B4e955C716647c7BB2C35Ab63`

- Documentation on the `nft.trades` table: `https://dune.com/docs/tables/spells/nft.trades/`

- The links to the Dune community blog with more information on wash trading: `https://community.dune.com/blog/nft-wash-trading-on-ethereum` and `https://dune.com/blog/wash-trading-2-blur`

- Mukhopadhyay, Mayukh and Ghosh, Kaushik. (2021). *Market Microstructure of Non-Fungible Tokens*. SSRN Electronic Journal. 10.2139/ssrn.3934676. URL: `https://www.researchgate.net/publication/356192381_Market_Microstructure_of_Non_Fungible_Tokens`

- *Study of the Facilitation of Money Laundering and Terror Finance through the Trade in Works of Art*: `https://home.treasury.gov/system/files/136/Treasury_Study_WoA.pdf` Page 25

- Furneaux, Nick. *Investigating Cryptocurrencies, Chapter 10*. Understanding, Extracting, and Analyzing Blockchain Evidence, Wiley, 2018

- Some of the best Reach, Retention, and Revenue analyses can be found at `https://0xatomist.notion.site/`

- An excellent Dune user to follow for NFTs analysis is @hildobby: `https://dune.com/hildobby`

5
Exploring Analytics on DeFi

There are two groups of products that drive the most transactions in the current state of Web3: NFTs, as we discussed in *Chapter 4*, and **decentralized finance** (**DeFi**), which we will explore in this chapter.

DeFi takes its name in opposition to the centralized characteristic of the current financial system. According to the book *How to DeFi: Beginner*, by CoinGecko, "*Decentralized Finance or DeFi is a movement that allows users to utilize financial services such as borrowing, lending, and trading without the need to rely on centralized entities.*" DeFi is not a single product but a series of projects trying to address financial demand in the Web3 space.

These projects make use of the concept of **composability**, which involves building upon parts created by other parties. It is often illustrated as building with Lego blocks, where developers combine various components to construct new infrastructures.

DeFi has introduced products that were once exclusive to central banks, such as the minting of new coins. Currently, some protocols enable the lending and borrowing of funds for a fee purely dependent on the liquidity of the pool and not external factors. These projects offer varying degrees of decentralization. For example, in the minting offer explained previously, we can encounter a stablecoin issued by a centralized entity named Tether or a decentralized option such as DAI, a protocol composed of a set of smart contracts with no central authority.

DeFi has also expanded its offerings to other native Web3 businesses, such as bridges between chains and flash loans. We will explain these in more detail in the subsequent sections:

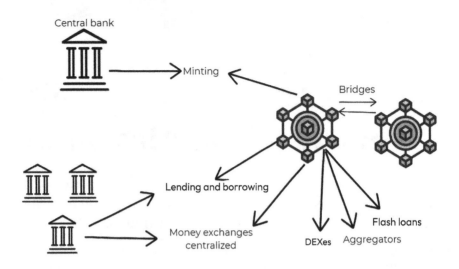

Figure 5.1 – Bank services and blockchain services

The disparities in financial services across the population are nothing new, and many of these DeFi projects aim to expand the reach of financial services wherever there is internet access. As Web3 analysts, we can leverage one of the main characteristics of Web3 – **transparency** – to unlock more value and help make these projects sustainable. Financial data that was traditionally limited to VIP analysts or released to the market at different times is now open for us to read, combine, and extract valuable insights to work on. Blockchain has democratized access; it is on us to learn how to read it and extract actionable insights.

To generate value with our work, it is essential to understand not only the data generated but also the DeFi business flow. As we did in *Chapter 4*, we will delve into fundamental protocol metrics, offering quick insights into each protocol's structure and user composition, but also those metrics that explain how a project generates revenue, reaches customers, deals with potential threats, and other relevant aspects.

In this chapter, we will explore the data structure and the business rationale of the following:

- ERC-20 tokens and stablecoins
- DEXs and aggregators
- Lending and borrowing (with a comment on flash loans)
- Bridges

This list of products is not exhaustive of the DeFi space. There are many other offers, such as decentralized derivatives, insurance, governance, lotteries, and more.

Technical requirements

The technical requirements listed in *Chapter 4* also apply to this chapter. We will be using indexed data available in SQL table services like **Dune Analytics**, **Increment**, and **Flipside**. To follow along, please open an account on any of these platforms by following the links provided in *Chapter 2*. Transactional data is queried with SQL services, and the syntax varies, depending on the query engines.

You can find Jupyter notebooks containing the examples discussed in this chapter in this book's GitHub repository at `https://github.com/PacktPublishing/Data-Science-for-Web3/tree/main/Chapter05`. We recommend reading through the code files in the `Chapter05` folder to follow along.

Stablecoins and other tokens

According to Coinbase, "*A stablecoin is a digital currency that is pegged to a "stable" reserve asset such as the US dollar or gold.*" Given that unpegged cryptocurrencies such as Bitcoin or Ethereum are so volatile, stablecoins have become a reliable medium of exchange. The main stablecoins, according to their market cap at the time of writing, are listed in *Figure 5.2*:

All	Fiat-backed	Crypto-backed	Hybrid	Algorithmic		
# Symbol	Mechanism	Price	Volume 24h	Market Cap ↓	7d %
1 USDT	Fiat-backed	$1.000	$14,690,385,099	$83,650,374,602	-0%
2 USDC	Fiat-backed	$1.001	$1,629,201,996	$27,299,501,274	-1%
3 DAI	Crypto-backed	$1.001	$49,056,353	$4,287,102,528	-0%
4 BUSD	Fiat-backed	$1.000	$1,278,935,022	$3,968,516,424	-2%
5 TUSD	Fiat-backed	$1.000	$883,204,329	$2,844,004,827	-3%
6 FRAX	Hybrid	$1.001	$3,563,941	$1,005,435,036	-0%

Figure 5.2 – Crypto panic stablecoins ranking

Stablecoins are a specific category of tokens that are linked to the value of external assets, providing price stability. There are various types of stablecoins, including those whose value follows the value of a government-issued currency such as the US dollar (named fiat currencies), cryptocurrencies, and commodities such as gold. To maintain the "peg," stablecoin teams have explored many paths. This can be seen in the "Mechanism" column in *Figure 5.2*.

The main stablecoins are pegged to fiat ("fiat-backed"), meaning that the companies issuing such tokens only do so if they have the backup money deposited in financial institutions. Examples of such stablecoins are USDT and USDC.

Crypto-backed stablecoins rely on smart contract protocols that issue stablecoins backed by a basket of other cryptocurrencies. These protocols balance offer and demand to ensure price stability by controlling interest loan rates to influence buyers' and borrowers' behavior. The system is overcollateralized to ensure price stability when there is high volatility and mainly works as a lender system. The main example of this mechanism is the token named DAI. It is issued by MakerDAO and is currently backed by a mixture of centralized and decentralized assets, such as USDC, Ethereum, Wrapped Bitcoin, and others.

Stablecoins can be created to mirror the value of the cryptocurrencies supporting them or to mimic the value of a fiat currency. An example of the former is the **wrapped** version of an asset, often referred to as a "wrapped token," which is a representation of an underlying asset, typically a cryptocurrency or digital asset, that has been tokenized and made compatible with a specific blockchain or network. The process of "wrapping" involves locking the original asset (for example, Bitcoin) on its native blockchain and then issuing the corresponding equivalent token on another blockchain, such as Ethereum. This is what happens with **Wrapped Bitcoin** (**WBTC**), which represents Bitcoin on the Ethereum blockchain, allowing Bitcoin to be used within the Ethereum ecosystem for decentralized applications, DeFi platforms, and other purposes.

Even though non-stable tokens emerged historically before stablecoins, it is easier to understand the concept of a token by learning about stablecoins. A **token** is simply a representation of value on the blockchain and such value can be derived from any rationale. For instance, some tokens represent ownership in a particular project, access to services, or even serve as part of a meme or cultural movement. Notably, some tokens, such as Dogecoin, which started as a meme, have achieved significant market capitalization, demonstrating the diversity of tokens in the cryptocurrency space. Today, such a meme coin is the eighth cryptocurrency in the market cap.

Now that we know the business case, let's delve into the data structure.

Understanding tokens, native assets, and the ERC-20 data structure

Cryptocurrency serves as the native asset of a blockchain, such as BTC in the Bitcoin chain, ETH in the Ethereum chain, and RBTC on the Rootstock chain. Its primary function is often to pay transaction fees on the network (gas fees) and incentivize validators/nodes to maintain the security of the cryptocurrency's network.

In contrast, tokens are created over an existing blockchain and are not native to the blockchain itself. Stablecoins, pool tokens, and all ERC-20 tokens in the Ethereum ecosystem are examples of tokens.

To build tokens, developers utilize the ERC-20 standard and its subsequent evolutions, which introduces a standard for functional tokens and ensures their fungibility. Recall that fungible refers to assets or tokens that are identical in value and can be exchanged on a one-to-one basis, with no distinction between individual units of the same type. The ERC-20 standard was initially introduced in 2015 and gained official recognition through an **Ethereum Improvement Proposal** (**EIP**) authored by Ethereum founder Vitalik Buterin and Ethereum developer Fabian Vogelsteller in 2017.

The smart contract that follows those methods and events is called ERC-20-compliant and is the contract that will maintain the registry of the tokens emitted, which is why it is very relevant for the analyst to learn about its basic characteristics.

The function methods we will encounter are as follows:

- `totalSupply()`: To return the total supply of tokens in the contract.
- `balanceOf()`: To read the address balance.
- `transfer()`: To transfer tokens from the sender's account to another.
- `transferFrom()`: To spend an allowance. This is a function that's called by the spender that implies two operations – that is, transferring the amount being spent and reducing the allowance by such an amount.
- `approve()`: To allow the spender to withdraw from the token owner's account multiple times, up to the approved value amount.
- `allowance()`: To return the amount allowed for withdrawal from the token owner's account.

It is possible to find the `mint` and `burn` functions, which modify the total supply of tokens according to a specific business logic. Here are some optional functions:

- `name()`: Returns the name of the token
- `symbol()`: Returns the symbol of the token
- `decimals()`: Returns the number of decimals the token uses

Here are some important events:

- `transfer`: This event is triggered by the `transfer()` function. The same considerations explained in *Chapter 4* regarding minting and burning apply, if a transfer originates "from" an address such as `0x0000`, we can interpret this as a minting event. If this address or `0x000dEad` is found in the `to` part of the transaction, it can be considered a burning transfer. Minting signifies their creation while burning means they are sent to an unrecoverable address, removing them from circulation. The function's hash is `0xddf252ad1be2c89b69c2b068fc378daa952ba7f163c4a11628f55a4df523b3ef`.
- `approval`: This event is triggered by the `approve()` function with the allowance value and the spender address.

Hands-on example

Now that we know the basics, let's go to the Jupyter notebook (`Chapter05/Stablecoins.ipynb`) where we will connect to the DAI contract (`0x6B175474E89094C44Da98b954EedeAC495271d0F`) and extract the public view information.

A **view** function means that it does not change the state data, so it can be executed on a single node instead of having every node in the blockchain run it. This kind of function does not generate a transaction and does not cost gas.

To inspect the DAI contract, we will use DAI's ABI, which can be found in this book's repository. Let's start by extracting the balance of a certain address with the following code snippet:

```
daiContract.functions.
balanceOf('0x60FaAe176336dAb62e284Fe19B885B095d29fB7F').call()*10**-18
```

The relevant ERC-20 events are stored in the transaction logs. Let's analyze the `0x2a9317882853dc5e0193a76dab76b29e4dc8045718af7925d8d166cdb0eec637` transaction, which involves a transfer of 120 DAIs between two addresses:

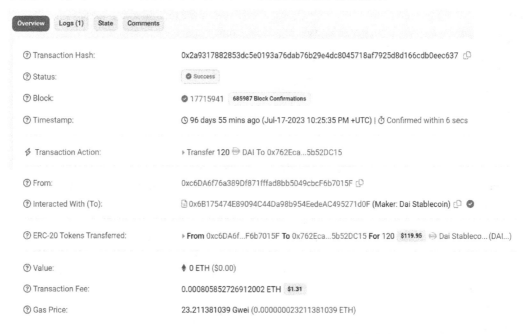

Figure 5.3 – DAI transfer transaction (source: https://etherscan.io/
tx/0x2a9317882853dc5e0193a76dab76b29e4dc8045718af7925d8d166cdb0eec637)

If we search for the transaction logs, we'll receive the following information:

Figure 5.4 – DAI transfer transaction logs (source: https://etherscan.io/
tx/0x2a9317882853dc5e0193a76dab76b29e4dc8045718af7925d8d166cdb0eec637)

The data we can see here is within the Ethereum **logs** associated with the smart contract address of
DAI: `0x6b175474e89094c44da98b954eedeac495271d0f`.

The raw log structure looks like this:

Event name or Topic [0]	Transfer (or `0xddf252ad1be2c89b69c2b068fc378daa952ba7f163c4a11628f55a4df523b3ef`)
From - Topic [1]	`0xc6DA6f76a389Df871fffad8bb5049cbcF6b7015F`
To - Topic [2]	`0x762EcaaF67097b3eb66a9a6904f42b835b52DC15`
wad - Topic [3]	`0x000000000000000000000000000000000000000000000068155a43676e00000` (or `120000000000000000000`)

Table 5.1 – The raw log structure

A **wad** is a decimal number with 18 digits of precision that is represented as an integer. In this
transaction, it represents the number of tokens transacted, which is 120. If we paste the wad value
in a hexadecimal-to-decimal converter such as the one at `https://www.rapidtables.com/
convert/number/hex-to-decimal.html`, it will show the decimal representation with 18 digits.

All the data suppliers we studied in *Chapter 2* have special tables that store transaction logs with
varying levels of preprocessing. The most basic versions are the raw logs to more filtered versions,
which display only ERC 20 token transfers and the prices of the tokens at the time of the transfer.
One example is Flipside, which has a specific table named `core__fact_token_transfers`
that contains all the events on the Ethereum blockchain with the name `'Transfer'`; that refers to
a token address. Similarly, Dune Analytics spells enable a similar table named `erc20_ethereum.
evt_Transfer`, and Increment has a model named `token balance`.

By aggregating this data, we can derive a wide variety of metrics. Let's see the calculation of the DAI current supply by leveraging the `erc20_ethereum.evt_Transfer` table:

```
WITH current_supply AS
(
    SELECT
    cast (tr.value as double)/ 1e18 AS supply
    FROM erc20_ethereum.evt_Transfer tr
    WHERE "contract_address" =
0x6b175474e89094c44da98b954eedeac495271d0f -- DAI
    and tr."from" = 0x0000000000000000000000000000000000000000
UNION ALL
    SELECT
  - cast (tr.value as double)/ 1e18 AS supply
    FROM erc20_ethereum.evt_Transfer tr
    WHERE "contract_address" =
0x6b175474e89094c44da98b954eedeac495271d0f -- DAI
    and tr."to" = 0x0000000000000000000000000000000000000000
)
select sum (supply)/1000000000 as supply
from current_supply
```

In this query, we calculate the DAI current supply by aggregating the transfers within the DAI contract address. Here, we do the following:

- The query uses a **Common Table Expression (CTE)** named `current_supply` to structure the data.

- The first part of the CTE calculates the total supply increase by summing the transferred amounts (converted from wei to DAI), where DAI is transferred *from* the zero address (`0x000000000 0000000000000000000000000000000`). This represents the creation of new DAI tokens.

- The second part of the CTE calculates the total supply decrease by summing the transferred amounts (also converted from wei to DAI), where DAI is transferred *to* the zero address. This represents the burning or removal of DAI tokens from circulation.

- The main query then calculates the final total supply by subtracting the total supply decrease from the total supply increase (that is, supply increase – supply decrease).

- The result is divided by 1,000,000,000 to convert it into a billion DAI.

In summary, this query finds the net change in the total supply of DAI tokens by taking into account both minting and burning transactions and then converting the result to a billion DAI.

We propose an additional metrics logic in the following dashboard: `https://dune.com/ gabriela/dai-cockpit`. Additionally, there is a great open source stablecoin dashboard available at `https://dune.com/hagaetc/stablecoins`.

This same analysis can be applied to any ERC-20 token; it's not necessarily limited to stablecoins. For instance, if we take the MKR token as an example, an excellent open source dashboard can be found at `https://dune.com/livethelife/mkr`.

A pivotal aspect of ERC-20 tokens is their seamless interchangeability within the Ethereum network. This characteristic of ERC-20 tokens plays a crucial role in the operation of **decentralized exchanges** (**DEXs**). DEXs leverage the ERC-20 standard to provide users with the ability to trade a myriad of tokens directly from their wallets, without the need for intermediaries. This connection between ERC-20 tokens and DEXs forms the cornerstone of the DeFi space, empowering users to trade, invest, and participate in financial activities.

Understanding DEX

Cryptocurrencies can be exchanged through various methods, including **peer-to-peer** (**P2P**) trading, **centralized exchanges** (**CEXs**), and DEXs. Each method has its advantages and characteristics:

- **P2P**: In this method, two parties directly buy and sell cryptocurrencies among themselves without intermediaries. It prioritizes privacy and enables a wide range of payment options, making it accessible to users worldwide. However, to ensure the completion of the transfer, certain players have appeared that may act as intermediaries for a small fee, such as escrow services, rating platforms, or dispute resolution services.

- **CEX**: This method offers cryptocurrency exchange services to users who have an account on their platform. It primarily matches buyers with sellers using an order book, where market makers and takers place their orders. The CEX's revenue is generated through transaction fees on each facilitated trade. Major CEXs include Binance, OKX, Coinbase, and Crypto.com. The CEX also verifies the identity of each person opening an account, following the regulations of the relevant country. These exchanges are user-friendly and offer liquidity and a wide range of trading pairs. They generally act as the entry point for many users starting in crypto. The term "centralized" refers to the exchange's control over the funds exchanged within it. This has several implications: as users are not in custody of their assets, if the CEX is attacked or becomes insolvent for any reason (such as a bank run), there is a risk of losing funds.

- **DEX**: A DEX operates through smart contracts without the involvement of third-party entities and prioritizes user control, privacy, and security. It allows users to exchange assets while keeping control of their funds in their wallets until the trade is completed. DEXs have gained popularity and, during the 2021 bull run, surpassed the amount of money traded in CEXs. However, liquidity on DEXs is often lower compared to CEXs.

Now, let's analyze some characteristics of DEXs further:

- **Custody of funds**: Users do not delegate the custody of their funds to a third party.

- **No identification required**: Users can freely interact with a DEX without the need for any form of identification. All that is required is an address to connect to the DEX.

- **High gas fees**: DEX transactions often incur higher gas fees on the blockchain compared to CEX trades.

- **Liquidity problems and slippage**: Slippage refers to the difference between the expected price of an asset and the actual price at which the trade is executed. As liquidity is provided by users rather than a centralized entity, the size of a trade can impact the asset's price. When a large trade is executed, it may cause the price to move unfavorably, resulting in slippage. This means the trader ends up paying a slightly higher price when buying or receiving a slightly lower price when selling than what they anticipated. Slippage is a reality in DeFi trading, especially in less liquid markets.

- **Impermanent loss**: This is a potential risk that's faced by liquidity providers in **automated market maker** (**AMM**) platforms. When a liquidity provider adds funds to a liquidity pool, they contribute assets to be traded on the platform. As trades occur, the relative value of the assets in the pool can change due to market fluctuations. If the price of one asset in the pool moves significantly compared to the other asset, the liquidity provider may experience an impermanent loss. This loss is "impermanent" because it only materializes if the liquidity provider decides to withdraw their funds from the pool.

- **Complex user experience and learning curve**: Interacting with DEX protocols can still be challenging for DeFi users, and the overall user experience may require improvement. Concepts such as slippage or impermanent loss still affect the trading experience.

- **Bugs and exploits**: Like any smart contract-based system, DEXs may be susceptible to bugs and security exploits.

To analyze the analytics of a DEX, we need to understand where the liquidity is locked, how trading pairs are organized, and how the smart contract generates revenue. This way, we will be able to approach the relevant smart contract swiftly.

Hands-on example – pools and AMM

To understand DEXs, two important concepts need to be introduced: liquidity pools and AMM. DEXs use liquidity pools and AMM to facilitate trading activity, also known as **swaps**.

Liquidity pools are token reserves that enable the user to exchange tokens with it. Anyone can open a pool by providing the necessary funds and without the need to seek permission from any central authority. The liquidity is allocated within a curve price and an algorithm places the bids and asks to execute the swaps. Chainlink defines **AMMs** as *"algorithmic "money robots" to make it easy for individual traders to buy and sell crypto assets. Instead of trading directly with other people as with a traditional order book, users trade directly through the AMM."*

One prominent DEX is **Uniswap**, which uses liquidity pools and AMM. The landing page looks as follows:

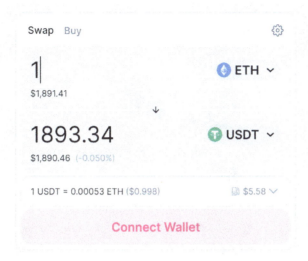

Figure 5.5 – The home page of Uniswap (source: https://app.uniswap.org/#/swap)

Uniswap has a pool dashboard at `https://info.uniswap.org/#/pools` that contains some basic analytics of the active liquidity pools. At the time of writing, the first pool in **TVL** and **Volume** is the USDC/ETH pair (`https://info.uniswap.org/#/pools/0x88e6a0c2ddd26feeb64f039a2c41296fcb3f5640`):

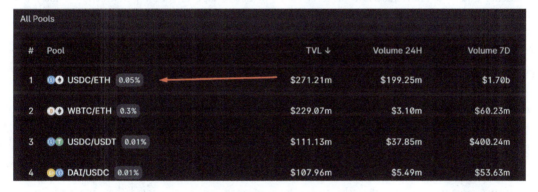

Figure 5.6 – The All Pools dashboard

The smart contract address of the pool is `https://etherscan.io/address/0x88e6a0c2ddd26feeb64f039a2c41296fcb3f5640`.

By programmatically exploring the pool's state data on `Chapter05/Liquidity_pool.ipynb`, we can identify the tokens that compose the pool by using the Pool ABI and reading the smart contract data with the following code snippet:

```
poolContract.functions.token0().call()
poolContract.functions.token1().call()
```

The result is as follows:

- Token 0: `0xA0b86991c6218b36c1d19D4a2e9Eb0cE3606eB48` or USDC

- Token 1: `0xC02aaA39b223FE8D0A0e5C4F27eAD9083C756Cc2` or wETH

Both are stablecoins, with one following the US dollar and the other representing the native Ethereum asset in wrapped form.

To obtain the balance locked of each token, we can use `erc_20.abi`, which is available in this book's GitHub repository, and query the pool with the following code snippet:

```
web3.eth.contract(address=token0, abi=erc_abi)
```

More on the available view functions can be found in the documentation: `https://docs.uniswap.org/contracts/v3/reference/core/interfaces/pool/IUniswapV3PoolState`.

To extract information from transactional data, we need to dig deeper into logs. Let's review a swap transaction and try to understand how the information we need is logged. The swap transaction to analyze is `0x78490143b8a80b23752bd305b51c7796add5373af089059beb3920c8e431ae78` and is executed in the `0x3041cbd36888becc7bbcbc0045e3b1f144466f5f` pool, which swaps between USDC and USDT.

On Etherscan (`https://etherscan.io/tx/0x78490143b8a80b23752bd305b51c7796add5373af089059beb3920c8e431ae78/`), we can see the following:

- From or sender: `0xaDAf0dA2F42bf54E2Ccf455F795A04ECD744138B`

- To: `0x3fC91A3afd70395Cd496C647d5a6CC9D4B2b7FAD` (Uniswap: Universal Router)

Nowadays, most swaps do not directly impact the pool smart contract. Instead, they interact with a Router smart contract, such as a Uniswap Universal smart contract. The router's mission is to take user-defined parameters (such as maximum slippage or swap recipient) and execute the necessary swaps to reach the trader's goal. The router can combine multiple pools and even NFT marketplaces and is optimized to find the lowest prices and lowest gas cost.

The transaction summary is as follows:

⚡ Transaction Action: ▸ Swap 182,509 ◉ XPR For 186.682219 💚 USDT On 🦄 Uniswap V2

▸ Swap 186.682219 💚 USDT For 186.134745 Ⓢ USDC On 🦄 Uniswap V2

Figure 5.7 – Transaction swaps

From *Figure 5.7*, we can interpret that the user, in one transaction, carried out a swap of XPR for USDT and later interacted with the pool under analysis to swap USDT for USDC.

Figure 5.8 shows a partial snapshot of the transaction logs page. The last log in particular contains valuable information:

Figure 5.8 – Swap log

Figure 5.8 shows that the relevant information for the swap is located in the logs of the pool address. As you may recall from *Chapter 2*, `topic_0` is the function signature. In this case, `0xd78ad95fa46c994b6551d0da85fc275fe613ce37657fb8d5e3d130840159d822` is the **swap** function.

Additional relevant functions are the mint or add liquidity function, which has a signature of `0x4c209b5fc8ad50758f13e2e1088ba56a560dff690a1c6fef26394f4c03821c4f`, and the burn or remove liquidity function, which has a signature of `0xdccd412f0b1252819cb1fd330b93224ca42612892bb3f4f789976e6d81936496`.

When liquidity is added or removed, the **liquidity providers (LPs)** receive LP tokens that represent their stake in the pool. These LP tokens can be traded in a secondary market, accrue interest, and sent to the pool when you're looking to extract the liquidity back to the LP.

If we interact with the `ethereum.logs` table in Dune, we can extract the number of swaps carried out by the pool, as follows:

```
select count (*) as n_trades
from ethereum.logs
where contract_address= 0x3041cbd36888becc7bbcbc0045e3b1f144466f5f
and topic0=0xd78ad95fa46c994b6551d0da85fc275fe613ce37657fb8d5e3d13
0840159d822
```

Another important piece of information to compare a pool with another that may offer the same token exchange is the strength of the pool for high liquidity trades. When large trades impact the reserves of the pool, there is a problem of slippage that, as we saw, can impact the final paid price. Here, it is important to study metrics related to the TVL, the liquidity of the pool, and so on. These metrics are typically calculated from aggregated transaction data. We propose some metrics logic in the following dashboard: `https://dune.com/gabriela/pool-basic-metrics`.

As we have been mentioning, in *Chapter 2*, we studied special tables that store transaction logs, with varying levels of preprocessing that adapt to the needs of the analyst. Some on-chain data providers even offer models that allow us to query the blockchain without writing code. Examples of such decoding services include the `dex.trades` tables on Dune or the Increment platform on Covalent, which has a drag-and-drop analytics service. Both Dune and Footprint are developing natural language queries to simplify the basic analysis of transaction data.

These tables and decoded data can vary between providers but what matters most is understanding the logic behind each query and familiarizing ourselves with the structure of log data. This will allow us to extract information or adapt queries to different table formats if needed, even controlling that the results returned by an NLP model are correct no matter the platform with which we are working. If we know the logic of the business and how the data is logged on the blockchain, we can solve the data questions using every platform.

Leveraging what we've already learned and the Dune Analytics tables listed here, we can create metrics that track the activity and revenue of the USDC/USDT pool under analysis. The tables are as follows:

- A raw data table named `ethereum.logs`
- An intermediate processed table named `erc20_ethereum.evt_Transfer` that includes logs signed as transfers
- An advanced decoded table named `dex.trades`

Here is a brief explanation of the logic behind the metrics displayed in the dashboard at `https://dune.com/gabriela/pool-basic-metrics`:

Name in the Dashboard	Logic
Number of trades	Count the number of swaps with the specified signature within the pool smart contract logs.
Traders logs 24 hs	Count the distinct addresses that appear in topic 2 of the Pool smart contract log with a "swap" as topic 0.
Average swap volume 24 hs	Using the `dex.trades` table, sum the amount in USD within the Pool smart contract and divide it by the number of transactions executed within 24 hours.
Pool TVL	Sum all the transfers where the pool was the recipient of the deposit and subtract all the transfers where funds left the pool.
Pool revenue	The revenue of a pool is generated by fees. The fee is deducted from the volume of the pair swap.

Table 5.2 – Dune dashboard query logic

Historically, DEXs incentivized the inflow of funds with higher yields, which led to the creation of professional funds that look for those advantages. Additionally, to avoid high slippage, big trades may need to be routed through different pools to be more cost-efficient. Routing multiple liquidity pools in a single transaction enables gas savings and minimizes slippage. In conclusion, aggregators were built as routers for liquidity and swappers.

DEX aggregators

DEX aggregators source liquidity from different DEXs, providing users with better token swap rates compared to any single DEX. These aggregators can optimize costs derived from slippage, swap fees, and token prices, resulting in more favorable rates for users when executed effectively. DEXs are generally interested in integrating with DEX aggregators as it helps attract more users and volume. One prominent example of a DEX aggregator is **1Inch**.

A map of the smart contracts that constitute the protocol and are maintained by the 1Inch team is available at `https://dune.com/queries/2238512`. There is a great dashboard that contains aggregated metrics at `https://dune.com/1inch/token`.

Additionally, **Increment**, a no-code product built by Covalent, has a model named Dex, which includes all 1Inch smart contracts across different chains, making the analysis easier. One valuable feature of this product is the "normalization" event, which consists of translating event signatures into human-readable words and their standardization. Each smart contract may have different names for similar events, and knowing the exact name is necessary for querying them. However, Increment standardizes the names, making querying more straightforward and cross-platform. Another noteworthy feature is that it opens up the query generated by the models, allowing customization and easier explanation to third parties of the logic taking place in the model.

In traditional finance, access to credit, loans, and collateral-based financial services has long been a cornerstone of the industry. DeFi also has a chapter on credit and collateralization that now offers users the ability to access credit without the need for intermediaries such as banks. We will analyze this in the next section.

Lending and borrowing services on Web3

The bank receives deposits, saves part of them to be able to repay in case the owner wants the cash back, and offers the other part as a loan in the market at a certain interest rate. The loan can be collateralized or non-collateralized, depending on the risk of the loan taker. The interest rate is set high enough to generate revenue for the bank and the depositor. Certain protocols on-chain reproduce a similar mechanism, as we will describe in this section.

At the time of writing, the main lending and borrowing protocols only work with collateralized loans. The process resembles a mortgage where the user provides the house as collateral as insurance for the loan payment. If the loan is not repaid in full, the bank keeps the house. In this case, if the collateral ratio of the loan is not maintained, the protocol liquidates the collateral.

Let's imagine that Alice wants to invest in a project in USD stablecoin but her collateral is in ETH. She is confident that ETH will increase in price, so she would rather not sell it for stablecoin. The solution is a protocol that takes Alice's ETH and lends her a USD-pegged stablecoin such as DAI. A protocol that does exactly that is Maker, which we have already mentioned previously. For the protocol to issue DAI, it requires 1.5 times the value of the issued DAI in collateral (ETH); this is called over-collateralization. The ratio between the collateral and the loaned asset is the collateral ratio. Usually, these protocols have a liquidation fee to disincentivize getting liquidated.

Another well-established protocol is **Compound**, which operates like a liquidity pool where liquidity providers supply funds to the pool in exchange for interest and borrowers take a loan against interest on the debt. The interest rate is known as **Annual Percentage Yield** (**APY**) and varies from pool to pool, depending on the liquidity and demand within the pool.

When funds are deposited in Compound, the market maker receives cTokens, which represent the percentage of the funds in the pool and accrue interest. A cToken is a type of cryptocurrency token that's used within the ecosystem. They are interest-bearing tokens that represent the amount of cryptocurrency a user has deposited into the Compound platform. The list of cTokens contracts can be found at `https://docs.compound.finance/#developer-resources`.

Let's explore the protocol in **Polygon**. The user page is at `https://app.compound.finance/markets?market=usdc-polygon`. The cToken contract is 0xF25212E676D1F7F89Cd72fFEe66158f541246445 and is called cUSDCv3.

The contract has many view functions, all of which are explored in the `Lending_borrowing.ipynb` notebook.

Some of the main functions are as follows:

- `numAssets()`: The number of assets that can be used as collateral. In the case under analysis, there are three assets, namely, ETH, wBTC, and Matic.
- `baseToken()`: The token that can be borrowed against the collateral – in our case, USDC.
- `getAssetInfo()`: This returns the collateral asset information, such as the collateral address or the price feed address on Chainlink.
- `Totalsupply()`: The total supply of base tokens plus interest accrued to suppliers.
- `getReserves()`: The balance of the base or collateral asset, which protects users from bad debt. We will analyze bad debt shortly.
- `getUtilization()`: Protocol utilization of the base asset – that is, USDC. The function for such a calculation is `TotalBorrows / TotalSupply`.

More functions to query state data are available; please refer to the documentation for more details.

Transaction data is also very useful for extracting insights. For example, it is possible to calculate the TVL and further collateral information by querying the logs of the collateral assets. The syntax follows the one we reviewed in the *Understanding DEX* section. A dashboard example can be found at `https://dune.com/datanut/Compound-Finance-Deposits-and-Loans`.

Lending and borrowing protocols make revenue out of the interest rate paid by the borrower. An important metric to measure revenue generated is the utilization ratio of a protocol, which is the result of the Borrowing Volume / TVL. This ratio tells us how efficient a protocol is to put the value that's been locked to work. The higher the utilization ratio, the better.

Specifically, in Compound, part of said interest goes to its reserves, which act as insurance, but such revenue distribution can be modified by the governance of the protocol, who are the COMP holders. COMP is an ERC-20 token that enables the community governance of the Compound protocol. A COMP token holder may participate and debate, propose, and vote on the changes to the protocol.

Within this industry, there is a crypto-native product that came to life to enable fast loans with zero collateralization: the flash loan.

Flash loans

Flash loans are crypto-native products, with **AAVE** being one of the most famous protocols in this category. A flash loan allows the borrower to take a loan with zero collateral, on the condition that the loan and any additional interest are repaid within the same transaction. If the borrower fails to repay the loan within the transaction, the entire transaction is reverted. Flash loans serve two main use cases: arbitrage and liquidations.

Arbitrage involves the simultaneous purchase and sale of the same or different assets in different markets, where the prices vary. The arbitrageur profits from the small price differences, but it usually requires a substantial amount to make a noticeable difference. This practice helps bring the market back to equilibrium, ensuring that the prices of the same asset remain stable across multiple markets.

In situations where a collateralization ratio is lost and the loan defaults, a third-party liquidator gains access to the collateral for liquidation purposes. The liquidator sells the collateral in the market on behalf of the borrower, pays back the debt, and receives a liquidation bonus for the job. All these steps can be executed in one transaction with flash loans and without requiring any collateral. These complex transactions are typically carried out by bots, which contribute to maintaining liquidity in the DeFi ecosystem and keeping prices stable across markets.

For further insights on flash loan transaction data, open the queries in the following dashboard: `https://dune.com/hildobby/flashloans`.

A note on protocol bad debt

Flash loans have been used to carry out attacks on DeFi protocols that resulted in these protocols having bad debt. Bad debt arises when users who provide liquidity to a pair are unable to withdraw their funds upon deciding to leave the pool. Let's consider an example:

1. The attacker obtains a flash loan for token A.

2. The attacker deposits token A into a DEX or CEX and swaps it for token B, leading to an increased supply of token A and decreased liquidity of token B, causing token B's price to rise.

3. The revalued token B is later used as collateral in a lending protocol to borrow token A. Due to the inflated collateral B price, the protocol lends more of token A than it would if the collateral were at its equilibrium price.

4. The attacker repays the loan in the form of A tokens, keeping the surplus of token A. When prices return to normal, liquidators try to liquidate token B at market price, but it is insufficient to cover the loan of token A. As a result, bad debt is incurred, leaving the last supplier of A tokens to bear the loss.

These attacks are facilitated when the price is sourced from a single oracle, making it susceptible to manipulation. Additionally, the lower cost associated with flash loans, which do not require collateral, makes such attacks more feasible.

An interesting dashboard created by the Risk DAO tracks the bad debt of protocols using on-chain data. You can explore it here: `https://bad-debt.riskdao.org/`.

The world is moving toward a multi-chain environment, where successful chains offer differentiated products and attract distinct ideas that become **dApps**. For example, Near, with its low fees, has developed the Sweat economy, while Avalanche subnets enable games to build their on-chain ecosystem without competing for gas slots on the main chain. As more protocols open up their services on multiple chains, they aim to leverage the benefits of each chain and reach a diverse range of users.

The increasing demand for transferring funds between different chains has led to the emergence of crypto-native products called bridges, which we will explore in the next section.

Multichain protocols and cross-chain bridges

A bridge is a structure that facilitates the transfer of funds and information between different chains. The market recognizes three groups of chains:

- **L1 chains** are the well-known blockchains, such as Bitcoin and Ethereum. It is called Layer 1 as the core team generates a layer of solutions over the foundation layer to increase scalability. An example of the evolution of L1 is the Ethereum merge, which occurred in September 2022.

- **L2 chains** are integrations that run on top of a blockchain to improve specific aspects, often focusing on scalability. These scaling solutions allow the main chain to offload data to a parallel architecture, processing it there and saving only the results on the main chain. Successful L2 chains include Optimism, Arbitrum, and Polygon zkEVM.

- **Sidechains** are new blockchains that are connected to a major blockchain. For instance, **Rootstock** is linked to Bitcoin, enabling EVM smart contract programming with the decentralization and security of Bitcoin. Sidechains are separate chains, meaning that consensus methods, gas rules, and other aspects may vary.

Given the ongoing availability of diverse blockchain offerings and the absence of any apparent halt to this trend, users will continue to explore transitioning from one blockchain to another to capitalize on the unique advantages offered by each. This underscores the persistent demand for bridge connections between these blockchains, which is expected to remain robust.

Depending on how a bridge operates, the transaction structure and the data points required for analysis may vary. Generally, there are two main types of bridges: centralized bridges and trustless bridges. **Centralized bridges** have a central entity responsible for bridge security. Examples include the Ronin bridge and the Multichain bridge. On the other hand, **trustless bridges** rely solely on smart contracts, such as the Near bridge and the Hop bridge.

Hands-on example – Hop bridge

Let's delve into how a Multichain bridge such as Hop works. Hop describes itself in `https://hop.exchange/` as a *"scalable rollup-to-rollup general token bridge."* It enables bridging between ETH and its L2 solutions, such as Polygon, Gnosis, Optimism, and Arbitrum.

The Hop bridge operates with three core products:

- A Hop token, which is pegged to the value of the underlying asset that's minted in each of the chains, where Hop is active and redeemable in the L1 chain

- A bonder or liquidity provider

- Automatic market makers, which allow us to swap between the Hop token and the native token in the destination chain

Let's consider an example transaction:

1. Alice wants to use a dApp active on Optimism but her funds are in ETH. So, to be able to interact with the dApp, she needs **oETH**, which is wrapped ETH on Optimism.

2. Alice bridges her ETH to Optimism by doing the following:

   I.   A bridge transaction is issued on ETH and will be executed on the native bridge after the waiting time and exit time have passed.

   II.   The bonder deposits hop-ETH or **hETH** in Alice's address on Optimism for the bridged amount minus fees and gas costs.

3. Alice can swap hETH for oETH and interact with the dApp.

4. After the exit time has passed, the bonder receives the funds previously provided to Alice along with a small fee.

This is a bridge transaction where the user can transfer funds between chains swiftly, sending an asset in one chain and receiving the equivalent (minus a fee) in another chain. In this example, we mentioned tokens such as oETH and hETH, which are minted and burned in each chain to represent the flow of funds between chains. This is known as a Lock and Mint type of bridge.

To analyze bridge contracts, refer to the complete list available at `https://github.com/hop-protocol/hop/blob/develop/packages/core/src/addresses/mainnet.ts`. There are a few `view` functions in it.

A useful view function is `l1CanonicalToken()` that provides information about the locked token in the bridge. Knowing this information, we can calculate the TVL, as explained in the `Bridges.ipynb` notebook.

For aggregated transactional data analysis, understanding the transaction's structure is essential. For instance, let's analyze the transaction under the 0xaf6089e3d7377b5b0c4ad86e486406a19e29280410402aab71195b0995608e81 hash, which involves transferring 0.4378 ETHs to the same address on Optimism:

⚡ Transaction Action: ▶ Deposit 0.4378 Ether to 🔴 Optimism via 🌀 Hop Protocol

Figure 5.9 – Transaction details (source: https://etherscan.io/
tx/0xaf6089e3d7377b5b0c4ad86e486406a19e29280410402aab71195b0995608e81)

To locate this data in the `raw_transactions` table of any data provider of those listed in *Chapter 2*, look for the signature or `TransferSentToL2` event, which includes the amount transferred, the bonder, and the user:

Figure 5.10 – Bridge cross transaction logs – ETH side

The transaction has its correlation in the Optimism chain. The relevant information is on the logs of the `l2canonical` token, as per the documentation. For wETH, this is `'0x4200000 0000000000000000000000000000000006'`. The transaction in Optimism is `https://optimistic.etherscan.io/tx/0x4e76ee9b997868ba894ea9362347bfa9ed64c 2aaf5b4482d6482940efbe3e738`, and the relevant log looks like this:

Figure 5.11 – Bridge cross transaction logs – OPT side

Most of these main protocols are already indexed and translated by major data providers, making analysis more accessible. For example, explore the very interesting dashboard at `https://dune.com/rchen8/Hop-Exchange`, which leverages events from the reviewed smart contracts.

Hop also offers a subgraph, and examples of queries can be found in the documentation: `https://docs.hop.exchange/v/developer-docs/subgraphs/queries`.

A note on DeFi risks and challenges

DeFi is a young, growing business with multiple challenges ahead. Data practitioners play a crucial role in preventing hacks, identifying unusual activities, measuring the risks associated with certain decisions, and handling damage control.

There may be instances where we find ourselves supporting governmental efforts to establish a regulatory framework for the activity, paving the way for a more substantial flow of funds into this ecosystem. As of today, regulatory uncertainty and diverse rules prevail. Although there are multiple initiatives aiming to create uniformity in legislation, it remains a work in progress. This situation directly impacts the industry, where concepts such as deposit guarantees are not applied, resulting in many users irrecoverably losing their funds after a hack.

The DeFi experience is still in its early stages, and data practitioners may also find themselves studying product experiences to enhance user interactions or educate users on better interacting with these products. Initiatives such as the SAFE wallet aim to bridge the gap between Web2 and Web3 experiences. This company leads in expanding what a wallet can do to match the experience of our traditional home banking.

The opportunities for creation in this space are vast, and data-driven decisions are imperative.

Summary

In this chapter, we delved into the world of DeFi, exploring its core components and the primary products offered in the sector. Our analysis covered a wide array of areas, including tokens, stablecoins, and DEXs with a focus on pools and DEX aggregation, lending and borrowing protocols, and the significance of bridges in facilitating cross-chain transactions.

In each case, we analyzed the business flow and how it generates revenue, and leveraged some of the data providers to generate aggregated metrics.

While the landscape of DeFi is ever-evolving, with new players emerging and innovative services being introduced, our focus remains on comprehending the underlying business models and mechanisms. Understanding the essence of these protocols enables us to effectively trace transactional details to construct informative metrics for further analysis.

Analytics companies play a vital role in simplifying this domain. Leveraging both on-chain and off-chain data and collaborating with protocol developers, these companies provide invaluable insights. By starting our analysis with well-established analytics firms, we can expedite our understanding of the DeFi landscape. However, the knowledge we've acquired in this chapter empowers us to establish our own criteria, delve into the code and the mathematical rationale, and tailor metrics to suit our unique requirements. This flexibility allows us to gain deeper insights into the DeFi space and make informed decisions based on our specific needs.

In the next chapter, we'll dive into the details of data preparation.

Further reading

To complement this chapter, the following sources may help:

- Lau, D., Lau, D., Jin, T. S., Kho, K., Azmi, E., Fang, L., Hor, B., & Win, K. W. (2021). *How to DeFi: Beginner*. CoinGecko.

- Fang, L., Hor, B., Azmi, E., Khor, W. W., & Gecko, C. (2021). *How to DeFi: Advanced*. CoinGecko.

- *A deep dive into automated market maker decentralized exchanges* (Uniswap v1). (n.d.). LearnWeb3: `https://learnWeb3.io/degrees/ethereum-developer-degree/sophomore/a-deep-dive-into-automated-market-maker-decentralized-exchanges-uniswap-v1/`.

- *The maker protocol white paper* | Feb 2020. (n.d.). MakerDAO | An Unbiased Global Financial System: `https://makerdao.com/en/whitepaper#abstract`.

- Fabian Vogelsteller <fabian@ethereum.org>, Vitalik Buterin <vitalik.buterin@ethereum.org>, *ERC-20: Token Standard*, Ethereum Improvement Proposals, no. 20, November 2015. [Online serial]. Available at `https://eips.ethereum.org/EIPS/eip-20`.

- Ori Pomerantz. (n.d.). *ERC-20 contract walk-through*. ethereum.org: `https://ethereum.org/developers/tutorials/erc20-annotated-code/#the-actual-contract`.

- *Introducing Permit2 & universal router*. (2022, November 17). Uniswap Protocol: `https://blog.uniswap.org/permit2-and-universal-router#universal-router-unified-token-and-nft-swaps`.

- Finematics. (n.d.). *What is DeFi? Decentralized Finance Explained* (Ethereum, MakerDAO, Compound, Uniswap, Kyber) [Video]. YouTube: `https://www.youtube.com/watch?v=k9HYC0EJU6E`.

- *Helper functions*. (n.d.). Compound III Documentation: `https://docs.compound.finance/helper-functions/`.

- *Dune Analytics*. (n.d.). How to Write SQL to Get TVL & Diversification Metrics such as HHI and Weighted Volatility [Part 4] [Video]. YouTube: `https://www.youtube.com/watch?v=UiETadtYaLY`.

- *Flash loans*: `https://docs.aave.com/faq/flash-loans`.

- Jp12. (2022, June 17). *Optimism bridge comparison*. Medium: `https://jp12.medium.com/optimism-bridge-comparison-453fa1f476f6`.

- Dogecoin. (n.d.). *Do only good everyday*. Dogecoin – An open-source peer-to-peer digital currency: `https://dogecoin.com/#what-is-dogecoin`.

- More Hop stats:

  - `https://dune.com/eliasimos/Bridge-Away-(from-Ethereum)`

  - `https://dune.com/queries/417810`

  - `https://dune.xyz/rchen8/Hop-Exchange`

  - `https://DeFillama.com/protocol/hop-protocol`

  - `https://cryptofees.info/`

  - `https://vfat.tools/polygon/hop/`

  - `https://explorer.hop.exchange/`

  - `https://app.hop.exchange/stats`

  - `https://volume.hop.exchange/`

- Hop Bridge. (n.d.). *Hop transfer diagram*. GitHub: `https://github.com/hop-exchange/contracts/blob/master/assets/Hop_Transfer_Diagrams.jpg`.

- The following is a list of very valuable dashboards and analytical resources:

CoinStats	`https://coinstats.app/`
DeFillama	`https://DeFillama.com/`
Debank	`https://debank.com/`
DeFiPulse	`https://www.DeFipulse.com/`
LoanScan	`https://linen.app/interest-rates/`
Nansen	`https://www.nansen.ai/`
Token Terminal	`https://tokenterminal.com/terminal/markets/lending`
Zapper	`https://zapper.xyz/dashboard`
Zerion	`https://zerion.io/`
DEXTools	`https://www.dextools.io/app/en`
GeckoTerminal	`https://www.geckoterminal.com/`
Into the Block	`https://www.intotheblock.com/`
Messari	`https://messari.io/`
Stablecoin dashboard	`https://stablecoins.wtf/`

Table 5.3 – A list of valuable dashboards

Part 2
Web3 Machine Learning Cases

In this part of the book, we will apply common artificial intelligence tasks to Web3-related data. This approach offers us an overview of the tools commonly used in the Web3 space, building upon the data and sources explored in *Part 1* of the book.

This part comprises the following chapters:

- *Chapter 6, Preparing and Exploring Our Data*
- *Chapter 7, A Primer on Machine Learning and Deep Learning*
- *Chapter 8, Sentiment Analysis – NLP and Crypto-News*
- *Chapter 9, Generative Art for NFTs*
- *Chapter 10, A Primer on Security and Fraud Detection*
- *Chapter 11, Price Prediction with Time Series*
- *Chapter 12, Marketing Discovery with Graphs*

6
Preparing and Exploring Our Data

Data preparation is a common theme in data science, extending beyond its association with the machine learning pipeline. It takes on various monikers such as data wrangling, data cleaning, and data preprocessing for feature engineering.

Here, we emphasize that significant time will be invested in data cleaning, feature engineering, and exploratory analysis, and we recognize the positive impact of robust preprocessing on outcomes, whether for a presentation for business stakeholders or its integration to a machine learning model.

Data cleaning encompasses tasks focused on identifying and rectifying data issues, particularly errors and artifacts. Errors result from data loss in the acquisition pipeline, while artifacts arise from the system that generates the data. Cleaning involves addressing missing data, handling outliers, removing duplicates, and performing necessary translations for data readability and conversion.

Data preparation spans tasks such as understanding and transforming received data to align with subsequent pipeline steps. This chapter delves into common scenarios that arise when working to understand, preprocess, and extract information from on-chain data. Specific topics include decimal treatment, approaches to smart contract evolution, and checksum validation. Additionally, the chapter introduces the **Exploratory Data Analysis (EDA)** concept and employs techniques for summary statistics and outlier detection to illustrate its advantages and insights.

This chapter explores the intricacies of preparing on-chain data and introduces the concept of EDA, facilitating the transition from analytics to machine learning. It does not aim to provide an exhaustive overview of all tools and methods, due to the extensive nature of this field of data science.

In summary, this chapter will cover the following topics:

- On-chain data preparation
- Introduction to Exploratory Data Analysis

Technical requirements

We extensively use the Pandas library, a popular and useful Python library for working with DataFrames and series. Pandas offers numerous functions to analyze, summarize, explore, normalize, and manipulate them. Series are one-dimensional array-like objects, and DataFrames are two-dimensional table structures with rows and columns. We use Pandas throughout this book's exercises to perform the aforementioned activities.

If you haven't installed Pandas yet, you can do so with the following code snippet:

```
pip install pandas.
```

The documentation for Pandas is available at `https://pandas.pydata.org/docs/`.

For data visualization, we use the Matplotlib and Seaborn libraries. Matplotlib provides a wide range of tools and control over the images we build. Seaborn is built on top of Matplotlib and is more user-friendly but has less flexibility.

The documentation for both libraries can be found at `https://seaborn.pydata.org/` and `https://matplotlib.org/`, respectively.

You can find all the data and code files for this chapter in the book's GitHub repository at `https://github.com/PacktPublishing/Data-Science-for-Web3/tree/main/Chapter06`. We recommend that you read through the code files in the `Chapter06` folder to follow along.

Data preparation

When dealing with information collected from diverse data sources, it is crucial to ensure consistency and uniformity across all records and fields before extracting insights or feeding the data into a machine learning model. In this section, we will explore various data preparation tasks that are particularly relevant to on-chain data.

Hex values

Hexadecimal notation is a base 16 system, utilizing symbols to represent numerical values from 0 to 9 and letters from A to F. In contrast, our everyday decimal notation employs 10 symbols to represent numerical values (0–9). Hexadecimal notation extends the range by including A to F, representing values from 10 to 15. This notation is often used for data storage purposes due to its efficiency in representing binary numbers with each hex digit representing 4 bits.

In the example presented in `Chapter06/Preparation`, we retrieve the latest block number from the Rootstock public node by following the documentation available at `https://developers.rsk.co/rsk/public-nodes/`.

The resulting value is presented in the form of a hex number, such as `0x4e07d0`:

```
block_number=data.get('result')
block_number
```

```
'0x4e07d0'
```

Figure 6.1 – Hexadecimal block number

This hex number can be decoded into a decimal number providing the base (`16`) using the following code snippet:

```
decimal_number = int(block_number, 16)
decimal_number
```

```
5113808
```

Figure 6.2 – Hexadecimal block number decoded

Following those steps, we are able to translate the hex response from the RSK node into our decimal system. To verify the accuracy of the translated information, we can compare our findings with the chain explorer available at `https://explorer.rsk.co/blocks` or `https://rootstock.blockscout.com/`. We will see that the block was added to the chain just a moment ago:

Figure 6.3 – Block explorer

Certain SQL database engines have the capability to convert hex values into a human-readable format directly within the query. For example, the ClickHouse system used by Covalent provides the `unhex` method. You can find more details in the documentation at `https://clickhouse.com/docs/en/sql-reference/functions/encoding-functions#unhex`.

Checksum

Checksum is an algorithm that hashes the address, enabling Ethereum to verify whether it is a valid address. In Ethereum, a checksummed address contains both uppercase and lowercase letters in a specific pattern.

Checksum address	Non-checksum address
0x95222290DD7278Aa3Ddd389Cc1E1d165CC4BAfe5	0x95222290dd7278aa3ddd389cc1e1d165cc4bafe5

Table 6.1 – Difference between addresses

Ethereum treats both lowercase and checksummed addresses as valid, and funds sent to either version will be directed to the same recipient. However, using a checksummed address provides an additional layer of security by preventing the accidental sending of funds to non-existent addresses.

This section holds significance on two fronts. Firstly, Python, like many SQL engines, is case-sensitive. So, it becomes imperative to manage the differentiation between lowercase and checksummed addresses when comparing or merging data from diverse sources. This guarantees compatibility and precision in data analysis. The second dimension pertains to the differentiation between valid and invalid addresses, a crucial aspect in maintaining data integrity and making our queries faster to run.

In `Chapter06/Preparation`, we test whether an address is a valid checksummed Ethereum address. For this purpose, we utilize the **eth-utils** library, which we explain more comprehensively in *Chapter 10*. The `test()` function allows us to convert a lowercase address into its checksummed version.

For another example, please refer to `Chapter10/EDA`, where we demonstrate the application of checksum addresses within a filter to remove invalid Ethereum addresses.

Decimal treatment

Solidity is the most commonly used smart contract programming language for EVM-based blockchains, but it does not support floats. To express decimals in Solidity, we use integers with the **fixed-point** methodology. The fixed-point methodology can be understood as the division of a variable numerator and a fixed denominator. If we review `Chapter04/Art` in Jupyter Notebook, in the *Chainlink* section, we can see the response from the oracle expressed in the following way:

```
latestData = contract.functions.latestRoundData().call()
latestData[1]
```

68600000000000000000

68600000000000000000

Figure 6.4 – Chainlink floor price response

Such a large number is not meaningful in an economic context and cannot be directly included in a dashboard or report. Therefore, it is necessary to translate it into our decimal system to make it more useful.

Smart contracts provide the number of decimals through a specific function. In the case of Chainlink's data-feed smart contract, the decimals() function informs us about the fixed point, or, in practical terms, how many decimal places we have to shift the comma to the left to convert the response into our decimal system. The steps to query the smart contract are explained in the *Chapter 2* section *Exploring state data*, and as shown in the Jupyter Notebook, the result is 18:

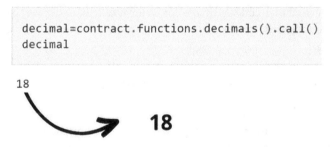

```
decimal=contract.functions.decimals().call()
decimal
```

18

18

Figure 6.5 – The data-feed decimal

The following figure showcases the transformed number that we can use in subsequent parts of a data pipeline:

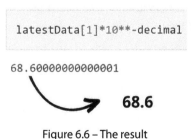

```
latestData[1]*10**-decimal
```

68.60000000000001

68.6

Figure 6.6 – The result

The same result can be achieved by applying the `fromWei()` function as per the following code snippet:

```
Web3.fromWei(latestData), 'ether')
```

The decimal treatment we just explored is also relevant for tokens. **Ethereum Request for Comment 20 (ERC-20)** is a technical standard for fungible tokens created on Ethereum. This standard defines a set of functions and events that developers must implement to ensure compliance with it. One of the optional functions in this standard is `decimal()`, which *returns the number of decimal places the token uses, for example 8, which means to divide the token amount by 100000000 (10 to the power 8) to get its user representation.*

More of this standard was analyzed in *Chapter 5*.

> **Note on decimals**
>
> The most common decimal denominator for Ethereum smart contracts is 18, while Bitcoin uses 8 and USDT utilizes 6 decimals.

In this section, we have learned that consuming on-chain data often requires extensive transformations. If our dataset contains excessively large strings that lack economic meaning, we may need to search for the smart contract's decimal value to properly position the decimal point. Additionally, if our dataset includes hex values, we need to decode them into our decimal system. Lastly, we have discovered how to transform lowercase addresses into checksum addresses to ensure compatibility with case-sensitive programming languages.

From Unix timestamps to datetime formats

Unix timestamps are commonly used in data analysis, but for visualization purposes in dashboards and reports, it is necessary to convert them into a human-readable format. Unix time represents the number of seconds that have passed since January 1, 1970, providing a system to track time using a single integer value.

In most SQL engines, the `truncate` function can be utilized to extract the relevant date part from the timestamp.

In Python, we can use the `datetime` module's `fromtimestamp()` function, which converts Unix timestamps to local datetime, and the `utcfromtimestamp()` function, which converts them to UTC datetimes.

In the Jupyter Notebook's `Chapter06/Preparation` section, we translate a Unix timestamp with the following code:

```
tm= 1678301971
print(datetime.utcfromtimestamp(tm))
```

```
2023-03-08 18:59:31
```

Figure 6.7 – Datetime translation

To validate our results, we can compare them with those obtained from `https://www.unixtimestamp.com/`, a popular tool that shows the same information:

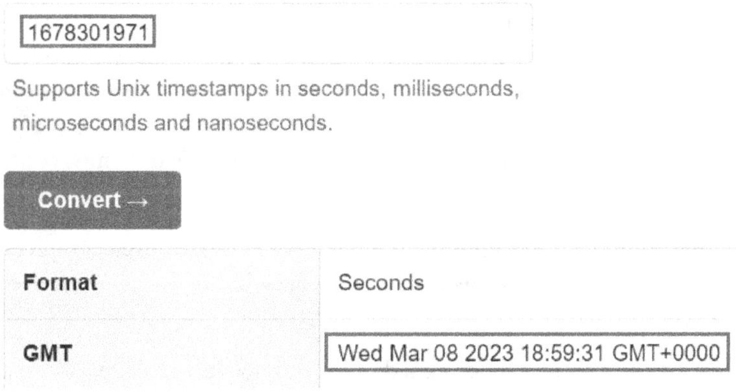

```
1678301971
```

Supports Unix timestamps in seconds, milliseconds, microseconds and nanoseconds.

Convert →

Format	Seconds
GMT	Wed Mar 08 2023 18:59:31 GMT+0000

Figure 6.8 – Unix timestamp translator

Evolution of smart contracts

Smart contracts, like any software product, may undergo changes and require upgrades for various reasons such as business necessity, security incidents, or to reduce gas costs. However, by design, everything deployed on the blockchain is immutable. The following information, sourced from `Ethereum.org`, outlines multiple approaches to enable an upgrade. The content is quoted under the **Creative Commons Attribution 4.0 International** (**CC BY 4.0**) license, in compliance with the terms of use. The original document can be found in the *Further reading* section of this chapter.

Smart contract upgrades can be achieved via the following methods:

- Creating multiple versions of a smart contract and migrating state (i.e., data) from the old contract to a new instance of the contract
- Creating separate contracts to store business logic and state

- Using proxy patterns to delegate function calls from an immutable proxy contract to a modifiable logic contract

- Creating an immutable main contract that interfaces with and relies on flexible satellite contracts to execute specific functions

- Using the diamond pattern to delegate function calls from a proxy contract to logic contracts

In conclusion, the ways to upgrade a smart contract do not involve modifying the deployed code. Rather, it entails substituting one contract for another. Currently, the most popular method for upgrading smart contracts is the **proxy pattern**. This pattern involves a separation between the proxy contract and the execution contract that holds the logic. The proxy acts on behalf of the logic smart contract redirecting transactions from the frontend to the correct smart contract in the backend. It is possible to swap the logic smart contract in the backend and update the proxy to start redirecting transactions to the newly deployed smart contract with the latest logic.

The fact that contracts may change implies that our queries need to adapt to reflect those changes. For example, if a smart contract starts emitting an event at a certain block, we need to be aware of it to capture the new information. As we saw in *Chapter 2*, we need the **Application Binary Interface** (**ABI**) to decode smart contracts that need to be duly updated to decode transactions after an upgrade. Not being aware that the contract we are parsing has changed may cause us to miss certain events and may negatively impact our analysis.

When analyzing a specific project, it's important to follow press releases, project representatives, and official information channels for news of any development launched to direct our queries to the smart contract that is less prone to changes.

In conclusion, while smart contracts are designed to be immutable, there are circumstances where upgrades and changes become necessary, and we need to be prepared to adapt our queries or code to these changes. For example, if we were analyzing Ethereum, we would need to be aware that the entire chain changed with the Merge, which occurred in September 2022 and has an impact at the data level.

Exploratory Data Analysis

Between the data cleaning phase and the modeling or formal statistical analysis, there exists an intermediate step known as EDA, which is a fundamental aspect of data science. EDA serves as the primary approach to understanding and making sense of a dataset, providing insights into the "population out of the sample" and transforming raw data into actionable information for businesses. EDA can include various techniques and methods:

- **Data summary or descriptive statistics**: Used to summarize central tendencies within the dataset.

- **Data visualization**: Graphical techniques such as histograms, box plots, scatter plots, and line plots are employed to visualize the data, aiding in pattern identification, outlier detection, and understanding the relationship between variables. Furthermore, data visualization is particularly effective when presenting conclusions to a non-technical audience.

- **Data exploration**: Helps us understand the distribution of variables, assess their shapes and skewness, and identify the presence of anomalies.

- **Handling missing data**: This allows us to identify missing rows and assess their impact on the results. It helps to determine patterns in missing values and to develop strategies for handling them effectively.

- **Outlier detection**: Identifying values that significantly deviate from the rest of the dataset and evaluating their influence on the analysis. These outliers can result from various causes, which we will discuss in the subsequent section.

- **Correlations and patterns**: Explores the relationships between variables using techniques such as correlation analysis and scatter plots. Additionally, they help identify trends or seasonality in the data over time.

A concise description of EDA can be found at `https://towardsdatascience.com/exploratory-data-analysis-8fc1cb20fd15`: *"Exploratory Data Analysis refers to the critical process of performing initial investigations on data so as to discover patterns, to spot anomalies, to test hypothesis and to check assumptions with the help of summary statistics and graphical representations."*

In this chapter, we will provide a brief introduction to summary statistics and outlier detection with the aid of graphical representations. We chose those two topics as they are probably transversals to all the datasets we will encounter in our journey. For further exploration of EDA topics, feel free to refer to the books in the *Further reading* section that are very useful.

To exemplify the concepts learned in this section, we will use the **Witches** dataset available on Kaggle (`https://www.kaggle.com/datasets/harrywang/crypto-coven?select=witches.csv`). It contains information about the Crypto Coven NFT project, where each row represents one witch NFT. The Witches project's main page can be found at `https://www.cryptocoven.xyz/`.

Summarizing data

Our datasets will contain categorical or quantitative variables. Categorical variables are those that can be divided into groups, such as colors or brands. On the other hand, quantitative variables represent numerical amounts, such as prices or the number of sales. The `df.describe()` code snippet returns the quantitative variables and their distribution.

Calculating the distribution of categorical data involves determining the frequency of each category. This analysis can provide meaningful insights. For example, in marketing, understanding the distribution of categorical variables such as age groups, income levels, or consumer preferences can help businesses segment their target audience effectively and create more targeted and successful campaigns. Another example is in fraud detection, where categorical variables such as transaction types or user behavior patterns can be crucial in detecting fraudulent activities. By studying the distribution of these variables, anomalies or unusual patterns can be identified, enabling organizations to develop effective fraud-detection models and strategies.

An application in the NFT space is to help determine whether a collection is owned by the retail public or whether it is held by a small group of collectors (centralized). This knowledge about an art collection's ownership characteristics can help an investor assess whether a project's price aligns with the market value or whether it is susceptible to manipulation. A more decentralized ownership structure implies a price closer to the market value.

In `Chapter06/EDA.ipynb`, we investigate the distribution of NFTs by creating two categories of holders: those with more than three NFTs of the same collection, which we name *collectors*, and those with fewer than three NFTs, that is, the *general public*. We follow three steps:

1. We count how many NFTs each address has, equivalent to a GROUP BY operation in a SQL query. This allows us to understand the holdings of each address.

2. We create a list of addresses that hold more than three NFTs from the same collection. The number of NFTs per address criteria is part of our analysis and a decision we make during the EDA. These micro-decisions impact the final result, and it is good practice to document them.

3. We build two separate `collectors_df` and `distributed_df` datasets depending on whether the address is in the list from Step 2.

With these straightforward steps, we can calculate the percentage of collectors and distributed owners for the project. *Figure 6.9* reveals that the collector percentage is only 32%, while the remaining 68% is held by the public.

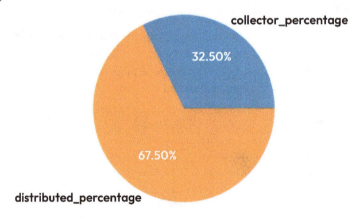

Figure 6.9 – Collector and distributed percentages

To summarize quantitative variables, we introduce concepts such as the mean, average, deviations, outliers, and others. Let's start with measures of central tendency or summary statistics, which are used to describe a set of values with a single value. These include the mean, median, and mode.

The **mean**, or average, is the most commonly used measure. It is calculated by summing all the values in a dataset and dividing it by the number of values:

```
Formula: Mean = (Sum of all values) / (Total number of values)
```

For example: if we have 5, 7, 2, 10, and 6 as values, the mean would be $(5 + 7 + 2 + 10 + 6) / 5 = 6$.

Pandas provides the `mean()` function, which returns the mean value for a column passed. If we calculate the mean of prices in the Witch dataset, we will add all prices and divide the result by the number of rows. Please see the following code snippet in `Chapter06/EDA.ipynb`, where we calculated the mean for the `price` column:

```
df['price'].mean()
```

To calculate the mean, all values are considered, but the resulting number may not be in the analyzed sample. Another important aspect is that the mean value is heavily influenced by outliers. Therefore, it is necessary to clean the dataset and remove outliers before calculating it.

The mean value is not a perfect measure of central tendency when the data is skewed. A better alternative is the median.

The **median** is defined as the middle value of a column when arranged in order of magnitude, from smallest to largest. To manually calculate the median, we would follow these steps:

1. Take all values from the `price` column and order them from smallest to largest.

2. Find the number situated in the center that divides the dataset into two equal parts:

   ```
   Formula (odd number of values): Median = Middle value
   ```

   ```
   Formula (even number of values): Median = (Sum of two middle
   values) / 2
   ```

   For example: for the 5, 7, 2, 10, and 6 dataset, when arranged in ascending order, the median would be 6.

Pandas provides the `median()` function to perform this calculation. For instance, to calculate the median for the `price` column, we can use the following code snippet, which is also shown in `Chapter06/EDA.ipynb`:

```
df['price'].median()
```

The median is often preferred over the mean when dealing with skewed data or data with outliers.

In `Chapter04/Art.ipynb`, when summarizing the data to find the floor price from multiple marketplaces over a set period of time, we chose to show the median instead of the average and the result is the following:

Figure 6.10 – Median floor price by marketplace

If we had used the average, the graphic would have shown significant variations between marketplaces, as depicted in *Figure 6.11*. Analyzing the floor price based on the average would not have been accurate, especially when referring to the OpenSea offer.

Figure 6.11 – Average floor price by marketplace

The **mode** is another measure of central tendency that represents the most frequently occurring value in the dataset. Graphically speaking, it is represented by the highest bar in the histogram. It can also be used with categorical variables. To calculate the mode manually, we would identify the most repeated price in our dataset:

Formula: No specific formula

For example, in the 15, 20, 18, 22, 15, 20, 18, 20, 22, and 25 dataset, the value that appears most frequently is 20. It appears three times.

Pandas provides the mode() function to calculate the mode for a column, as shown in the following code snippet from Chapter06/EDA.ipynb:

```
df['price'].mode()[0]
```

> **A note on missing prices**
>
> Measures of central tendency not only assist us in summarizing our dataset but also prove helpful in addressing missing values within the dataset.
>
> For instance, during periods of extreme volatility, certain trading houses may suspend commercialization. This holds true for both traditional markets and centralized crypto exchanges. If our database happens to source prices from such an exchange, it is possible that there will be missing rows of data. In such scenarios, pandas functions such as `fillna()` or `interpolate()` can be employed to impute missing values. With the `fillna()` function, we can specify whether to complete the NaN values with the mean or the median.

In conclusion, in our EDA, we have explored measures of central tendency such as the mean, median, and mode, which provide insights into the distribution and characteristics of our data.

Building upon our exploration of central tendency, we now turn our attention to outlier detection. Outliers are data points that deviate significantly from the overall pattern of the dataset, and they can have a substantial impact on our analysis and interpretation. In the next section, we will delve into various techniques and approaches for identifying outliers.

Outlier detection

According to the book *Introduction to Data Science* by Rafael A. Irizarry, outliers are defined as *"data samples with a value that is far from the central tendency."* While outliers are not inherently good or bad, they can significantly impact our analysis and lead to incorrect conclusions. This is particularly true when working with prices, where market volatility can distort the true value of assets transacted. Prices are used as proxies for value, but it's important to recognize that some prices deviate significantly from the actual value, making them outliers.

In certain instances, the primary goal is to identify and analyze outliers, which is typically the focus in anomaly detection techniques such as those discussed in *Chapter 4*, specifically for uncovering fraud or money laundering.

There are several reasons why outliers may occur:

- An instrument measurement error such as a disconnected API or an unbalanced scale

- Data entry errors

- Working with samples or populations that are less homogeneous than initially assumed

Let's explore some techniques to identify outliers in our dataset:

- **Box plot (whisker plot)**: This graphical representation summarizes the data using five important numbers: minimum, first quartile, median, third quartile, and maximum. We can identify outliers as those that are far from the box:

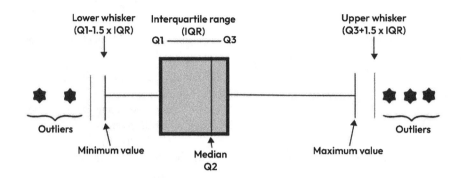

Figure 6.12 – Parts of the box plot

This image can be automatically generated by Pandas with the following code snippet:

```
df.boxplot(column=['ETH_price'])
```

Alternatively, we can use the Seaborn library, as shown in our Jupyter notebook (`Chapter06/Outliers`).

- **IQR method** (**Interquartile range**): This method is also used by box plots. Quartiles (Q) are the four points that divide data into same-sized groups. In IQR, we use them as limits against which we will define whether a value is too far from the set and has to be considered an outlier. If a data point is more than 1.5 times the lower quartile (Q1) or more than 1.5 times the upper quartile (Q3), it is considered an outlier.

Pandas helps to calculate the quartiles with the `df.quantile()` function. Once we have them, we can calculate other parts of this formula.

In `Chapter05/Outliers`, we calculate the IQR, bottom, and upper limits in this part of the code:

```
q25,q75 = df.ETH_price.quantile([0.25,0.75])

iqr = q75-q25
outlier_bottom_lim = q25 - 1.5*iqr
outlier_top_lim = q75 + 1.5*iqr
```

Figure 6.13 – Calculation of IQR and limits

The 1.5 multiplier is common practice but can be adjusted to adapt to our case.

- **Three-sigma rule** (**Z-score**): The three-sigma rule states that 99.7% of data falls within three standard deviations (three-sigma) of the mean in a normal distribution. This rule is used for outlier detection because data points outside the three sigmas can be considered outliers.

This method uses the mean as a starting point, which can be influenced by outliers. A more robust modified Z-score method can be employed, which incorporates the median and median absolute deviation in its formula. The metric is a statistical measure that helps identify outliers in a dataset by comparing each data point to the median and median absolute deviation. It provides a robust way to detect extreme values, especially in datasets with skewed distributions.

Summary

This chapter has addressed various preparation methods applicable to on-chain data scenarios. We explored techniques such as unhexing data, decimal treatment, handling checksum addresses, and converting Unix timestamps to datetime formats. These methods have proven foundational in preparing the on-chain data for subsequent analysis.

Moreover, we introduced the concept of EDA as a crucial step in understanding and summarizing datasets, with a specific focus on central tendency metrics. Additionally, we delved into outlier detection techniques, such as box plots and the IQR method, aiding in the identification of extreme observations deviating significantly from the majority of the data.

By applying these cleaning and EDA techniques, we have equipped ourselves with essential tools for the effective analysis and interpretation of on-chain data. These foundational concepts serve as building blocks for more advanced techniques and methodologies as we continue this journey. For more insights into these methodologies, please refer to the *Further reading* section.

Further reading

The following links may help to complement this chapter:

- Technical requirements:

  - *10 minutes to pandas, pandas 1.5.3 documentation, pandas - Python Data Analysis Library:* `https://pandas.pydata.org/docs/user_guide/10min.html#min`

- Evolution of smart contracts:

  - *Upgrading Smart Contracts, ethereum.org:* `https://ethereum.org/en/developers/docs/smart-contracts/upgrading/`

- Exploratory Data Analysis:

  - *Introduction to Data Science: A Python Approach to Concepts, Techniques and Applications,* Laura Igual, Santi Seguí, Springer

  - *Three Ways to Detect Outliers, Colin Gorrie, Colin Gorrie's Data Story:* `https://colingorrie.github.io/outlier-detection.html#modified-z-score-method`

- *Python for Data Analysis: Data Wrangling With Pandas, NumPy, and Jupyter,* Wes McKinney, O'Reilly Media

- *Box Plot Review, Khan Academy:* `https://www.khanacademy.org/math/statistics-probability/summarizing-quantitative-data/box-whisker-plots/a/box-plot-review`

- *Hands-On Exploratory Data Analysis With Python: Perform EDA Techniques to Understand, Summarize, and Investigate Your Data,* Usman Ahmed, Suresh Kumar Mukhiya, O'Reilly Media: `https://www.packtpub.com/product/hands-on-exploratory-data-analysis-with-python/9781789537253`

- *The Data Science Design Manual,* Steven Skiena, Springer

- Cleaning:

  - *RSK Explorer:* `https://explorer.rsk.co/blocks`

  - *More on Time on the Blockchain, Nick Furneaux, Wiley,* Chapter 9, Investigating Cryptocurrencies, Understanding, Extracting, and Analyzing Blockchain Evidence, Page 156 to Page 161

7

A Primer on Machine Learning and Deep Learning

Before applying any machine learning algorithm, having a comprehensive understanding of the dataset and its key features is essential. This understanding is typically derived through **exploratory data analysis** (**EDA**). Once acquainted with the data, we must invest time in feature engineering, which involves selecting, transforming, and creating new features (if necessary) to enable the use of the chosen model or enhance its performance. Feature engineering may include tasks such as converting classes into numerical values, scaling or normalizing features, creating new features from existing ones, and more. This process is tailored for each specific model and dataset under analysis. Once this process is completed, we can proceed to modeling.

The goal of this chapter is to review introductory concepts of machine learning and deep learning, laying the foundation for *Part 2* of this book. In *Part 2*, we will delve into various use cases where artificial intelligence is applied to Web3 data. While not covering every possible model in detail, we will provide brief descriptions of project motivations, the models themselves, and the tools used, and include useful references for further reading.

We will explore the main concepts of machine learning and deep learning, discussing two typical machine learning pipelines – one using scikit-learn and the other using Keras. Additionally, we have compiled an extensive *Further reading* section for each theme covered in this chapter to encourage continued learning.

Specifically, the following topics will be addressed:

- Basic concepts of machine learning and deep learning
- Machine learning pipeline with scikit-learn and Keras

Technical requirements

We will be using **scikit-learn**, a popular Python library specially designed for machine learning tasks. It offers algorithms and tools for data preprocessing, feature selection, model selection, and model evaluation.

If you have not worked with scikit-learn before, it can be installed by using the following code snippet:

```
pip install scikit-learn
```

The documentation for scikit-learn can be found at `https://scikit-learn.org/stable/`.

For deep learning, we have the option to use **TensorFlow** or **Keras**. TensorFlow is a powerful open source library for numerical computation that provides solutions to train, test, and deploy a variety of deep learning neural networks. It serves as the infrastructure layer, which enables low-level tensor operations on the CPU, TPU, and GPU. On the other hand, Keras is a high-level Python API built on top of TensorFlow. It is specially prepared to enable fast experimentation and provides informative feedback when an error is discovered. According to the 2022 survey *State of Data Science and Machine Learning*, by Kaggle, Keras reached a 61% adoption rate among machine learning developers and data scientists.

If you have not worked with TensorFlow or Keras before, they can be installed with the following code snippet:

```
pip install tensorflow
pip install keras
```

For deep learning, a large amount of computational power is required; our normal CPU may not be fully prepared for the task, resulting in slow training and inference. The alternative is to run a GPU locally or in the cloud – hosted using Kaggle Kernel or Google Colab. They have a similar UI that resembles the structure of a Jupyter notebook, making it easy to run the code from the repository on any of these platforms.

You can find all the data and code files for this chapter in this book's GitHub repository at `https://github.com/PacktPublishing/Data-Science-for-Web3/tree/main/Chapter07`. We recommend that you read through the code files in the `Chapter07` folder to follow along.

Introducing machine learning

The definition of machine learning, as provided by Computer Science Wiki, is "*a field of inquiry devoted to understanding and building methods that "learn" – that is, methods that leverage data to improve performance on some set of tasks. It is seen as a part of artificial intelligence. Machine learning algorithms build a model based on sample data, known as training data, in order to make predictions or decisions without being explicitly programmed to do so.*"

(Source: `https://computersciencewiki.org/index.php/Machine_learning`)

Professor Jason Brownlee defines deep learning as *"a subfield of machine learning concerned with algorithms inspired by the structure and function of the brain called artificial neural networks."* Deep learning is distinguishable from other machine learning methods because it uses artificial neural networks as a basis for its methods.

The relationship between these two fields is generally represented as follows:

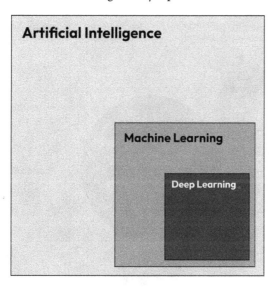

Figure 7.1 – Venn diagram of artificial intelligence

Let's analyze the definition of machine learning further:

- Machine learning models create their own rules based on the data we provide, as stated by the phrases *"understanding and building methods that learn"* and *"make predictions or decisions without being explicitly programmed to do so."* Previously, we used filters in our queries or *if statements* in our programs. With machine learning, particularly supervised learning, we feed data and let the model infer the rules. In the book *Python Data Science Handbook*, the author challenges the idea that the model learns by itself, instead suggesting that it tunes the parameters we provide by adapting to the observed data. Once it fits those parameters to the seen data, it can infer results as needed from unseen data.

- *"Machine learning algorithms build a model based on sample data, known as training data."* Data passed to machine learning algorithms needs to be split at least into two: training and test data. The training dataset is used to build the model. The test dataset is used to evaluate the model's capacity to make predictions with data it has not seen before. The model's predictions are then compared to the ground-truth data and the evaluation metrics are calculated.

Machine learning techniques can be classified as supervised learning, unsupervised learning, and reinforcement learning. Common tasks that are solved by machine learning techniques are shown in *Figure 7.2*:

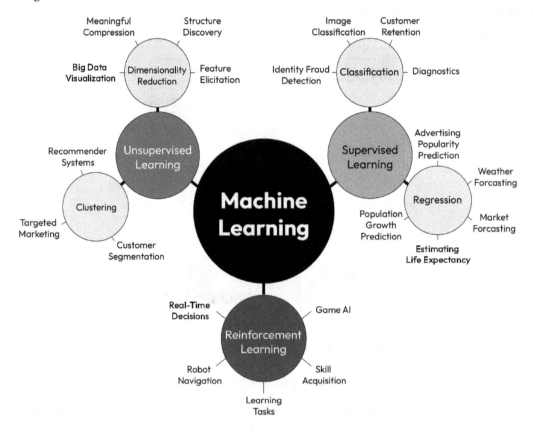

Figure 7.2 – Machine learning applications

Supervised learning consists of creating a function that can map inputs to outputs, allowing the model to infer outputs from unseen or similar inputs. In this process, we use features to describe the characteristics of a variable and labels or tags to identify the predicted variable. Through this, our model can learn the relationship between the features and the labels or tags.

In Web3 analysis, **tagging** plays a crucial role as it allows us to attribute an identity to addresses that are a combination of numbers and letters and have no direct connection to the outside world. However, creating a library of tagged addresses can be a challenging task and just recently, it has become the business of a company named Arkham that incentivizes the "*de-anonymizing of the blockchain*" with public data. Tagged addresses are one of the main leverages for companies such as Nansen, which have made significant progress in tagging hundreds of addresses on Ethereum and other chains, enabling machine learning techniques and data analysis reports.

Tagging can also be found in Etherscan, where important projects tag their addresses to enable public audits. Also, Dune and Flipside have tables with labels where their research teams add relevant information that can help with queries. If you want to learn more about identity attribution, Nick Fourneaux, in the book *Investigating Cryptocurrencies*, teaches how to extract addresses from websites such as forums or software-sharing sites, download HTML as raw text, and execute a regex analysis.

Supervised learning can be further divided into regression and classification techniques. In classification techniques, we have a discrete set of categories as labels (such as fraudulent transactions or non-fraudulent transactions). In regression, we have quantitative labels, such as the price of NFT art or tokens.

Unsupervised learning consists of trying to identify the structure or patterns of a dataset that may not be explicit. The tasks that fall under unsupervised learning typically include the following:

- Clustering – that is, identifying groups within a given dataset

- Dimensionality reduction – that is, attempting to represent the dataset with a smaller amount of features

- Novelty detection – that is, trying to identify when a change has occurred in the data

Reinforcement learning teaches a model to find the optimal solution for a problem by leveraging what the model already knows and what it can learn via a cumulative reward after interacting with its environment. The model receives feedback from the environment in the form of rewards or penalties, and its goal is to maximize its total reward. The idea behind reinforcement learning is to mimic the way humans learn by trial and error:

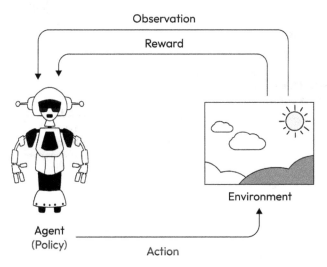

Figure 7.3 – Agent-environment loop (adapted from https://gymnasium.farama.org/content/basic_usage/)

To make a project come to life, there are some initial business/data steps that must be undertaken:

- *Defining a Web3 data science problem* means stating what we want to solve with the data we have with precision. In such a definition, we have to be able to describe the problem we want to solve, why we want to solve it, and what assumptions are considered.

- *Getting the data* means getting our hands on the dataset we will work with. It is possible that the dataset has already been built with all the rows and columns of interest, or that we have to build it by combining multiple sources of data. An initial list of data sources is listed in *Chapters 2* and *3*. More data sources may be needed, depending on the problem we will tackle.

- *EDA* is used to make sense of the dataset using summary statistics and data visualization techniques. *Data preparation* is a preprocessing step where we transform the dataset to improve its quality or make it digestible to the model. On-chain data may need a lot of transformations. We analyzed some of those methods in *Chapter 6*.

Now, let's analyze the steps to select, train, and evaluate a model.

Building a machine learning pipeline

After cleaning the data and selecting the most important features, the machine learning flow can be summarized into steps, as shown in *Figure 7.4*:

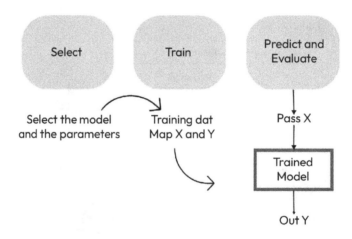

Figure 7.4 – Machine learning pipeline

To carry out this process, we must do the following:

1.   Select a model and its initial parameters based on the problem and available data.

2.   Train: First, we must split the data into a training set and a test set. The process of training consists of making the model learn from the data. Each model's training process can vary in time and computational consumption. To improve the model's performance, we must employ hyperparameter tuning through techniques such as grid search or random grid search.

3.   Predict and evaluate: The trained model is then used to predict over the test set, which contains rows of data that have not been seen by the algorithm. If we evaluate the model with the data that we used to train it, the model will always predict well, and we will not be able to improve it. Model performance is assessed using task-specific evaluation metrics.

When we achieve a good model, we must save it so that we can use it when we receive unseen data. We can use tools such as *Pickle* and *Keras Tokenizer* to accomplish this. Pickle serializes the trained model and converts it into a file, allowing it to be used in another environment. To produce a result, we must pass data with the same structure that it is ready to receive so that the model can make predictions.

Let's apply this pipeline with a hands-on example. In `Chapter07/ML_warmup`, we aim to identify fraudulent transactions on the Ethereum network using a Kaggle dataset named *Ethereum Fraud Detection Dataset*, where only 17% of its rows are fraudulent. This is a typical supervised classification task.

Model

Based on the problem at hand, we must select a model or a couple of models to test which one performs better on our data. If we are unsure about the model to select, we can examine similar structured problems solved on Kaggle. In the Jupyter notebook, we selected a random forest classifier with the following code snippet:

```
random_forest = RandomForestClassifier(random_state=42)
```

Many algorithms are available for training and the choice can be difficult. One way to choose among many models is to reduce the reducible error. Literature usually refers to this matter as the bias-variance trade-off. Before addressing that trade-off, we need to understand the different types of errors that exist. The prediction error for any machine learning algorithm can be classified as follows:

- **Noise** or **irreducible error**: This type of error cannot be deleted, no matter how well we implement the model.

- **Bias error**: This can be reduced. Wikipedia defines it as "*an error from erroneous assumptions in the learning algorithm.*" A model with high bias oversimplifies reality and leads to a high error between the prediction and the ground-truth value. High-bias models oversimplify, which means that they do not have enough parameters to capture the complexity of the data they learn from, resulting in underfitting. More on this concept will be covered in the next section.

- **Variance error:** This can also be reduced. Wikipedia defines it as an error derived from *"sensitivity to small fluctuations in the training set."* This means that the model is learning the particularities of the training dataset so well that it will not generalize enough to predict on unseen data. These models are highly dependent on the exact training data and are unable to generalize. We encounter this error when the model performs well on training data but poorly on test/validation data, indicating an overfitting problem.

Low variance with high bias algorithms train less complex models with a rather simple or rigid underlying structure – for example, linear regression. On the other hand, high variance with low bias algorithms train complex, flexible models that can be exact on training data but inconsistent in prediction – for example, KNN.

If we understand bias and variance and recognize that both are derived from the choice of the model we make, to make an optimal decision we will have to choose the model that reduces the total error with a trade-off between both:

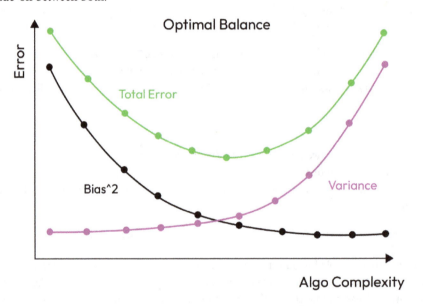

Figure 7.5 – The bias-variance trade-off

Another criterion for selecting a model is its performance, which is measured by the evaluation metric of choice. We can run multiple models and evaluate them all with the same metric, and the model that performs better is the one we continue tuning. We will discuss evaluation metrics in subsequent sections.

In `Chapter07/ML_warmup`, we selected a random forest classifier. This algorithm looks to reduce the variance of the model without compromising bias and performs well in the evaluation metric known as recall. More about the random forest algorithm can be found in the *Further reading* section.

Training

To begin the training process, we split the data into a training dataset and a test dataset. This allows us to keep part of the data unseen by the model during training, and we can evaluate its performance afterward:

```
X_train, X_test, y_train, y_test = train_test_split(X, y,\
    test_size=0.33, random_state=42)
```

The training process consists of passing the features and labels to the algorithm so that it learns from them. The learning algorithm will try to find patterns in the training data that map the attributes of the input data to the target. The trained model captures these patterns.

In `Chapter07/ML_warmup`, we instruct the model to learn with the following code snippet:

```
random_forest.fit(X_train, y_train)
```

Underfitting and overfitting

Let's consider three scenarios, where the model is represented by a black line. Which scenario performs classification better?

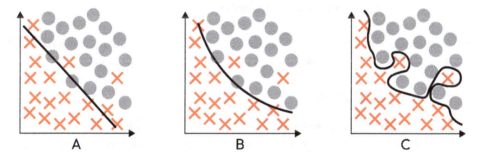

Figure 7.6 – Three classification scenarios

Let's understand the scenarios:

- **Scenario A**: The model is very simple and unable to capture the boundary between the two classes. This is called **underfitting**.

- **Scenario B**: The model was able to find an acceptable boundary between both classes, although it may misclassify some of the border samples. In general, it captures the complexity of the dataset.

- **Scenario C**: The model adapted too much to the training dataset and learned all the details, not just the relevant characteristics that differentiate one class from another. It was unable to generalize. This is called **overfitting**.

Figure 7.7 – What a model does when overfitting (source: https://twitter.
com/MaartenvSmeden/status/1522230905468862464)

We aim for scenario B, where the model is complex enough to capture the important features but does not adapt too much to the training data so that it performs well on unseen samples.

Prediction and evaluation

Here, we pass unseen data to our trained model and evaluate how accurate its predictions are compared to the ground truth. If the result is acceptable, we keep the model; otherwise, we tune hyperparameters and train again. *A hyperparameter is a variable that is set before the training process and cannot be changed during learning. Parameters are those that are fine-tuned during training.*

In the Jupyter notebook, we use the following code snippet to predict and evaluate the model:

```
y_test_pred = random_forest.predict(X_test)
print(classification_report(y_test_pred,y_test))
conf_mat=confusion_matrix(y_test_pred,y_test)
```

To evaluate whether the result is acceptable and we can keep the model, we can use the confusion matrix for a binary classification task. The resulting confusion matrix for the dataset we analyzed in the Jupyter notebook is shown in *Figure 7.8*:

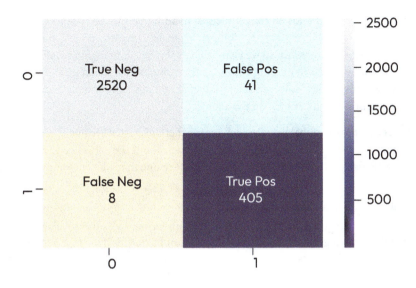

Figure 7.8 – Confusion matrix

Let's understand the components of the confusion matrix:

- **True negative (TN)**: The model predicted negative, and it is true. These transactions are not fraudulent.

- **True positive (TP)**: The model predicted positive, and it is true. These transactions are fraudulent.

- **False negative (FN)**: The model failed to predict and they were fraudulent.

- **False positive (FP)**: The model flagged these transactions as fraudulent, but they were not.

Based on these numbers, we can calculate precision and recall. **Precision** answers the question, of all the classes we predicted as positive, how many were actually positive?

$$\frac{TP}{TP + FP}$$

Our precision is 0.91.

Recall answers the question, of all the fraudulent classes, how many did our model predict correctly? The formula for this is as follows:

$$\frac{TP}{TP + FN}$$

Our recall is 0.98.

The evaluation of the results depends on the problem at hand. Selecting the metrics correctly is very important as it will impact the subsequent decisions we make. In `Chapter07/ML_warmup`, we are working to find fraudulent transactions, so we value models that result in higher recall than precision. We prefer recall because the cost of missing a fraudulent transaction is much higher than flagging a potentially harmless transaction. However, the number of FP flags cannot be enormous because of the cost of the transaction and its impact on the client.

Real-world datasets are mostly imbalanced, which means that the classes are not equally represented. It is our job to apply techniques that enable the model to learn about the existence and characteristics of both classes, particularly when the less frequent class is the one that we are trying to detect.

> **A note on balanced and imbalanced datasets**
>
> **Accuracy**, as the percentage of correct predictions, is another commonly used evaluation metric. However, it will not yield good results if the dataset is not balanced. If we take accuracy as an evaluation metric in an imbalanced dataset, the model only needs to identify the majority class to return a good result, and that does not guarantee that this is a good model.
>
> In our EDA, we will examine the proportion of each class and determine whether we are dealing with a balanced or imbalanced dataset. For example, in `Chapter07/ML_warmup`, we know that the proportion of fraudulent stances is 17%.
>
> We can solve this by using oversampling or undersampling techniques in the feature engineering preprocessing step. This must be done with caution as it may alter the underlying relationships in our data or remove some critical information.
>
> We can also use algorithms that have already been optimized for imbalanced datasets and allow the user to add that information to the training process – for example, by using the `class_weight` parameter in the random forest algorithm.
>
> Additionally, we can optimize the split by considering the unequal representation of the classes by using `stratify` in `train_test_split`.

Introducing deep learning

In *Part 2* of this book, we will also use deep learning methodologies when solving the use cases. Deep learning models employ multiple layers of interconnected nodes called neurons, which process input data and produce outputs based on learned weights and activation functions. The connections between neurons facilitate information flow, and the architecture of the network determines how information is processed and transformed.

We will study three types of neural network architectures in detail in their corresponding chapters. For now, let's introduce the framework and terminology that we will use in them.

The neuron serves as the fundamental building block of the system and can be defined as a node with one or more input values, weights, and output values:

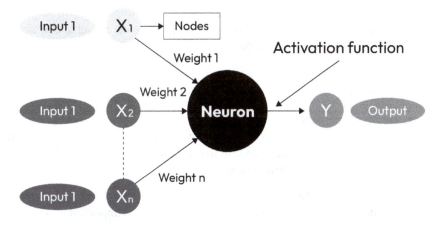

Figure 7.9 – A neuron's structure

When we stack multiple layers with this structure, it becomes a neural network. This architecture typically consists of an input layer, hidden layers, and an output layer:

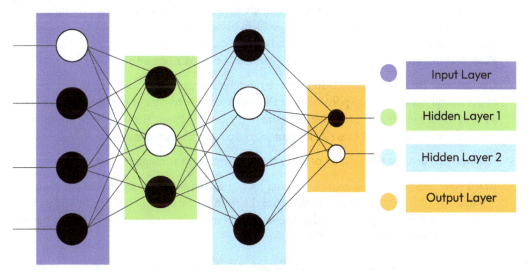

Figure 7.10 – Neural network structure

The input layer initiates the network and passes data to the hidden layers, which perform calculations on the features and patterns. The more hidden layers there are, the more complex calculations are executed.

The output layer receives the processed information from the hidden layers and provides a result or output summarizing the information that's been processed within the network.

The connections between nodes contain weights that carry information on how to solve a specific problem. During model training, we calibrate these weights to adapt the model to our dataset. The weights represent the learnable parameters of the model.

This flexible structure allows users to tune numerous hyperparameters to enhance the model's performance. The fundamentals are as follows:

- **Learning rate**: This hyperparameter controls how much a model changes in response to weight updates. Finding the correct value is crucial as a very small learning rate may result in a lengthy training process, while a higher one can lead to sub-optimal weight sets and altered results. The learning rate is closely related to the optimizers.

- **Activation functions**: These functions determine whether a neuron should be activated or not, meaning they decide whether the neuron's input to the network is important for the prediction process using simple mathematical operations. The activation function derives output from a set of input values fed into each layer. A list of activation functions in Keras can be found at `https://keras.io/api/layers/activations/`.

- **Cost functions**: These functions quantify the error between the predicted and expected values, summarizing the model's performance in a single value to be minimized during training. The choice of the cost function depends on the problem being solved, with common examples being mean squared error for regression tasks and categorical cross-entropy for classification tasks. Keras lists the various losses at `https://keras.io/api/losses/`.

- **Optimizers**: These algorithms help improve model performance by adjusting the attributes of the neural network. Its responsibility in the architecture is to change the learning rate and weights of the neurons to reach the minimum of the loss function. The supported optimizers in Keras are listed here: `https://keras.io/api/optimizers/`.

- **Epochs**: This denotes the number of times the algorithm runs through the entire dataset.

- **Batch size**: This refers to the number of samples considered to update the model parameters. A batch size of N means that N samples from the training dataset will be used to update the model parameters. Keep in mind that these samples are held in memory, so a higher batch size requires more memory.

All the models we use, will be analyzed within the Keras framework, which has excellent documentation.

Model preparation

In `Chapter07/DL_warmup`, we will work with the same dataset as in the previous section – *Ethereum Fraud Detection Dataset*. This time, we will select fewer columns and standardize the numbers using `RobustScaler()` from sklearn.

As in all prediction problems, we want to separate the test and training datasets with `train test split ()`.

Model building

We'll create a sequential model with Keras. The structure of sequential models consists of a stack of the same or different layers, where the output of one layer goes into the other.

The following code snippet sets the input layer to expect rows of data with the number of columns of the dataset. In this case, we are only working with 11 columns:

```
model.add(Input(shape=(X_train.shape[1],)))
```

We add three hidden layers, each with a decreasing number of nodes. All of them use `relu` as the activation function. The `Dense` layer is a fully connected layer and is one of the many types of layers, such as `Convolutional` or LSTM:

```
model.add(Dense(30, activation='relu'))
model.add(Dense(10, activation='relu'))
model.add(Dense(5, activation='relu'))
model.add(Dense(1, activation='sigmoid'))
```

Since this is a binary classification task, in the last layer, we will use the `sigmoid` activation function and `1` in the output layer:

```
model.add(Dense(1, activation='sigmoid'))
```

Before training the model, it needs to be compiled with the optimizer, the loss functions, and the metrics. The compiler configures the learning process. It's worth mentioning that as this is an imbalanced dataset, we are interested in precision and recall, so we must build the metric by leveraging the `keras` library, as follows:

```
metrics = [
    keras.metrics.Precision(name="precision"),\
    keras.metrics.Recall(name="recall"),
]
```

Now, we must add it to the compiler:

```
model.compile(optimizer=keras.optimizers.Adam(1e-2), \
    loss=loss_function, metrics=metrics)
```

Training and evaluating a model

Once the model has been built, we have to feed it our dataset, which means we have to train it. This is done with `fit()`, and in this case, we decided to do it for 90 epochs.

Once training has been performed, it is necessary to evaluate the model by predicting data that has not been part of the training. We can do this with `X_test` and `y_test`.

The classification report shows that recall for the minority class is 95%, which is very good. With more data preprocessing and by applying techniques for imbalanced datasets and hyperparameter tuning, we could further improve the results.

In this particular exercise, one of the Zen of Python principles applies perfectly. *Simple is better than complex* – a simpler machine learning model performed better than a complex neural network.

Now that we have explored both methodologies, we will highlight additional characteristics of each field:

Machine learning	Deep learning
Can train and make inferences from smaller datasets	Requires large amounts of data
Shorter training and can be done with a CPU	Longer training and needs a GPU to train effectively
Makes simple correlations	Makes non-linear complex correlations
Mostly explainable	Opaque model, complex to explain

Table 7.1 – Differences between machine learning and deep learning

A note on the ethical and social impact of artificial intelligence

Discussions regarding ethics and social impact may appear distant from our daily work, but given that our projects typically unfold within a business environment, it is advisable to consider their broader implications. The ethical and social ramifications of machine learning and deep learning encompass diverse dimensions, including the following:

Bias: Similar to the bias error, which oversimplifies its learning outcome, machine learning models can inherit biases present in training data, potentially leading to discriminatory outcomes. Bias can be introduced at various stages of the machine learning life cycle, from data collection to model deployment. It is important to obtain unbiased data to train our models and regularly audit them to detect and rectify bias.

Transparency: The opacity of complex machine learning models poses challenges for regulators and may undermine user trust. Many DeFi ventures are actively seeking regulatory approval to facilitate the flow of funds from traditional banking systems into the DeFi world. Given the highly regulated nature of the finance sector, data scientists working in this domain must make efforts to enhance model interpretability and provide explanations for their decisions to regulatory authorities.

Addressing these ethical considerations necessitates a multidisciplinary approach that involves technology developers, policymakers, ethicists, and more. As professionals working with models, we need to keep these challenges in mind, especially when selecting datasets, preprocessing them, or evaluating their results in the real world.

Summary

In this chapter, we delved into the fundamental concepts of artificial intelligence, which will serve as the foundation for our journey in *Part 2* of this book. We explored various types of tasks, including supervised learning, unsupervised learning, and reinforcement learning. Through a hands-on example, we gained insights into the typical machine learning process, which encompasses model selection, training, and evaluation.

Throughout this chapter, we acquired essential knowledge related to common challenges in machine learning, such as striking the right balance between underfitting and overfitting models, the existence of imbalanced datasets, and which metrics are relevant to evaluate models that are trained with them. Understanding these concepts is vital for any successful machine learning project.

Moreover, we progressed into the basics of deep learning, where we explored the key components of a neural network using Keras. Additionally, we implemented a pipeline to tackle a supervised problem to see all the concepts duly applied.

In the next chapter, we will discuss an important topic, sentiment analysis.

Further reading

To learn more about the topics that were covered in this chapter, take a look at the following resources:

- Definitions:

  - Igual, L. and Seguí, S. (2017). *Introduction to data science: A python approach to concepts, techniques and applications.* Springer.

  - Ertel, W. (2018). *Introduction to artificial intelligence.* Springer.

  - Skansi, S. (2018). *Introduction to deep learning: From logical calculus to artificial intelligence.* Springer.

  - Ian Goodfellow, Yoshua Bengio, and Aaron Courville. (2016). *Deep Learning.* Available at `https://www.deeplearningbook.org/`.

  - Chollet, F. (2017). *Deep Learning with Python.* Manning Publications.

  - Müller, A. C. and Guido, S. (2016). *Introduction to Machine Learning with Python: A guide for data scientists.* O'Reilly Media.

  - VanderPlas, J. (n.d.). *What Is Machine Learning?* Pythonic Perambulations. Available at `https://jakevdp.github.io/PythonDataScienceHandbook/05.01-what-is-machine-learning.html`.

  - *What is Deep Learning?*: `https://machinelearningmastery.com/what-is-deep-learning/`.

- Mining addresses from websites: Furneaux, Nick. *Investigating Cryptocurrencies, Chapter 9*. Understanding, Extracting, and Analyzing Blockchain Evidence, Wiley, 2018. Page 125.

- James, G., Witten, D., Hastie, T., and Tibshirani, R. (2022). *An Introduction to Statistical Learning: With Applications*. In R. Springer.

- Gymnasium documentation: `https://gymnasium.farama.org/`.

- *Introduction – Spinning up documentation*. (n.d.). Welcome to Spinning Up in Deep RL! Spinning Up documentation. Available at `https://spinningup.openai.com/en/latest/user/introduction.html#what-this-is`.

- *Nansen Wallet Labels and Emojis: What Do They Mean?* (2023, March 14). Nansen – Crypto, DeFi and NFT Analytics. Available at `https://www.nansen.ai/guides/wallet-labels-emojis-what-do-they-mean#alpha-labels`.

- Pipelines:

  - EliteDataScience. (2022, July 8). *WTF is the Bias-Variance Tradeoff?* (Infographic). Available at `https://elitedatascience.com/bias-variance-tradeoff`.

  - *Sklearn.ensemble.RandomForestClassifier*. (n.d.). scikit-learn. Retrieved March 14, 2023, from `https://scikit-learn.org/stable/modules/generated/sklearn.ensemble.RandomForestClassifier.html`.

  - *SMOTE oversampling*. (n.d.). Machine Learning Mastery. Available at `https://machinelearningmastery.com/smote-oversampling-for-imbalanced-classification/`.

  - Nyuytiymbiy, K. (2022, March 28). *Parameters and Hyperparameters in Machine Learning and Deep Learning*. Medium. Available at `https://towardsdatascience.com/parameters-and-hyperparameters-aa609601a9ac`.

  - Heatmap on `Chapter07/ML_warmup`: T, D. (2019, July 25). *Confusion matrix visualization*. Medium. Available at `https://medium.com/@dtuk81/confusion-matrix-visualization-fc31e3f30fea`.

  - Tutorial to use a Kaggle dataset on Colaboratory. Useful to follow along with `Chapter07/ML_warmup`: Gupta, K. (2022, August 24). *How to Load Kaggle Datasets into Google Colab?* Analytics Vidhya. Available at `https://www.analyticsvidhya.com/blog/2021/06/how-to-load-kaggle-datasets-directly-into-google-colab/`.

  - Pramoditha, R. (2022, January 26). *How to Choose the Right Activation Function for Neural Networks*. Medium. Available at `https://towardsdatascience.com/how-to-choose-the-right-activation-function-for-neural-networks-3941ff0e6f9c`.

- Gupta, A. (2022, May 24). *A Comprehensive Guide on Deep Learning Optimizers*. Analytics Vidhya. Available at `https://www.analyticsvidhya.com/blog/2021/10/a-comprehensive-guide-on-deep-learning-optimizers/`.

- *PEP 20 – The Zen of Python*. (2022, March 15). PEP 0 – Index of Python Enhancement Proposals (PEPs) | peps.python.org. Available at `https://peps.python.org/pep-0020/`

- Keras Team. (2020, April 17). *Keras documentation: Imbalanced classification: credit card fraud detection*. Keras: Deep Learning for Humans. Available at `https://keras.io/examples/structured_data/imbalanced_classification/`.

- Ramchandani, P. (2021, April 10). *Random Forests and the Bias-Variance Tradeoff*. Medium. Available at `https://towardsdatascience.com/random-forests-and-the-bias-variance-tradeoff-3b77fee339b4`.

- Tuning with Bayesian optimization: Rendyk. (2023, August 17). *Tuning the Hyperparameters and layers of neural network deep learning*. Analytics Vidhya. Available at `https://www.analyticsvidhya.com/blog/2021/05/tuning-the-hyperparameters-and-layers-of-neural-network-deep-learning/`.

- *How to Grid Search Hyperparameters for Deep Learning Models in Python with Keras*. (2022, August). Machine Learning Mastery. Available at `https://machinelearningmastery.com/grid-search-hyperparameters-deep-learning-models-python-keras/`.

8

Sentiment Analysis – NLP and Crypto News

Natural language processing (**NLP**) falls under the umbrella of artificial intelligence and is concerned with the comprehension of text by computers. Recent advancements in this field, exemplified by the emergence of tools such as ChatGPT, have become an integral part of our daily lives. Yet, the financial sector has been leveraging NLP for quite some time, particularly for fundamental analysis.

Fundamental analysis seeks to ascertain the intrinsic value of assets such as stocks, tokens, or NFT art based on publicly accessible information. In traditional finance, textual data is sourced from periodic submissions to the SEC (such as Form 10K or 10Q), including financial statements, specialized media news, social media platforms such as X (formerly Twitter), and other avenues. Web3 has fostered a similar environment where market activities are continuous, and X and news platforms serve as predominant textual resources. It's worth noting that while most Web3 companies may not yet be obligated to file regulatory reports, it's probable that such data sources will eventually become available for most companies.

NLP in the financial sector encompasses various applications, including the following:

- **Sentiment analysis**: Determining the positivity, negativity, or neutrality of text, which could be news articles, social media posts (tweets, Reddit, and so on), and more. These algorithms can also provide insights into polarity and subjectivity, aiding in assessing sentiments toward companies, industries, markets, government decisions, crypto developments, and more.

- **Topic modeling**: This helps classify and organize large volumes of financial documents based on the underlying topics they cover. This aids in efficiently managing and accessing relevant information.

- **Summarization**: In a world where content is being created at a non-stop rate, there simply is not enough time and/or resources to analyze and give hierarchy to all of it. NLP techniques are being applied to collect and create short summaries of documents that are easy to process by analysts.

- **Fraud detection**: Scrutinizing emails, chats, financial documents, transcribed conversations, and more using NLP techniques to uncover patterns that are potentially indicative of fraudulent activities.

- **Trading**: Incorporating NLP tools into trading strategies to signal or predict market trends, or enhance the decision-making process of fundamental analysis traders.

The data source for NLP techniques is text that is categorized as unstructured. We are surrounded by it, with more being produced every second. We explored some text sources in *Chapter 3*; we will explore some others in this chapter.

In this chapter, we will analyze the sentiment of the news sourced from Crypto Panic. To do so, we will build a **neural network (NN)** and explain the concept and use of pre-trained embeddings. A crypto news dataset and a traditional finance news dataset will be employed to train our model. Additionally, we'll learn the essentials of how to pre-process text for NN utilization and how to evaluate the results of such a model.

At the time of writing, ChatGPT is a tangible reality. Publicly accessible information reveals its training on an extensive multilingual corpus, utilizing reinforcement learning to progressively enhance its performance. We'll learn how to incorporate ChatGPT for sentiment analysis on the Crypto Panic dataset. This can be useful to implement as a ready-to-use tool while we build a specialized corpus to train our models.

In this chapter, we will cover the following main topics:

- A deep learning pipeline for sentiment analysis, encompassing preparation, model construction, training, and evaluation phases.

- Integrating ChatGPT for sentiment analysis

Technical requirements

In this chapter, we'll utilize tools from the libraries that were introduced in *Chapter 7* – that is, scikit-learn and Keras. Additionally, we will employ **NLTK**, a Python library that proves valuable for working with human language data. NLTK includes a range of modules and functions that empower us to execute tasks such as tokenization, stemming, and part-of-speech tagging on our selected databases. This library streamlines the process of processing extensive text datasets so that they're ready to be integrated with machine learning or deep learning models.

If you have not worked with NLTK before, it can be installed with the following code:

```
pip install nltk
```

The documentation for `nltk` can be found at `https://www.nltk.org`. Another essential library when handling text manipulation and cleaning is **re**, short for **Regular Expression**. A regular expression is a sequence of characters that defines a search pattern. Here's an example:

Pattern	Search Criteria
[a-z]	Any single character in the range a-z
[0-9A-Fa-f]	Match any hexadecimal digit

Table 8.1 – Example of a "re" pattern

The `re` library provides functions and methods to employ the aforementioned patterns. For instance, `re.sub` replaces all characters that match the pattern with a specified string. A comprehensive list of functions is available at `https://docs.python.org/3/library/re.html#module-re`.

Throughout our work, we will utilize Google's Colaboratory platform, which already includes the core library imports. However, for specific tasks, additional imports will be required.

You can find all the data and code files for this chapter in this book's GitHub repository at `https://github.com/PacktPublishing/Data-Science-for-Web3/tree/main/Chapter08`. We recommend that you read through the code files in the `Chapter08` folder to follow along.

Example datasets

We will merge two headline datasets in this chapter; you can find links to the relevant sources in the *Further reading* section and the code. The datasets are as follows:

- **Financial Phrase Bank**: This dataset is also available on **Kaggle** and contains a headline accompanied by sentiment analysis labels from the viewpoint of a retail investor. It comprises multiple datasets, each of which categorizes sentences based on the level of consensus regarding the sentiment of the phrase. For this exercise, we will utilize the *Sentence_AllAgree* dataset.

- **CryptoGDELT2022**: Presented in the paper *Cryptocurrency Curated News Event Database From GDELT*, this dataset comprises news events extracted from the **Global Database of Events, Language, and Tone** (**GDELT**). It covers news events between March 31, 2021, and April 30, 2022. The dataset includes various sentiment scores and manual labeling methods. In this exercise, we will exclusively employ manual labeling.

Let's get started with building our pipeline.

Building our pipeline

In an NLP pipeline, preparation generally encompasses a pre-processing step where we clean and normalize the data. Following that, a feature representation step translates the language into input that can be consumed by our chosen models. Once this is completed, we are ready to build, train, and evaluate the model. This strategic plan will be implemented throughout the subsequent sections.

Preparation

Language manifests in numerous variations. There are formatting nuances, such as capitalization or punctuation; words that serve as linguistic aids without true semantic meaning, such as prepositions; and special characters, including emojis, further enrich the landscape. To work with this data, we must transform raw text into a dataset while following a similar criterion as numeric datasets. This cleaning process enables us to eliminate outliers, reduce noise, manage vocabulary size, and optimize data for ingestion by NLP models.

A basic flow diagram of the data cleaning pipeline can be seen in the following figure:

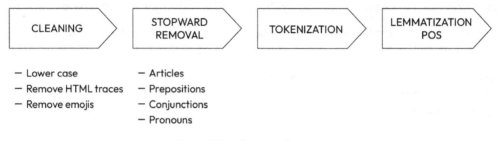

Figure 8.1 – Cleaning diagram

Let's delve into some of these steps.

Normalization

Normalization encompasses a series of tasks, including lowercasing and removing HTML traces, links, and emojis. Our objective is to clean our database so that only words remain.

Furthermore, this process involves eliminating words that lack informativeness for our model or that could potentially introduce bias, leading to suboptimal predictions. Depending on the task, we will select words that we may have to delete. This step also addresses the process of removing words that may have escaped the *stop words* cleaning process.

We can also convert Unidecode text into ASCII text. Unidecode accommodates characters from diverse languages, allowing them to be translated into their nearest ASCII counterpart. For instance, the Spanish character "ñ" becomes "n" in ASCII. We implement this transformation in `Database_and_Preprocessing.ipynb` using the following code snippet:

```
text = unidecode.unidecode(text)
```

Normalization fosters uniformity by rendering all text in a consistent format, directing the model's focus toward content rather than superficial differences.

Stop words

Our objective here is to exclude words that contribute minimal semantic value or meaning to our model. Frequently employed words such as articles ("a," "the," "an"), prepositions ("on," "at," "from," "to"), conjunctions ("and," "so," "although"), and pronouns ("she," "he," "it") play functional roles in language but lack substantial semantic content that the model can leverage.

Consequently, this collection of words is generally filtered out during preprocessing. The stop words collection can be downloaded by language and directly applied to our cleaning process using NLTK. In `Database_and_Preprocessing.ipynb`, we downloaded the English stop words with the following code snippet:

```
nltk.download('stopwords')
stop_words = set(stopwords.words('english'))
```

This process reduces the noise in the data and helps improve the efficiency of the model.

Tokenization

Tokenization involves splitting the text within our database into smaller units of meaning referred to as tokens. These units can take the form of sentences or words. For instance, let's take a look at the following headline:

"SEC investigating Coinbase for its Earn product, wallet service, and exchange activity"

When tokenized into words, this yields the following output:

```
['SEC', 'investigating', 'Coinbase', 'Earn', 'product', ',', 'wallet',
'service', 'exchange', 'activity']
```

Tokenization results in a structured input that the NLP model can process effectively, facilitating data analysis. Such analysis guides decisions on vocabulary size for dimensionality reduction, a demonstrated example of which can be found in `Database_and_Preprocessing.ipynb`. This showcases the top recurring words in the analyzed dataset. Such analysis gives the following result:

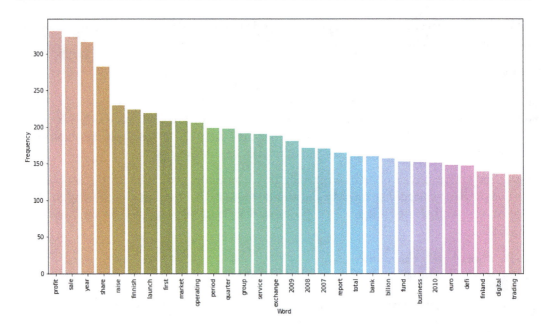

Figure 8.2 – Top recurring words in analyzed headlines

Lemmatization and part-of-speech (POS) tagging

These techniques reduce words to their base or root form. It allows us to reduce the diversity of words we have to process by selecting those words that are conjugated and replacing them with their root word. In our example sentence ("SEC investigating Coinbase for its Earn product, wallet service, and exchange activity"), the word *investigating* will change to *investigate*.

The accuracy of lemmatization hinges on the library's comprehension of the word's context or function within the sentence. POS tagging contributes this contextual information to our analysis. Here's an example:

```
nltk.pos_tag
```

POS tagging helps us programmatically assign a context to each word, depending on its position in the sentence or document. Here's an example:

```
word= ['SEC', 'investigating', 'Coinbase', 'Earn', \
    'product', ',', 'wallet', 'service', 'exchange', 'activity']
[nltk.pos_tag([w]) for w in word]
[[('SEC', 'NNP')], [('investigating', 'VBG')], [('Coinbase', 'NN')],
[('Earn', 'NN')], [('product', 'NN')], [(',', ',')], [('wallet',
'NN')], [('service', 'NN')], [('exchange', 'NN')], [('activity',
'NN')]]
```

The result of cleaning the sentence looks like this:

```
investigate coinbase earn product wallet service exchange activity
```

Let's look at some additional preprocessing techniques:

- **Stemming**: This involves removing prefixes and suffixes from words to derive a common base form, known as the "stem." The resulting stem may not always form a valid word, but it aims to capture the core meaning.

- **Named entity recognition** (**NER**): This technique automatically identifies and classifies named entities (for example, names of people, places, organizations, and dates) in text. NER extracts structured information from unstructured text, categorizing entities into predefined classes. An example of this approach is offered by the X (formerly Twitter) dataset, which we covered in *Chapter 3*.

- **Dependency parsing**: This technique analyzes a sentence's grammatical structure to establish relationships between words. It creates a hierarchical structure where each word is linked to its governing word (the "head") and assigned a grammatical role (the "dependency label").

> **Checkpoint**
>
> A step-by-step version of this pipeline is detailed in `Database_and_Preprocessing.ipynb`. If you want to skip this section, the resulting `.csv` file has been uploaded to this book's GitHub and is accessible at `preprocessed.csv`.

Feature representation

Following the preprocessing phase, the next step involves transforming the resultant raw text data into features that the model can utilize for statistical inference. The goal is to extract relevant information from the text and encode it in a way that algorithms can understand. There are multiple ways to achieve this, but they generally involve representing words as vectors and measuring the frequency of words in a document. Some common techniques are bag of words, **term frequency-inverse document frequency** (**TF-IDF**), and word embeddings. Let's briefly describe them.

Bag of words

This technique builds a vector that represents all the words in the document by the number of times that word appears. It ignores the order of the sentence or the context of the word. Its implementation can be accomplished using `sklearn.feature_extraction.text.CountVectorizer` from the scikit-learn library. This approach is basic and loses important contextual information, and it may also create a very sparse matrix because the vocabulary is vast:

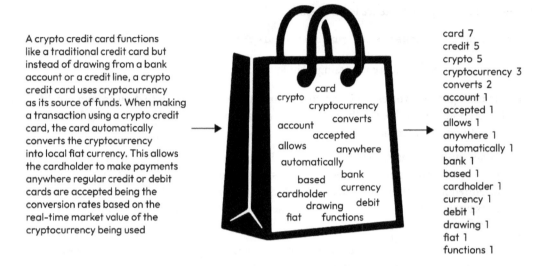

A crypto credit card functions like a traditional credit card but instead of drawing from a bank account or a credit line, a crypto credit card uses cryptocurrency as its source of funds. When making a transaction using a crypto credit card, the card automatically converts the cryptocurrency into local fiat currency. This allows the cardholder to make payments anywhere regular credit or debit cards are accepted being the conversion rates based on the real-time market value of the cryptocurrency being used

crypto card
cryptocurrency
converts
account
accepted
allows anywhere
automatically
based bank
cardholder currency
drawing debit
fiat functions

card 7
credit 5
crypto 5
cryptocurrency 3
converts 2
account 1
accepted 1
allows 1
anywhere 1
automatically 1
bank 1
based 1
cardholder 1
currency 1
debit 1
drawing 1
fiat 1
functions 1

Figure 8.3 – Bag of words. Text extracted from https://rif.technology/content-hub/crypto-credit-card/

Moreover, this approach can be enhanced by incorporating n-grams, which involve concatenating two or more words that hold contextual meaning together. For example, "natural language", "machine learning," and "press release" encapsulate specific concepts when combined, but in isolation, they do not retain the concept. Incorporating n-grams into bag of words can expand the vocabulary further.

TF-IDF

This is an alternate technique where **TF** signifies **term frequency,** meaning that this method also counts the number of occurrences of a word in a text. **IDF,** or **inverse document frequency** implies that it also downscales those words that appear with high frequency. This way, we can score words that are distinct in a given document and therefore are considered informative. This approach can be achieved with `sklearn.feature_extraction.text.TfidfVectorizer`.

Word embeddings

Word embeddings represent words as dense vectors within a continuous space. This approach retains information about context and semantic meaning by capturing relationships between words. **Word2Vec** and **GloVe** (`https://www.tensorflow.org/tutorials/text/word2vec`) are popular algorithms that generate word embeddings. These embeddings can either be pre-trained on large text corpora or fine-tuned for specific tasks. In our model, we employ Glove (`https://nlp.stanford.edu/projects/glove`) vectors.

Glove, in particular, is a pre-trained vector that's developed via an unsupervised learning algorithm. This method leverages linear substructures prevalent in texts and gauges semantic similarity by measuring vector distances. The GloVe website provides a classic example illustrating the relationships discerned by the model:

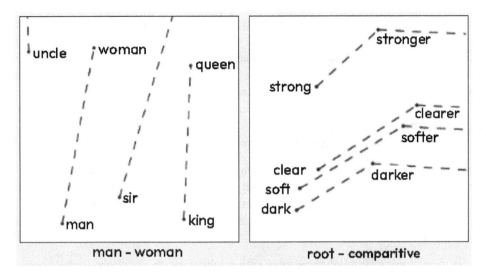

Figure 8.4 – Example of structures found in the words by GloVe
(source: https://nlp.stanford.edu/projects/glove/)

Model building

We are working on a supervised task to classify Crypto Panic headlines into positive, negative, and neutral. For this purpose, we will employ the **LSTM** model, an abbreviation for **long short-term memory**. The entire process outlined in this section can be followed through the `Modeling.ipynb` file.

LSTM is a type of **recurrent neural network** (**RNN**) that's capable of learning long-term dependencies that significantly outperform regular RNNs with text tasks. This structure is commonly used in NLP tasks as it can model sequences of input data well and retain dependencies between words in a sentence or document. Consequently, it can predict not only based on the current input but also consider long-distance information – that is, the context – and not just specific words. It is important to note that while LSTMs can be more effective in capturing long-term dependencies, their performance can also depend on factors such as the specific task, the size of the dataset, and the model's architecture. In some cases, other advanced architectures such as transformer-based models (such as BERT and GPT) have also demonstrated superior performance in certain NLP tasks.

Christopher Olah provides a great introduction to the model in his blog, describing it as follows:

"Humans don't start their thinking from scratch every second. As you read this essay, you understand each word based on your understanding of previous words. You don't throw everything away and start thinking from scratch again. Your thoughts have persistence."

LSTM serves as a specialized form of RNN that's designed to detect patterns in data sequences, whether they arise from sensor data, asset prices, or natural language. Its distinct feature lies in its capacity to preserve information over extended periods compared to conventional RNNs. RNNs have a short-term memory that retains information in the current neuron, resulting in a limited ability to predict with longer sequences. When the memory is exceeded, the model simply discards the oldest data and replaces it with new data, without considering whether the discarded data was important or not. LSTM overcomes this short-term memory problem by selectively retaining relevant information in the **cell state** in addition to the traditional short-term memory stored in the **hidden state**.

At the beginning of each computational step, we have the current input, *x(t)*, the previous state of the long-term memory, *c(t-1)*, and the previous state of the short-term memory stored in the hidden state, *h(t-1)*. At the end of the process, we obtain an updated cell state and a new hidden state. The cell state carries information along with the timestamps of our dataset, allowing it to extract meaning from the order of the input data.

These three inputs navigate through three gates, each serving a specific function:

- **Forget gate**: This gate determines which current and previous information is retained and which is discarded. It integrates the previous status of the hidden state and the current input, passing them through a sigmoid function. The sigmoid function outputs values between 0 and 1, with 0 indicating that the previous information is considered irrelevant and can be forgotten, and 1 indicating that it should be preserved. The result is multiplied by the current cell state.

- **Input gate**: This gate determines the importance of the current input in solving the task. It quantifies the relevance of the new information carried by the input, *x(t)*. The current input is multiplied by the hidden state from the previous run. All information deemed important by the input gate is added to the cell state, forming the new cell state, *c(t)*. This new cell state becomes the current state of the long-term memory and will be used in the next run.

- **Output gate**: The output of the LSTM model is computed in the hidden state:

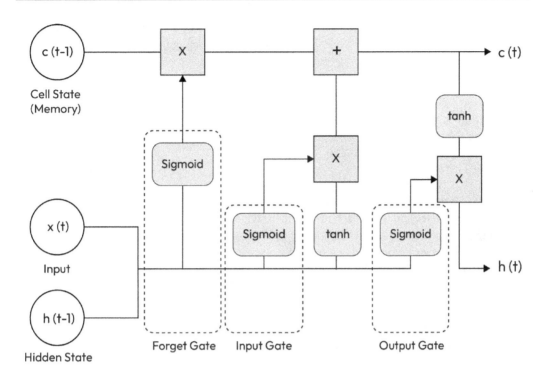

Figure 8.5 – Cell states

To interact with the LSTM, we need to input vectors with uniform lengths. To fulfill this requirement, we must encode the preprocessed input text sequentially, as follows:

- `tokenizer.texts_to_sequences(X_train)`: This step transforms each text into a sequence of integers using the tokenizer's most frequently encountered words. If the tokenizer lacks certain words in its vocabulary, a predefined <OOV> (out-of-vocabulary) token is employed.

- `pad_sequences`: This function transforms the previously converted sequences into a 2D array of shape: (number of sequences, length of the sequence desired). The length or `maxlen` argument can be user-defined or defaulted to the longest sequence in the list. Additionally, the user can select whether padding occurs at the sequence's beginning or end.

The model we have constructed features the embedding layer as its foremost element, with `trainable` = `False` to retain insights from Glove500. Should we opt for training from scratch, we have to set that parameter to `True`:

```
model = Sequential()
model.add(Embedding(input_dim = len(word_index) + 1 ,\
    output_dim = embedding_dim ,\
    weights = [embedding_vectors],\
    input_length = max_length ,\
    trainable = False))
```

Furthermore, our design incorporates an LSTM layer, a dense layer, and a dropout layer. The dropout layer, a regularization technique that's frequently employed to prevent overfitting, operates by randomly deactivating (that is, setting to zero) a fraction of neurons during each forward pass in training. This helps prevent the network from relying too heavily on specific neurons and encourages the network to learn more robust and generalized features:

```
model.add(Bidirectional(LSTM(embedding_dim, activation = 'relu',\
    dropout = 0.0 ,\
    recurrent_dropout = 0.0)))
model.add(Dense(embedding_dim, activation='relu'))
model.add(Dropout(0.3))
```

For the last dense layer, we use `'softmax'` activation, which assigns decimal probabilities to each trained class:

```
model.add(Dense(label_distinct, activation='softmax',\
    bias_initializer = 'zeros'))
```

We compile by utilizing the loss function of `'categorical_crossentropy'`, a standard choice for multiclass classification tasks encompassing more than two classes, as is the scenario here:

```
model.compile(loss = 'categorical_crossentropy',\
    optimizer = Adam(1e-3), \
    metrics = ['accuracy'])
```

> **Checkpoint**
>
> A step-by-step version of this part of the pipeline is shown in `Modeling.ipynb`. If you want to skip this section, the resulting model and tokenizer have been uploaded to this book's GitHub repository and are accessible via `chapter8_model.h5` and `text_tokenizer.json`.

Training and evaluation

We can train the model with the following code snippet:

```
model.fit(X_train_pad, y_train, batch_size = batch_size, \
    epochs = 10, validation_data = (X_test_pad, y_test), \
    verbose = 0, callbacks=[tensorboard_callback])
```

Upon completing the training, we assess its performance and outcomes through three distinct methods:

Mini test: We look for test samples, apply the model, and conduct evaluations. We must always remember to preprocess our samples and pass them to our model in the same shape as it is ready to consume.

TensorBoard: This visualization tool, enabled by TensorFlow, illustrates the model's performance during the learning process and the evolution of the loss function across epochs. The provided code establishes a `log` folder for storing the resulting training and validation outcomes:

```
tensorboard_callback = \
    tf.keras.callbacks.TensorBoard(log_dir="./logs")
```

This folder is referred to in the training instructions provided with `callbacks=[tensorboard_callback])`. TensorBoard then accesses this folder to display the results.

ROC AUC curve: According to Jason Brownlee's blog, "*A ROC curve is a diagnostic plot for summarizing the behavior of a model by calculating the false positive rate and true positive rate for a set of predictions by the model under different thresholds.*" The ROC curve is an evaluation metric for binary tasks. To apply it to our multiclass case, we must transform the multiclass problem into a binary one using either the **one-versus-one (OvO)** or **one-versus-all (OvA)/one-versus-rest (OvR)** approach. In OvR, we assess each class against the others. In OvO, we evaluate each class against every other class in pairs. Choosing between these techniques depends on specific problem nuances, class count, computational resources, and dataset characteristics. Certain machine learning libraries, such as scikit-learn, offer the choice between OvA and OvO strategies for multi-class classification algorithms.

In this case, we use the OvA approach, where we measure how well our model predicts each label, considering one as true and all the others as false. That way, we can plot the ROC AUC. The closer to 1, the better the model; the further it approaches 0.5, the less skillful it is:

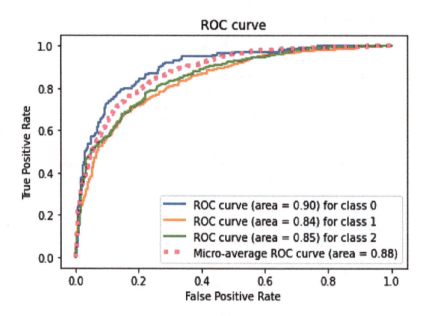

Figure 8.6 – ROC AUC curve applied

Both accuracy and the ROC AUC curve can be overly optimistic when dealing with imbalanced datasets.

F1 score: When addressing a multiclass classification problem through the OvA perspective, we acquire a binary set of values that allow us to calculate precision, recall, and the F1 score. The F1 score proves more suitable when the aim is to minimize both false positives and false negatives. This metric amalgamates information from both precision and recall and is their harmonic mean. The F1 score formula is as follows:

$$F1 \; Score \; = \; 2* \frac{Precision*Recall}{Precision + Recall}$$

This is succinctly summarized by Joos Korstanje in his blog:

- *A model will obtain a high F1 score if both precision and recall are high*

- *A model will obtain a low F1 score if both precision and recall are low*

- *A model will obtain a medium F1 score if precision or recall is low and the other is high*

The aforementioned metric can be generated with the subsequent code snippet:

```
classification_report(y_test, y_pred_onehot, target_names=target_names
```

The weighted average F1 score for the model is 0.72.

We can save the trained model for future use using the following code snippet:

```
text_tokenizer_json = tokenizer.to_json()
with io.open('text_tokenizer.json','w',encoding='utf-8') as f:
    f.write(json.dumps(text_tokenizer_json, \
        ensure_ascii=False))
model.save('chapter8_model.h5')
```

In the `Chapter08/app.py` file in this book's GitHub repository, we've developed an app that retrieves titles from the Cryptopanic API, applies the trained sentiment model, and displays the outcome in the console.

A note on NLP challenges

Due to the inherent complexities of human language, NLP faces several challenges that may significantly impact the performance and accuracy of its models. However, potential mitigation strategies exist to address these challenges:

Ambiguity: Words and phrases often carry multiple meanings, with the correct interpretation depending on the context. This complexity poses challenges, even for native and non-native speakers of a language, as seen in metaphors. Similarly, models encounter difficulties in interpreting user intent. To tackle this, models can be designed to incorporate broader contextual information, leveraging surrounding words and phrases for more accurate meaning inference.

Language diversity: Languages exhibit wide variations in grammar, syntax, and semantics. Additionally, slang, regional dialects, and cultural nuances further contribute to linguistic diversity. NLP models, trained on a specific type of data, may struggle to generalize to diverse linguistic contexts. To address this limitation, models can be trained on more extensive and diverse datasets encompassing various linguistic patterns.

Data sparsity: NLP models heavily rely on vast amounts of labeled data for training. However, acquiring labeled data for all conceivable language variations and applications proves challenging. Transfer learning techniques, such as pre-training on a large corpus and fine-tuning for specific tasks, offer a viable solution by mitigating the need for extensive labeled data.

Ethical considerations and bias: NLP models may inadvertently learn bias present in training data, resulting in biased outputs. Addressing this issue requires the curation of diverse and representative training datasets, regular audits of models for bias, and the implementation of fairness-aware training techniques.

While NLP faces numerous challenges, ongoing research and advancements in machine learning techniques contribute to overcoming these hurdles.

ChatGPT integration

When pressed for time and unable to gather the necessary data for training a new model to build a classifier, we can explore the option of utilizing pre-trained models, such as those offered by TextBlob, spaCy, or the Hugging Face libraries. Additionally, we can seamlessly integrate readily available models such as ChatGPT.

I asked ChatGPT to present itself and this is what it said:

"I'm ChatGPT, a large language model developed by OpenAI, based on the GPT-3 architecture. I'm trained on a vast amount of text data and can generate human-like responses to a wide variety of questions and prompts. My main purpose is to assist users in generating text, whether it's writing an article, answering questions, or completing creative tasks. I have a broad range of knowledge on various topics, including science, technology, history, and literature, among others. I'm designed to understand natural language and can respond to text-based input in a conversational manner."

Of particular relevance to this chapter is the final statement. This tool is well-versed in diverse vocabulary and is primed to process textual input.

ChatGPT has a different architecture compared to LSTM. It uses the **transformer** architecture, which allows it to understand and generate natural language text. Transformers use self-attention mechanisms to capture relationships between words in a sentence, allowing for parallel processing of words rather than sequential processing like in LSTMs. Transformers are used to translate languages, summarize long articles, answer questions, complete sentences, and even create stories. BERT and GPT are popular transformer models.

In the `Chapter07/chat_gpt integration` file, we've replicated the same use case as the previous segment, where we interacted with the Cryptopanic API to extract titles, apply the ChatGPT model, and display the output in the console, yielding excellent results. To facilitate this, an API key is required, which can be generated by following these steps on the OpenAI website:

1. Visit `https://platform.openai.com/docs/api-reference`, go to the sign-up section, and proceed to sign up on their website.

2. On the left-hand side, you will see a dropdown menu that says **View API keys**. Click on this to access the page for generating a new API key:

API keys

Your secret API keys are listed below. Please note that we do not display your secret API keys again after you generate them.

Do not share your API key with others, or expose it in the browser or other client-side code. In order to protect the security of your account, OpenAI may also automatically rotate any API key that we've found has leaked publicly.

You currently do not have any API keys. Please create one below.

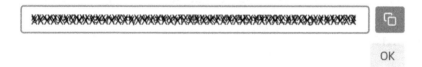

Figure 8.7 – ChatGPT – API keys landing page

3. It is essential to generate and securely store the generated API keys as they can't be retrieved once they've been generated:

API key generated

Please save this secret key somewhere safe and accessible. For security reasons, **you won't be able to view it again** through your OpenAI account. If you lose this secret key, you'll need to generate a new one.

XXXXXXXXXXXXXXXXXXXXXXXXXXXXXXXXXXXXXXXXXXXXXXXXXXXXXXXXXXX

OK

Figure 8.8 – Chat GPT – API key generated

The idea of this section is to recognize that ChatGPT exists and can do great work as well as solve the sentiment analysis problem by connecting the API, which may be a temporary solution if there is not enough data to train a specialized model.

It is possible to fine-tune ChatGPT for a specific task or domain using task-specific data. This process enables the model to adapt to the nuances and requirements of the target application. For instance, we can customize the model to generate shorter answers, reduce the amount of context required in a prompt for improved responses, and define how it handles edge cases. Let's imagine we would like to integrate a specialized bot into our company's internal communications system that delivers concise summaries of cryptocurrency news with a specific tone or format. This could be done with this training process. Detailed documentation for this process is available at `https://platform.openai.com/docs/guides/fine-tuning`, and a step-by-step tutorial can be found in the *Further reading* section.

Summary

The field of NLP is rapidly evolving, providing an effective means to extract insights from unstructured data such as text. Throughout this chapter, we introduced the field, illustrated a typical task within it, delineated the workflow, discussed pertinent data, and executed model training using embeddings. Additionally, we demonstrated the model evaluation process and showcased its integration into a program that sources headlines from the CryptoPanic API.

It's worth emphasizing that amassing a substantial volume of data is pivotal for high model accuracy. Nevertheless, in cases where constructing such a model isn't feasible, alternative solutions are available. We explored one such solution involving the ChatGPT API, which provides access to a text bot trained on a comprehensive corpus of data.

In the subsequent chapter, we will delve into the support that data teams can extend to artistic groups who are seeking to transform their artworks into unique products through the utilization of NFTs.

Further reading

To learn more about the topics that were covered in this chapter, take a look at the following resources:

- Introduction:

  - Bird, Steven, Edward Loper and Ewan Klein (2009), *Natural Language Processing with Python*. O'Reilly Media Inc. Available at `https://www.nltk.org/book/`.

  - Yordanov, V. (2019, August 13). *Introduction to natural language processing for text*. Medium. Available at `https://towardsdatascience.com/introduction-to-natural-language-processing-for-text-df845750fb63`.

  - Gabriel Doyle, and Charles Elkan. (n.d.). *Financial Topic Models*. Available at `https://pages.ucsd.edu/~gdoyle/papers/doyle-elkan-2009-nips-paper.pdf`.

  - Sigmoider. (2018, May 3). *Get started with NLP (Part I)*. Medium. Available at `https://medium.com/@gon.esbuyo/get-started-with-nlp-part-i-d67ca26cc828`.

- Suhyeon Kim, Haecheong Park, and Junghye Lee. (n.d.). *Word2vec-based latent semantic analysis (W2V-LSA) for topic modeling: A study on blockchain technology trend analysis.* Available at `https://www.sciencedirect.com/science/article/pii/S0957417420302256`.

- State of data science and machine learning (2022). *Kaggle: Your Machine Learning and Data Science Community.* Available at `https://www.kaggle.com/kaggle-survey-2022`.

- *Very good ChatGPT fine tuning tutorial: Tech-At-Work.* (2023, September 11). Easily Fine Tune ChatGPT 3.5 to Outperform GPT-4! [Video]. YouTube. Available at `https://www.youtube.com/watch?v=8Ieu2v0v4oc`.

- Example database:

  - Malo, P., Sinha, A., Korhonen, P., Wallenius, J., and Takala, P. (2014). *Good debt or bad debt: Detecting semantic orientations in economic texts.* Journal of the Association for Information Science and Technology, 65(4), 782-796. Available at `https://www.kaggle.com/datasets/ankurzing/sentiment-analysis-for-financial-news`.

  - Manoel Fernando Alonso Gadi, and Miguel Ángel Sicilia. (2022, October 10). *Cryptocurrency Curated News Event Database From GDELT* [pdf]. Research Square. Available at `https://assets.researchsquare.com/files/rs-2145757/v1_covered.pdf?c=1665769708`.

- Preprocessing:

  - Bird, S., Klein, E., and Loper, E. (2009). *Natural language processing with Python.* O'Reilly Media.

  - *Sklearn.feature_extraction.text.CountVectorizer.* (n.d.). scikit-learn. Retrieved March 24, 2023. Available at `https://scikit-learn.org/stable/modules/generated/sklearn.feature_extraction.text.CountVectorizer.html`.

  - *Sklearn.feature_extraction.text.TfidfVectorizer.* (n.d.). scikit-learn. Retrieved March 24, 2023. Available at `https://scikit-learn.org/stable/modules/generated/sklearn.feature_extraction.text.TfidfVectorizer.html`.

- Model:

  - Dudeperf3ct. (2019, January 28). *Force of LSTM and GRU.* Blog. `https://dudeperf3ct.github.io/lstm/gru/nlp/2019/01/28/Force-of-LSTM-and-GRU/#bag-of-words-model`.

  - Brandon Rohrer. (n.d.). *Recurrent Neural Networks (RNN) and Long Short-Term Memory (LSTM)* [Video]. YouTube. Available at `https://www.youtube.com/watch?v=WCUNPb-5EYI&list=PLVZqlMpoM6kaJX_2lLKjEhWI0NlqHfqzp`.

- Pennington, J. (n.d.). *GloVe: Global vectors for word representation*. The Stanford Natural Language Processing Group. Available at `https://nlp.stanford.edu/projects/glove/`.

- Jason Brownlee. (2020). *Deep Convolutional Neural Network for Sentiment Analysis (Text Classification)*. Machine Learning Mastery. Available at `https://machinelearningmastery.com/develop-word-embedding-model-predicting-movie-review-sentiment/`.

- Evaluation:

  - T., B. (2022, December 9). *Comprehensive guide on Multiclass classification metrics*. Medium. Available at `https://towardsdatascience.com/comprehensive-guide-on-multiclass-classification-metrics-af94cfb83fbd`.

  - Jason Brownlee (2021). *Tour of Evaluation Metrics for Imbalanced Classification*. Machine Learning Mastery. Available at `https://machinelearningmastery.com/tour-of-evaluation-metrics-for-imbalanced-classification/`.

  - Korstanje, J. (2021, August 31). *The F1 score*. Medium. Available at `https://towardsdatascience.com/the-f1-score-bec2bbc38aa6`.

9
Generative Art for NFTs

"I use data as a pigment and paint with a painting brush that is assisted by artificial intelligence."

– Refik Anadol

In this chapter, we'll take an artistic break and indulge in some creativity. While our previous focus was on analyzing content generated by others on the blockchain, in this chapter, we will be creating our own content to be added to the blockchain.

The inclusion of this chapter stems from the recognition that, as data scientists, we might encounter requests to produce or assist in crafting an NFT collection in collaboration with a group of artists. In *Chapter 4*, we studied the artistic applications of NFTs and explored notable collections, such as *Bored Ape*, which has a total traded volume of 978,382 ETH (approximately USD 1,800 million). We do not know whether they used AI to produce all the images, but they are a good use case of how art can be owned and traded on the blockchain. To be able to participate in that market, we will learn about the entire process, from crafting an image to listing it for sale on OpenSea.

One particular collection named *Artsy Monke* used AI to create images by combining the Bored Ape collection with 20 curated painting styles. You can find their OpenSea collection website at `https://opensea.io/collection/artsy-monke`. The image on the cover of the book is Artsy Monke #9937.

Another example is Refik Anadol's *Machine Hallucinations* collection, which is a collaboration with NASA that uses over two million raw images, recorded by space institutions such as the International Space Station, the Hubble and MRO telescopes across the world into six AI data-created paintings and one sculpture as input.

The complete spectrum of tools that AI has enabled is beyond the scope of this chapter. However, we will discuss three practical tools that may be useful if an artist group contacts us to help them build their NFT collection: colorizing, transfer style, and prompt generative art. We will go from edits that do not modify the content and progress to full creation of images. Finally, we will learn how to create a collection on the blockchain and list it for sale.

In this chapter, we will cover the following main topics:

- Creating with colors – colorization tool
- Creating with style – style transfer workflow
- Creating with prompts – text-to-image solutions
- Monetization – minting and selling NFTs

Technical requirements

In this chapter, we'll employ distinct tools for each section. For the *colorization* segment, we will work with a program named **Style2Paints**. Its documentation can be located at https://github.com/lllyasviel/style2paints (licensed under Apache 2.0). To download the program, simply go to https://drive.google.com/open?id=1gmg2wwNIp4qMzxqP12SbcmVAHsLt1iRE. This will download a .zip file onto your computer that needs to be extracted.

Moving to the *style transfer* segment, we will use a VGG19 model, whose documentation can be found at https://www.tensorflow.org/api_docs/python/tf/keras/applications/vgg19/VGG19. It follows the Keras example available at https://keras.io/examples/generative/neural_style_transfer/.

For the *text-to-image* segment, we will interact with a Leonardo AI platform for which we only need to create an account. Furthermore, we will interact with the OpenSea platform, which will require us to have an active wallet for minting purposes.

You can find all the data and code files for this chapter in this book's GitHub repository at https://github.com/PacktPublishing/Data-Science-for-Web3/tree/main/Chapter09. We recommend that you read through the code files in the Chapter09 folder to follow along. The NFT collection created in this chapter is accessible at https://opensea.io/collection/mysterious-library.

Creating with colors – colorizing

Colorizing an image involves a lot of work for the artistic team. As data scientists, we can assist them with a tool that allows us to paint easily while following their artistic direction. The tool we're referring to is named **Style2Paints**, a semi-automatic method for colorization that can produce automatic results when there is no need for color correction. It also provides a functionality to provide hints to the tool for more customized results.

Hands-on Style2Paints

Once Style2Paints has been installed, the main page looks like what's shown in *Figure 9.1*. There's a color style column on the left-hand side and a color palette on the right:

Figure 9.1 – Style2Paints main view

This tool can be used with color and black-and-white images. Follow these steps:

1. To upload an image for colorization, click on the 🔼 symbol.

2. Select the painting region of the image and click **OK**.

3. On the left, we will be offered a list of images that have already been pre-colored that can be clicked and downloaded. For instance, if we upload a basic sketch or "line art," the tool will suggest some color styles located at the left-hand side of the site.

Consider the following line art example:

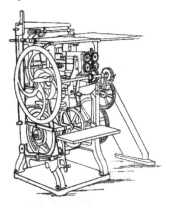

Figure 9.2 – Book binding machine, Joseph William Zaehnsdorf, public domain, via Wikimedia Commons

By using these color styles, we can create eight different colored images of the book binder from a single black-and-white image just by clicking on a color combination:

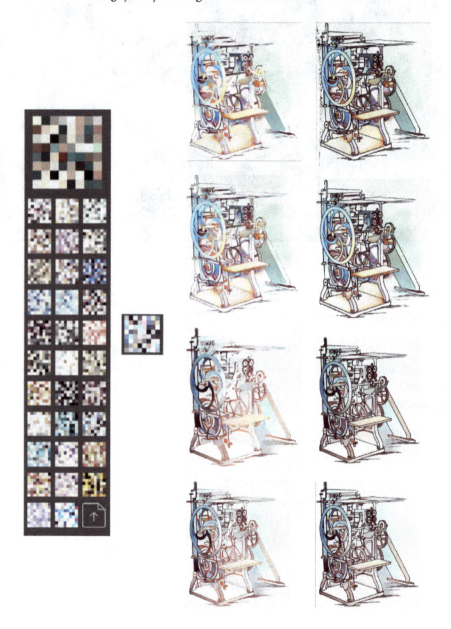

Figure 9.3 – Colorized versions of book binding

It is also possible to edit images that already have some color. For example, let's consider Artsy Monke #9937:

Figure 9.4 – Artsy Monke #9937

We can easily change the colors that are used by the image by using the color style offering located on the left-hand side of the tool. By clicking on each color combination, the images change. Some examples can be seen in *Figure 9.5*:

Figure 9.5 – Colorized Artsy Monke #9937

It is also possible to manually colorize without the color style suggestions and use a color palette with "hint points," as the documentation names it. A use case for hints is keeping a certain aesthetic the same or correcting some of the color style suggestions Follow these steps:.

1. Select one of the colors on the right-hand side of the tool by clicking on it.

2. Add a dot to the part of the image we want to colorize with the selected color. This is a "hint."

3. Click on the ⚡ icon; the image will reload, painting the selected area with the color we chose.

A step-by-step tutorial on how to use this intuitive tool can be found in the *Further reading* section.

Theory

A **convolutional neural network** (**CNN**) is a specialized type of deep neural network that's designed primarily for analyzing visual data. At a high level, CNNs are inspired by how the human visual system processes information. They consist of layers that automatically learn and detect various features, such as edges, corners, textures, and more complex patterns, from raw pixel data. These learned features are then used for tasks such as image classification, object detection, facial recognition, and more.

The following are the key components of a CNN:

- **Convolutional layer**: This is the core of a CNN. It applies a set of learnable filters (also called kernels) to the input image. The layer identifies the distinct features of an image in a process known as feature extraction.

- **Pooling layer**: This layer reduces the spatial dimensions of the feature maps while retaining important information. There are two types of pooling: max pooling and average pooling. It is usually applied after the convolutional layer to reduce the size of the feature map that was created in the previous layer. After several convolutional and pooling layers, the feature maps are flattened into a one-dimensional vector, which serves as the input to the fully connected layers.

- **Fully connected layers**: These layers are similar to those in traditional neural networks, connecting separate layers.

The components we've just detailed can be visualized in order in *Figure 9.6*:

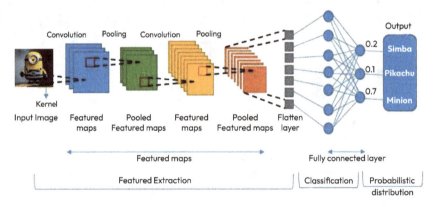

Figure 9.6 – Structure of a CNN. Photo by Alison Wang in Unsplash

CNNs are trained using labeled datasets. During training, the network's parameters (weights and biases) are updated using optimization algorithms such as gradient descent to minimize a loss function that quantifies the difference between predicted and actual labels.

The Style2Paints model is based on a CNN framework trained with the Danbooru database, which has two parts: the draft and refinement processes. According to the *Two-stage Sketch Colorization* paper,

"*The first drafting stage aggressively splashes colors over the canvas to create a color draft, with the goal of enriching the color variety (…) The second refinement stage corrects the color mistakes, refines details and polishes blurry textures to achieve the final output.*" This neural network has been trained to work with color sketches that, by definition, lack some important information, such as shades or textures.

It uses **generative adversarial networks (GANs)**, a type of CNN for generative modeling. This type of neural network works with two sub-models: a generator and a discriminator. The generator performs an unsupervised task, summarizing the distribution of the training dataset (generally images) and generating synthetic replicas to be analyzed by the discriminator. The discriminator receives the replicas, combined with some samples of the training dataset, and performs a supervised task, classifying between real (the ground truth sample) and fake (the generated by the generator). The model is considered trained when the discriminator cannot identify a generated image from a ground truth one. The generator is then kept to generate new samples of the problem domain.

The training process can be seen in the following figure:

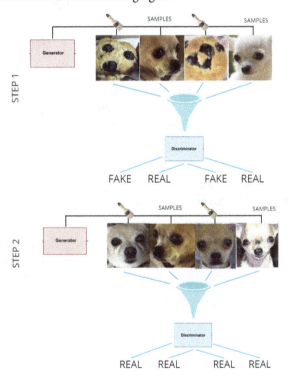

Figure 9.7 – Steps in the training process

This can be seen as two sub-models competing against each other and getting better at generating and discriminating. That is why the word "adversarial" is in its name. An overview of this structure can be found in the *Further reading* section.

Training GANs require large datasets and a lot of GPU. Videos from the Washington University of Saint Louis have been included in the *Further reading* section if you are interested in training your own GAN.

A note on training datasets

Better results will be yielded if the model that's being used has been trained with the same image style that we are trying to reproduce. For example, if we want to paint with a photographic style, we may try to avoid using anime-trained models.

As anticipated, Style2Paints was trained with the Danbooru dataset, which is a tagged anime dataset that has been evolving and expanding over time. Style2Paints was trained on the 2018 version, but at the time of writing, there is a 2021 version. This dataset contains images accompanied by a JSON file with metadata and tags. The anime art has some common characteristics, such as big expressive eyes with vibrant colors, heightened expressions, and a varied color palette to reflect the atmosphere present in the images.

The following are some commonly used image datasets:

- **ImageNet**: This is a compilation of images that follows the WordNet hierarchy. Each relevant concept in the WordNet collection is a "synonym set" that forms relations with other synsets, establishing a hierarchy of concepts: from general to abstract and specific. The ImageNet project is trying to provide 1,000 images per synset. This dataset is useful for object classification tasks. For more information, visit `https://www.image-net.org/`.

- **Common Objects in Context** (**COCO**): This is a large-scale dataset that's been annotated for object detection tasks. It contains over 33,000 images, organized into directories, and the annotations are in JSON format and contain the objects and the bounding box coordinates. For more information, visit `https://cocodataset.org/#home`.

- **MPII Human Pose Database**: This dataset has been prepared for use in human pose estimation tasks. It contains approximately 25,000 images reflecting over 410 everyday human activities. For more information, visit `http://human-pose.mpi-inf.mpg.de/`.

- **Frames Labeled in Cinema**: This dataset contains images that have been extracted from popular Hollywood movies. The images went through multiple processes (from selection to cleaning) before undergoing a final manual review and annotation of body joints. For more information, visit `https://bensapp.github.io/flic-dataset.html`.

- **Caltech-UCSD Birds-200-2011**: This dataset contains close to 12,000 images of 200 categories of birds with test and train subsets. Each image has detailed annotations, including one subcategory label, 15 part locations, 312 binary attributes, and one bounding box. The dataset is available on TensorFlow. For more information, visit `https://www.vision.caltech.edu/datasets/cub_200_2011/`.

- **Laion-5b**: This is the dataset over which Stable Diffusion (something we'll review shortly) was trained. It contains 5.85 billion CLIP-filtered image-text pairs via a general crawl of the internet that was done by the German entity LAION. For more information, visit `https://laion.ai/blog/laion-5b/`.

In this section, we learned how to use a tool that helps in the coloring workflow, automatically or manually. In the following section, we will dig deeper into coloring with a broader impact on the image by transferring a style from one image to the other with AI.

Creating with style – style transfer

Another way we can assist an artistic team is via style transfer, a process that involves combining two images:

- The style image or *root* image, from which we will learn the style
- The target image, which we will transform with the new style

The resulting image will retain the core elements of the target image but appear to be painted or printed following the style image.

There are several methods for performing style transfer, including leveraging GANs (described in the previous section), using **Visual Geometry Group** (**VGG**), and employing Stable Diffusion (which we will cover in the next section).

In `style_transfer.ipynb`, we will use VGG19, a special type of CNN with 19 layers that has been trained with over a million images from the ImageNet database to extract the style of a Picasso painting and transfer it to a photograph. Picasso belonged to the **cubism** movement, where the artists applied multiple perspectives, used geometric shapes, and flattened the picture plane. An interesting article on the defining characteristics of this artistic movement can be found in the *Further reading* section.

Let's go through the steps we must follow.

Preparation

First, we must obtain the tensor representations of the root and target images. The `preprocess_image()` function does this by leveraging the Keras library with the following code snippet:

```
def preprocess_image(image_path):
    img = keras.preprocessing.image.load_img(
        image_path, target_size=(img_nrows, img_ncols)
    )
    img = keras.preprocessing.image.img_to_array(img)
    img = np.expand_dims(img, axis=0)
    img = vgg19.preprocess_input(img)
    return tf.convert_to_tensor(img)
```

Model building

We build the VGG19 model by setting the ImageNet dataset weights, which means the model will be initialized with weights that have been pre-trained on the ImageNet dataset. The `include_top` parameter is set to `False`, which means the top layers that are responsible for classification are not included in the model. The reason is that we want to use the VGG19 model as a feature extractor rather than for classification purposes:

```
model = vgg19.VGG19(weights="imagenet", include_top=False)
```

The code also extracts the information that's generated by each layer of the model so that it can be used in the loss functions that we'll describe here.

We define three loss functions:

- The **total variation loss**, which seeks to ensure the coherence of the final image by measuring the spatial continuity between pixels in the resulting image.

- The **content loss**, which aims to minimize the difference between the target image and the resulting image, keeping the composition and high-level representation of the target image and the resulting image similar. The layer over which we calculate this loss is named `content_layer_name`.

- The **style loss**, which seeks to minimize the difference between the style image and the resulting image. As defined in the Keras documentation, it is *"the sum of L2 distances between the Gram matrices of the representations of the base image and the style reference image."* The style loss focuses on information related to color distribution, texture, brush strokes, and more. The layers over which we calculate this loss are defined in a list named `style_layer_names`.

The style loss uses a gram matrix (which is essentially a tensor multiplied by its transpose) and is calculated in the `gram_matrix()` function. The rationale behind the gram matrix of a convolutional layer is to combine the style features that are learned among them. For instance, Pablo Picasso's cubism is a combination of colors, shapes, and textures. A synthesis (the gram) of those features measuring the correlation between them will represent Picasso's style.

The `compute_loss` function summarizes the combination of the various losses defined previously, while `compute_loss_and_grads` runs the calculations.

Training and inference

The training process will reduce the style loss and the content loss, which make up the total variation loss. The training process uses **stochastic gradient descent** (**SGD**) as the optimizer to iteratively decrease the loss.

The proposed script saves the image every 100 iterations, allowing us to monitor image variation. The documentation proposes displaying the final image at the end of the training process, which we set at 4,000 steps.

By using the `util` function in the notebook named `deprocess_image()`, which rebuilds the image from a tensor into a `.png` file so that it's ready to be saved and displayed, we can see the style transfer of a Pablo Picasso painting to a photograph:

Figure 9.8 – A waterfall in Picasso's painting style

In the first section, we learned how to modify images automatically by applying color; in this section, we reviewed how to create images by combining a base image with a specific style. In both cases, we provided the images we wanted to modify. In the next section, we will learn how to create images with a text input or prompt.

Creating with prompts – text to image

In this section, we will introduce some services that enable images to be generated based on a **prompt**. A prompt is a set of natural language instructions that, when fed to the model, generates images. Whatever can be described in words can be transformed into an image. The more descriptive the prompt is, the more unique the output will be. The instructions can include some keywords that will enhance the originality of the created pieces of art, such as the style of the generated image, the aspect ratio, the resolution of the expected images, and more.

All of the services we will present use some form of **diffusion models**, combined with other models to make the image generation process more efficient, clean it from disturbing results (for example, for minor 18), and more. Diffusion models are generative models that try to replicate the training data. During training, the model adds noise to the training dataset and learns how to reverse it to recover the original image. By recovering from the training noise, the model learns the fundamental aspects of an image, as well as how to generate new data.

Let's briefly analyze them one by one.

DALL.E 2

OpenAI, the same research team that developed ChatGPT, developed DALL-E 2, an image generator from text descriptions. According to their documentation, "*DALL·E is a transformer language model. It receives both the text and the image as a single stream of data containing up to 1280 tokens, and is trained using maximum likelihood to generate all of the tokens, one after another.*" The model is a 12-billion parameter autoregressive transformer that's trained on 250 million image-text pairs collected from the internet.

DALL-E 2 not only generates images according to a predefined prompt but also enables the user to modify parts of the image or add contextual background to smaller pieces of images.

This same team also designed **contrastive language image pre-training** (**CLIP**), which allows us to map texts with images and returns the most appropriate caption for an input image. More information can be found at `https://openai.com/research/clip`. This takes image tagging and categorization to another level of speed.

Stable Diffusion

Stable Diffusion models are open source and contain code and checkpoints. To enable Stable Diffusion models to be trained on low GPU, they do not train on images but rather on the latent space of the dataset. The models learn from the underlying structure of the dataset instead of processing each image. Training with latent space enables us to feed the model with text and images in the same space that the model will use to regenerate the image.

The CLIP model mentioned in the previous section helped train the latest version of Stable Diffusion V2. The link to the repository is `https://github.com/Stability-AI/stablediffusion`.

Midjourney

The base models that are used by Midjourney are not disclosed, but they are likely a combination of diffusion models, as explained for DALL-E and Stable Diffusion. Midjourney is currently only accessible through a Discord bot on their official Discord server or by inviting the bot to a third-party server. It has no API.

This service became popular very fast.

Leonardo.Ai

The link to their page is `https://app.leonardo.ai/`. This tool offers off-the-shelf models that generate images specifically trained in some of the most common themes, such as **role-playing games (RPGs)** or realistic photographs. It also offers tools to fine-tune models so that they can be adapted to our training datasets and a liberal free tier. Finally, it is developer-friendly with an easy-to-interact API. Each model has a "base model" description based on Stable Diffusion releases.

To get started, sign up on their app and complete the **Get started** survey. There is no need to pay to interact with the basic service, but you must do so to get API keys:

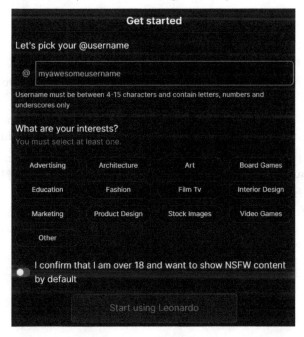

Figure 9.9 – Logging in to Leonardo.Ai for the first time

In the home page view, there is a list of models that we can interact with, depending on the type of image we want to generate. As mentioned earlier, each model is optimized for a specific purpose. For example, there is a model specially designed for vintage-style photography or RPG character portraits.

We can also see two tabs called **Community Feed** and **Personal Feed**, which show images generated by the community and our images, respectively.

If we move to the AI generation tool, we will see several options to choose from on the left-hand side of the view, including the following:

- **Number of images**: This allows us to select the number of images we want to generate with each run.

- **Prompt magic**: According to their description, *"Our experimental render pipeline may have better prompt adherence."* The images are more artistic with this enabled.

- **Prompt magic strength**: This option determines the weight of the render detailed previously.

- **Public images**: This option allows us to choose whether we want to share these images with the public feed.

- **Image dimensions**: This option lets us set the size of the images.

- **Guidance scale**: This option determines the weight of the prompt in the final image. It is suggested to keep it at 7 or 8.

We can also upload an image to be used as a prompt.

A note on good prompts

Vocabulary: Avoid the use of "very" or "super" for emphasis. Instead, opt for words that convey the same meaning. For instance, replace "very tired" with "exhausted."

Typos: Refrain from sending incorrectly spelled words, abbreviations, contractions, or slang as the model may struggle to align them with the dataset on which it was trained.

Specificity: Minimize ambiguity in word choices and unnecessary text. For improved results, opt for expressions such as "cheeseless pizza" instead of "pizza with no cheese." Utilize negative prompts to exclude specific objects or characteristics from the image.

Keywords to consider: Include hints about the image's background, style words (such as anime, realistic, paper art, cubism, charcoal painting, folk art, graffiti), lighting (soft, ambient, neon, studio lights), or time of day (morning, golden hour, midnight).

Furthermore, the application helps us with the prompt generation. Within the AI tool that we just described, we can see the **Prompt Generation** tab, which assists us in generating the prompt to obtain the desired image using AI.

Hands-on with Leonardo.Ai

Let's try an exercise with the API. The documentation is available at `https://docs.leonardo.ai/reference/getuserself`. It is an easy-to-use API that can be accessed with our well-known `request` library.

The API can help us build the entire pipeline from a prompt to a folder that we can submit to the artistic team for review. The `Leonardo_AI.ipynb` file contains the workflow we'll explore.

Although the API is under development and not all functionalities and models can be invoked programmatically, most of the options described previously can be added as parameters to the payload.

Let's review the following code snippet:

```
payload = {
    "prompt": prompt,
    "modelId":"6bef9f1b-29cb-40c7-b9df-32b51c1f67d3",
    "width": 512,
    "height": 512,
    "sd_version": "v2",
    "presetStyle": "LEONARDO",
     "public": False,
    "promptMagic": True
}
```

To interact with the API, we need to log in and obtain a set of API keys that will pass as authorization in the header.

It is important to read the parameters from the website as the documentation for this is not complete. For example, some models are trained with specific image dimensions, so it is better to input those preferred dimensions in the parameter payload. Additionally, not all the models can be called from the API, and there is no access to the prompt generator.

Despite these limitations, this is a great tool that can help us generate high-quality images rapidly.

Minting an NFT collection

The purpose of analyzing all the tools in this section is to create or modify images that we can sell or the artistic team we support will sell. Once we have generated the images, we want to "own" them in the Web3 sense, as explained in *Chapter 4*. To achieve this, we will create a collection in a marketplace.

Minting is the act of creating the digital trace of an item on the blockchain. As we saw when describing ERC 721, it means that the trace will point to a URL containing the stored image. Everything that is stored on the chain pays a gas fee.

The concept of lazy minting has emerged rather recently. **Lazy minting** involves authorizing the platform to mint the NFT at the moment of the NFT sale and not before. This is important because minting involves gas expenditure, and, in moments of high congestion, gas prices can be high. In addition, lazy minting helps reduce the risk of creating a collection that may not be sold high enough to cover the initial investment. At the time of writing, the main marketplaces, such as OpenSea and Rarible, offer the service.

The process consists of the following steps:

1. Creators mint an NFT *lazily* using a specific smart contract. The smart contract will mint and sell the NFT on our behalf. We provide the authorization.

2. The buyer pays a price that covers the minting costs and the NFT itself when purchasing our NFT.

This method defers the minting process until just before the NFT is sold, which is an incentive for creators to continue producing and showcasing their art without necessarily paying for gas.

Let's create a collection on OpenSea:

1. Go to `https://opensea.io/`. To interact with the platform, you will need a wallet.

2. Connect your wallet and go to the profile options:

Figure 9.10 – Connecting to your wallet

3. Click on **My Collections**:

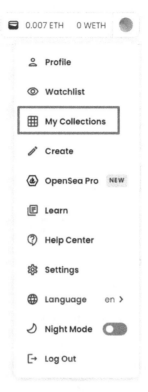

Figure 9.11 – The My Collections tab

4. Click on the blue **Create a collection** button:

My Collections

Create, curate, and manage collections of unique NFTs to share and sell. Learn more

Figure 9.12 – The My Collections page

5.   You will be offered two options: the traditional option (**Deploy your own contract**) and the lazy minting option (**Use the OpenSea contract**). Click on the second option:

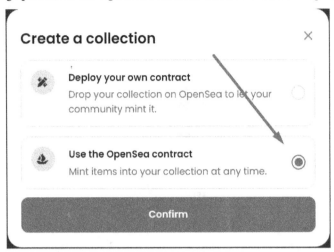

Figure 9.13 – Choosing the lazy minting option

6.   A page will open where you can complete the collection's details. Among them we will find the following details:

I.   The name of the collection.

II.   Description.

III.   The accepted currency.

IV.   Images for the collection page.

V.   Author earnings. As we mentioned in *Chapter 4*, it is possible to establish a percentage that the creator will retain each time the NFT is sold.

Once all the required details have been filled in, click **Save**. Now that we have a collection, we have to add pieces of art to it:

1.   Go back to your profile and click **Create**:

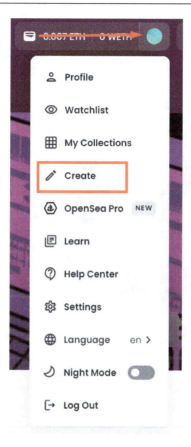

Figure 9.14 – Creating an NFT

2. You may require additional authorization to access this panel. If so, you will be taken to the **Create New Item** page: `https://opensea.io/asset/create`.

3. Upload the image, video, or audio that you want to mint. In this example, we will mint one of the images that was generated with the `Leonardo_AI.ipynb` notebook:

Create New Item

* Required fields

Image, Video, Audio, or 3D Model *

File types supported: JPG, PNG, GIF, SVG, MP4, WEBM, MP3, WAV, OGG, GLB, GLTF. Max size: 100 MB

Name *

Mysterious book #1

Figure 9.15 – Details of the new item

4. Start filling in the required fields:

    I.   Name

    II.   Description

    III. Connect it to the collection that was created in *step 4 previously*

    IV.   Identify the number of items of the same nature that can be minted

    V.   The network where this item will live

    Click **Create**; you will see the following output:

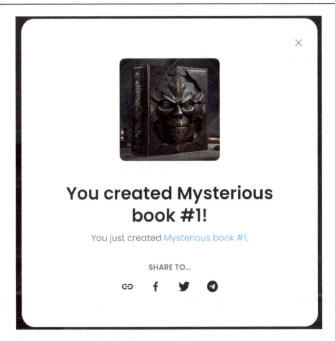

Figure 9.16 – Resulting message after signing the creation

5. Enable the sale. To do this, navigate to the page of the item and click on the **Sell** button:

Figure 9.17 – Sale details

New options will appear for you to choose from. It is possible to choose between a fixed price or an auction with a limited time. If we want to sell for a fixed price, we can follow the next steps.

6. Click on **Fixed price**:

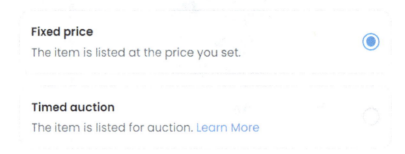

Figure 9.18 – The Fixed price option

7. Set a price in any of the coins or tokens that are acceptable according to what we decided when creating the collection.

8. Below this, we will find a summary of earnings and the fee that OpenSea charges (at the time of writing, this is 2.5%).

9. If we agree, we can click on **Complete listing**. To approve the listing, OpenSea requires our signature.

10. Once signed, we will receive a new notification, informing us that the item has been listed. Now, it is out there in the marketplace and can be purchased!

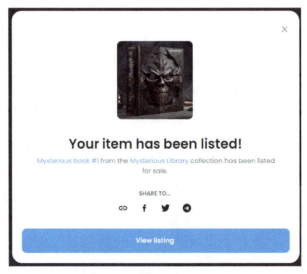

Figure 9.19 – The listing for sale has been enabled

All the illustrations that were generated in this section are available in The Mysterious Library Collection: `https://opensea.io/collection/mysterious-library`.

Summary

Throughout this chapter, we explored three different approaches to using AI tools in artistic projects. We examined the use of GAN models for colorizing sketches, explored the VGG19 model for transferring style, and discovered state-of-the-art applications of Stable Diffusion models for generating art based on prompts.

Moreover, we learned about the entire workflow, from the finished piece of art to listing the final image on a marketplace. By combining the power of AI and blockchain technology, we now have a range of new opportunities to explore and monetize artistic work in exciting and innovative ways.

It is worth noting that questions have arisen concerning the ownership of images generated using AI. This arises from the possibility that these models may have been trained on copyrighted pieces of art without the artist's consent. Respondents contend that the transformative nature of the model's outputs, coupled with the fair use argument, could potentially dismiss such accusations. This ongoing issue is yet to be definitively resolved by legal authorities and is likely to exhibit variations across different countries.

Having explored the area of NFTs, we'll now shift our focus to a critical aspect that underpins the integrity of this innovative landscape – fraud detection. In the following chapter, we will analyze another use case where machine learning can help us uncover anomalies and increase transaction security.

Further reading

To learn more about the topics that were covered in this chapter, take a look at the following resources:

- Crypto Grims: `https://twitter.com/cryptogrims`

- Artsy Monke collection: `https://opensea.io/assets/ethereum/0xa4bcd3b7f141ba1f08f36033fdfce691565561bc`.

- Mishra, M. (2020, September 2). *Convolutional neural networks, explained*. Medium. Available at `https://towardsdatascience.com/convolutional-neural-networks-explained-9cc5188c4939`.

- Fortis, S. (n.d.). *Google AI turns all 10,000 BAYC NFTs into machine-made art*. Cointelegraph. Available at `https://cointelegraph.com/news/google-ai-turns-all-10-000-bayc-nfts-into-machine-made-art`.

- Lllyasviel (n.d.). *style2paints.github.io*. Available at `https://style2paints.github.io/`.

- Lllyasviel/style2paints. (n.d.). GitHub. Available at `https://github.com/lllyasviel/style2paints`.

- Tang, J. (2020, October 20). *Attempt to understand an all-star auto-color project—Style2Paints (Part 1)*. Medium. Available at `https://medium.com/ai-innovation/attempt-to-understand-an-all-star-auto-color-project-style2paints-part-1-84d2e3d96da`.

- Lvmin Zhang, Chengze Li, Tien-Tsin Wong, Yi Ji, and Chunping Liu. (n.d.). *CUHK Computer Science and Engineering*. Available at `https://www.cse.cuhk.edu.hk/~ttwong/papers/colorize/colorize.pdf`.

- Nerdy Rodent. (2020, November 19). *Style2Paints – Easily colour any line art using AI* [Video]. YouTube. Available at `https://www.youtube.com/watch?v=cvN9oQfC3w0`.

- Overview of GAN structure. (n.d.). *Google for Developers*. Available at `https://developers.google.com/machine-learning/gan/gan_structure`.

- Prof. Jeff Heaton – Washington University of St. Louis. (2022, January 19). *Introduction to GANS for Image and Data Generation (7.1)* [Video]. YouTube. Available at `https://www.youtube.com/watch?v=hZw-AjbdN5k`.

- Prof. Jeff Heaton – Washington University of St. Louis. (2021, February 17). *Training a GAN from your Own Images: StyleGAN2 ADA* [Video]. YouTube. Available at `https://www.youtube.com/watch?v=kbDd51W6rkM`.

- Prof. Jeff Heaton – Washington University of St. Louis. (2021, May 12). *Training NVIDIA StyleGAN2 ADA under Colab Free and Colab Pro Tricks* [Video]. YouTube. Available at `https://www.youtube.com/watch?v=L3JLzoe-dJU`.

- *T81_558_deep_learning/t81_558_class_07_1_gan_intro.ipynb at master · jeffheaton/t81_558_deep_learning*. (n.d.). GitHub. Available at `https://github.com/jeffheaton/t81_558_deep_learning/blob/master/t81_558_class_07_1_gan_intro.ipynb`.

- *T81_558_deep_learning/t81_558_class_07_2_train_gan.ipynb at master · jeffheaton/t81_558_deep_learning*. (n.d.). GitHub. Available at `https://github.com/jeffheaton/t81_558_deep_learning/blob/master/t81_558_class_07_2_train_gan.ipynb`.

- Jason Brownlee PhD. (2019, July 19). *Machine Learning Mastery*. Machine Learning Mastery. Available at `https://machinelearningmastery.com/what-are-generative-adversarial-networks-gans/`.

- *4 characteristics of cubism and why they are important.* (n.d.). Artlex – Art Dictionary and Encyclopedia. Available at `https://www.artlex.com/art-movements/cubism/characteristics/`.

- *Neural style transfer*: `https://keras.io/examples/generative/neural_style_transfer/`.

- *DALL·E: Creating images from text.* (n.d.). OpenAI. Available at `https://openai.com/research/dall-e`.

- *Zero-shot text-to-Image generation.* (n.d.). arXiv.org. Available at `https://arxiv.org/abs/2102.12092`.

- Aleksa Gordić - The AI Epiphany. (2022, September 1). *Stable Diffusion: High-Resolution Image Synthesis with Latent Diffusion Models | ML Coding Series* [Video]. YouTube. Available at `https://www.youtube.com/watch?v=f6PtJKdey8E`.

- *Stability-AI/stablediffusion.* (n.d.). GitHub. Available at `https://github.com/Stability-AI/stablediffusion`.

- *How Stable Diffusion works? Latent Diffusion Models Explained.* (2022, December 3). Louis Bouchard. Available at `https://www.louisbouchard.ai/latent-diffusion-models/`.

- Arya, G. (2023, January 14). *Power of latent diffusion models: Revolutionizing image creation.* Analytics Vidhya. Available at `https://www.analyticsvidhya.com/blog/2023/01/power-of-latent-diffusion-models-revolutionizing-image-creation/`.

- *API Documentation.* (n.d.). Leonardo.Ai. Available at `https://docs.leonardo.ai/reference/getuserself`.

- Ashley, K. (2021). *Make art with artificial intelligence: Make and sell your art with AI, blockchain, and NFT.*

A Primer on Security and Fraud Detection

"All warfare is based on deception." - Sun Tzu

The history of fraud is as old as time. Fraud in the crypto world comes as no surprise, and as crypto gains mainstream adoption, it becomes increasingly necessary to be aware of the different forms of fraud in order to be able to identify it.

Fraud is a significant issue for businesses in general, for governments, and for the blockchain industry in particular. According to the 2022 PwC Global Annual Review on fraud, 46% of surveyed organizations reported experiencing some form of fraud or economic crime within the last 24 months.

Governments are aware of the issue for tax purposes, as well as to combat money laundering and terrorism financing. Relevant agencies have a mandate to enforce the law and combat such illicit activity even if cryptocurrencies are involved. Due diligence is required for all subjects associated with financial activity or money services businesses, a concept that has expanded to include centralized exchanges. That is the reason why major **centralized exchanges** (**CEXs**) only open accounts for new users when the person behind the ID is validated. Compliance with certain quality standards is essential, and failure to comply can lead to sanctions.

The crypto industry is also interested in solidifying trust in compliance with robust smart contracts and a seamless experience while transacting. Smart contract breaches, scam schemes, and the use of cryptocurrencies as payment for hacks have not helped in this pursuit. Data science has been helping to solve this issue for some time now. The challenge has been adapting the data science practice for the blockchain dataset, which is rather different and pseudo-anonymous. Some interesting companies such as Chainalysis, Elliptic, and CipherTrace are at the forefront of forensic data science in blockchain, helping authorities in investigations and supporting general user trust.

In this chapter, we will examine the transaction behavior of addresses to train a machine learning model that can determine whether or not we are dealing with a scammer.

Particularly, we will cover the following topics:

- What illicit activity looks like on Ethereum

- Exploratory data analysis of transactional data on Ethereum

- Preparation, model training, and evaluation to flag fraudulent transactions

Technical requirements

You can find all the data and code files for this chapter in the book's GitHub repository at `https://github.com/PacktPublishing/Data-Science-for-Web3/tree/main/Chapter10`. We recommend that you read through the code files in the `Chapter10` folder to follow along.

In this chapter, we will use the Ethereum Utilities library (`eth-utils`), which contains commonly used utility functions for Python developers working with Ethereum. Depending on our environment, we may need to import additional low-level libraries that are utilized by `eth-utils`.

If you haven't installed `eth-utils` yet, you can do so using the following code snippet:

```
pip install eth-utils
```

The documentation for `eth-utils` is available at `https://eth-utils.readthedocs.io/en/stable/`. If the installation fails due to a lack of supporting libraries, you can find the complete list of required libraries that need to be pre-installed in `Chapter10/EDA.ipynb`.

A primer on illicit activity on Ethereum

There is a technical difference between fraud and a scam. A scam is an act where we unknowingly pay for a fake item, transfer money, or provide our private keys to a criminal. Conversely, fraud refers to any suspicious activity on our address that we did not authorize. In this book, we will use both terms interchangeably.

The Ethereum Security blog has three key messages for anyone starting in the crypto industry:

- *Always be skeptical*

- *No one is going to give you free or discounted ETH*

- *No one needs access to your private keys or personal information*

As of today, some of the most common scams include the following:

- **Giveaway scams**: These basically work by criminals promising that if we send X amount of crypto to an address, it will be returned to us but doubled in amount. These schemes are often psychological, offering the victim only a limited amount of time to participate in this "opportunity," generating a **fear of missing out** (**FOMO**) effect. This scheme often uses high-profile X (formerly Twitter) accounts, videos of celebrities, and so on.

- **IT support scams**: These scammers impersonate IT support or admin personnel from blockchain services, such as wallets, exchanges, marketplaces, or even a chain. They may ask for some information from us or to validate our ID and, in general, will try to get the minimum necessary information to extract our funds. These sorts of scammers can be found mostly on Discord discussion channels or Telegram. It is very usual to see next to real people's names the phrase "*Never DM first.*" Scammers will write first, trying to generate a connection and trust. It is worth remembering that Web3 is a decentralized landscape, so it is unlikely that support teams will be scanning the internet to answer our questions. If we were interacting with a centralized platform with a support team in place, the team would always contact us through official channels.

- **Phishing scams**: This is a type of social engineering attack that uses impersonation through email to convince the victim to provide the necessary information to commit the fraud. The email will usually contain links that redirect to fake websites or download malicious malware. As we saw in *Chapter 3*, when detailing where to go for off-chain data, we should try to access websites following a trusted link – for example, through CoinMarketCap or CoinGecko. There are many ways to detect phishing, but the reality is that they are becoming more creative over time.

- **Broker scams**: These are trading brokers with a lot of followers on social media who allegedly generate outstanding profits. A real person is behind the account of a broker, who will interact with the victim until the latter sends their funds to be "managed" by the broker. Once sent, those funds are lost.

Each of these scams is further explained with real-life examples on this blog: `https://ethereum.org/en/security/`.

Regardless of the fraudulent scheme, money will be transferred through a transaction and saved in an account. In the next section, we will analyze account behavior to try to determine which account can be trusted and which should be flagged as a scam.

Preprocessing

We will be working with a balanced dataset that was used in the paper *Detection of illicit accounts over the Ethereum blockchain*. You can find the link to the paper in the *Further reading* section. This dataset is a balanced dataset, with 48 columns or features that combine licit and illicit accounts. The dataset was created by using the CryptoScamDB database and Etherscan; the latter is a tool that we are already familiar with. `cryptoscamdb.org` manages an open source dataset that tracks malicious URLs and their associated addresses.

The columns and their description as follows:

Feature	Description
`Avg_min_between_sent_tnx`	The average time between sent transactions for an account in minutes
`Avg_min_between_received_tnx`	The average time between received transactions for an account in minutes
`Time_Diff_between_first_and_last(Mins)`	The time difference between the first and last transaction
`Sent_tnx`	The total number of sent normal transactions
`Received_tnx`	The total number of received normal transactions
`Number_of_Created_Contracts`	The total number of created contract transactions
`Unique_Received_From_Addresses`	The total unique addresses from which the account received transactions
`Unique_Sent_To_Addresses`	The total unique addresses from which the account sent transactions
`Min_Value_Received`	The minimum value in Ether ever received
`Max_Value_Received`	The maximum value in Ether ever received
`Avg_Value_Received`	The average value in Ether ever received
`Min_Val_Sent`	The minimum value of Ether ever sent
`Max_Val_Sent`	The maximum value of Ether ever sent
`Avg_Val_Sent`	The average value of Ether ever sent
`Min_Value_Sent_To_Contract`	The minimum value of Ether sent to a contract
`Max_Value_Sent_To_Contract`	The maximum value of Ether sent to a contract
`Avg_Value_Sent_To_Contract`	The average value of Ether sent to contracts
`Total_Transactions(Including_Tnx_to_Create_Contract)`	The total number of transactions
`Total_Ether_Sent`	The total Ether sent for an account address

Feature	Description
`Total_Ether_Received`	The total Ether received for an account address
`Total_Ether_Sent_Contracts`	The total Ether sent to contract addresses
`Total_Ether_Balance`	The total Ether balance following enacted transactions
`Total_ERC20_Tnxs`	The total number of ERC20 token transfer transactions
`ERC20_Total_Ether_Received`	The total ERC20 token-received transactions in Ether
`ERC20_Total_Ether_Sent`	The total ERC20 token-sent transactions in Ether
`ERC20_Total_Ether_Sent_Contract`	The total number of ERC20 tokens transferred to other contracts in Ether
`ERC20_Uniq_Sent_Addr`	The number of ERC20 token transactions sent to unique account addresses
`ERC20_Uniq_Rec_Addr`	The number of ERC20 token transactions received from unique addresses
`ERC20_Uniq_Rec_Contract_Addr`	The number of ERC20 token transactions received from unique contract addresses
`ERC20_Avg_Time_Between_Sent_Tnx`	The average time between ERC20 token-sent transactions in minutes
`ERC20_Avg_Time_Between_Rec_Tnx`	The average time between ERC20 token-received transactions in minutes
`ERC20_Avg_Time_Between_Contract_Tnx`	The average time ERC20 token between sent token transactions
`ERC20_Min_Val_Rec`	The minimum value in Ether received from ERC20 token transactions for an account
`ERC20_Max_Val_Rec`	The maximum value in Ether received from ERC20 token transactions for an account
`ERC20_Avg_Val_Rec`	The average value in Ether received from ERC20 token transactions for an account
`ERC20_Min_Val_Sent`	The minimum value in Ether sent from ERC20 token transactions for an account
`ERC20_Max_Val_Sent`	The maximum value in Ether sent from ERC20 token transactions for an account
`ERC20_Avg_Val_Sent`	The average value in Ether sent from ERC20 token transactions for an account

Feature	Description
ERC20_Uniq_Sent_ Token_Name	The number of unique ERC20 tokens transferred
ERC20_Uniq_Rec_Token_ Name	The number of unique ERC20 tokens received
ERC20_Most_Sent_ Token_Type	The most sent token for an account via an ERC20 transaction
ERC20_Most_Rec_Token_ Type	The most received token for an account via an ERC20 transaction

Table 10.1 – An explanation of each dataset column (source – from page 10 of
the paper, Detection of illicit accounts over the Ethereum blockchain)

In `Chapter10/EDA.ipynb`, we analyzed the dataset and came to the following conclusions:

1. There are 4,681 accounts and 48 features. Within these addresses, there are five duplicated addresses and five invalid addresses.

   To determine whether an address is valid or invalid, we use part of the code of EIP-55, combined with a custom formula named `address_validation()`.

   Ethereum Improvement Proposal (**EIP**)-55 involves adding and checking for uppercase letters in Ethereum addresses. The original code can be found at `https://github.com/ethereum/EIPs/blob/master/EIPS/eip-55.md`. The code turns a hexadecimal address into bytes and checks the checksum encoding to confirm whether it is a valid Ethereum address. If not, it raises a warning.

   In the `address_validation()` function, we add an additional condition to count the characters of each address, discarding those that are not 42 characters.

   If both conditions are met, the address is considered valid, and the checksummed version is returned. Otherwise, a `not an ethereum address` flag is returned:

```
def checksum_encode(addr):
    hex_addr = addr.hex()
    checksummed_buffer = ""
    hashed_address = eth_utils.keccak(text=hex_addr).hex()
    for nibble_index, character in enumerate(hex_addr):
        if character in "0123456789":
            checksummed_buffer += character
        elif character in "abcdef":
            hashed_address_nibble = int(hashed_address[nibble_
index], 16)
            if hashed_address_nibble > 7:
                checksummed_buffer += character.upper()
```

```
            else:
                    checksummed_buffer += character
            else:
                raise eth_utils.ValidationError(
                    f"Unrecognized hex character {character!r} at
    position {nibble_index}"
                )
        return "0x" + checksummed_buffer


    def test(addr_str):
        addr_bytes = eth_utils.to_bytes(hexstr=addr_str)
        checksum_encoded = checksum_encode(addr_bytes)
        try:
           assert checksum_encoded == addr_str, f"{checksum_encoded}
    != expected {addr_str}"
        except AssertionError:
            return checksum_encoded
    def address_validation(addr_str):
        if len(addr_str) == 42:
                result = test(addr_str)
        else:
            result = "not an ethereum address"
        return result
```

2. There are some missing values from columns 25 to 49. The percentage of null values is 17.7%.
    We identify any missing values in the dataframe, calculating the percentage of missing values
    for each column in the dataframe.

    We use the following code snippet:

    ```
    percent_missing = df.isnull().sum() * 100 / len(df)
    ```

    There are several ways to proceed when dealing with null values, as we studied in *Chapter 5*.
    However, we will explore another approach that we have not yet tried, which is complementing
    the dataset. Given the open nature of on-chain data, this is feasible. We will further analyze this
    step in the subsequent section and `Chapter10/Rebuilding.ipynb`.

3. The fraudulent transactions and missing values are at the top of the dataset. The most fraudulent
    accounts seem to have missing values. Refer to the heatmap at `Chapter10/EDA.ipynb`.

4. There are 12 columns with little variance (and only one value, which is zero). Columns with little variance may not be helpful for our training. These columns are as follows:

    ```
    ['min_value_sent_to_contract', 'max_val_sent_to_contract', 'avg_
    value_sent_to_contract', 'total_ether_sent_contracts', 'ERC20_
    avg_time_between_sent_tnx', 'ERC20_avg_time_between_rec_tnx',
    'ERC20_avg_time_between_rec_2_tnx', 'ERC20_avg_time_between_
    contract_tnx', 'ERC20_min_val_sent_contract', 'ERC20_max_val_
    sent_contract', 'ERC20_avg_val_sent_contract']
    ```

    We identify these columns using the following code snippet:

    ```
    variance_df= df.nunique()
    ```

5. After cleaning duplicates and invalids, there are 2,497 non-fraudulent accounts and 2,179 fraudulent accounts.

6. We ran a correlation matrix and discovered that five columns are heavily correlated. These columns are as follows:

    ```
    ['ERC20_max_val_rec', 'ERC20_min_val_sent', 'ERC20_max_val_sent',
    'ERC20_avg_val_sent', 'ERC20_uniq_rec_token_name']
    ```

    Dropping columns with similar information is important because redundant information does not add value to our training; rather, it can make our algorithm learn slower and complicate the interpretability of our model if we have to explain it. Multicollinearity can also affect certain models, such as linear models. Refer to the heatmap for correlations at `Chapter10/EDA.ipynb`.

7. The two columns with categorical data (`ERC20_most_sent_token_type` and `ERC20_most_rec_token_type`) are heavily sparse, with most tokens appearing only once or being blank.

    When we group by ERC token, there is no clear category that could be useful. One-hot-encoding these columns may result in a heavily sparse training dataset. Additionally, new tokens are being minted every day, and adding this information to our model would create a variable that becomes outdated quickly.

Based on the conclusions reached from the preceding analysis, we cleaned up the data to adapt it to our needs. The following steps were taken:

1. We dropped duplicated addresses.
2. We tried to populate missing values from Etherscan.
3. We dropped low-variance columns.
4. We dropped columns with 0.95 or more correlation.

5. We dropped the `object`-type columns.

6. We dropped the `Address` column.

7. We refilled NaNs with the median.

Let's expand the preprocessing from *step 2*, which involves populating missing values from Etherscan. Real-life datasets tend to be incomplete. It is the job of data analysts or data scientists to complement those columns that are partially complete. There are several methodologies to do that, and we explored the traditional ones in *Chapter 5* when no further data is available.

In `Chapter10_Rebuilding`, we tried another methodology that involves going to the source and looking for the missing data. Throughout this book, we have listed multiple sources, and as more progress is made in this area, new sources of on-chain data will become available, helping us complete our datasets. Additionally, specialization in Web3 will enable us to make inferences over data because we can understand it. This is particularly helpful when the data point we need to reflect in the dataset is indirect or does not stem directly from on-chain data.

In the dataset extracted from the paper, *Detection of illicit accounts over the Ethereum blockchain*, 17% of the rows had missing data. To complement the paper, we used one of the data sources we have been analyzing for some time now – Etherscan. We leveraged the free tier of their API and were able to complement most of the rows. The link to the API documentation is `https://docs.etherscan.io/`. The steps to complement those columns are outlined in `Chapter10_Rebuilding`, where we extracted the missing data points and appended them to the dataframe. If Etherscan has no trace, we can infer that the address did not carry out such a transaction.

After this process, a few null rows remained that we complemented with the median of the column. With this final step, we have a complete dataset ready for training.

Checkpoint: If you want to skip this section, the resulting `.csv` file has been uploaded to the book's GitHub and is accessible at `final.csv`.

A note on great preprocessing

A great example of data building and preprocessing in this space is related to a dataset constructed for the paper *Exploiting Blockchain Data to Detect Smart Ponzi Schemes on Ethereum* (the link to the paper is provided in the *Further reading* section). The aim of the paper is to train a machine learning algorithm to classify Ponzi schemes' smart contracts. To achieve this, the researchers built a dataset comprising 200 Ponzi smart contracts and 3,580 non-Ponzi ones. For each contract, they extracted the bytecodes, transaction data, and internal transactions. Since internal transactions are not stored on-chain, the research team reran an Ethereum client to reproduce them. Additionally, to convert bytecodes into meaningful features or categories, the team translated them to opcode and included the frequency of each one in the smart contract.

Training the model

Once we have finished cleaning and preprocessing the data, we shuffle the dataset and then split it into separate train and test datasets. Then, we iterate through several models that have performed well on binary classification tasks, including `KNeighborsClassifier`, `DecisionTreeClassifier`, `AdaBoostClassifier`, `GradientBoostingClassifier`, and `RandomForestClassifier`.

However, just because a model performs well on one dataset doesn't mean it will work well on another. This is where tuning the model becomes important. Machine learning models have hyperparameters that need to be modified to adapt to the specific data. Customizing these hyperparameters to our dataset will improve the performance of the model. In order to execute this optimization, there are some available tools, such as scikit-learn GridSearchCV.

GridSearchCV is an exhaustive search through a range of hyperparameter values to find the best combination that maximizes the evaluation metric of our choice. It is really "exhaustive" in the sense that it will test each combination of estimators, so it can become a computationally consuming procedure and can take a lot of time. It is also worth mentioning that the search is limited by the search space that we arbitrarily choose, and therefore, `best_estimator_` returned by the `GridSearchCV` will be contained within it. In cases where we have no idea which parameters to choose, we can run **RandomizedSearchCV** to provide guidance on where to start the search. `RandomizedSearchCV` defines a search space and randomly tests it. The documentation for both classes can be found at `https://scikit-learn.org/stable/modules/generated/sklearn.model_selection.RandomizedSearchCV.html` and `https://scikit-learn.org/stable/modules/generated/sklearn.model_selection.GridSearchCV.html`.

Both `GridSearchCV` and `RandomizedSearchCV` have a `cv` parameter that refers to cross-validation. **Cross-validation** is a resampling method that partitions data into K bins of equal size to run K number of learning experiments. The results are then averaged to reduce the randomness of a model's performance and make it more robust. This class is typically contained in other implementations such as grid search. However, it can also be used independently.

There are variations such as Stratified *K* fold, which ensures that each split contains the same proportion of observations of each class, and Repeated *K* fold, which repeats the exercise for each fold but shuffles each partition to make it a new sample every time. The documentation for these procedures can be found at `https://scikit-learn.org/stable/modules/generated/sklearn.model_selection.KFold.html`.

The result of our training shows a best-performing model on `GradientBoostingClassifier`.

Evaluating the results

We will use a confusion matrix to show the model's performance, as it is highly useful for binary classification problems. The choice of evaluation metric will depend on the type of problem being addressed. In the case of fraud detection, we want to ensure that the false negative rate is minimized, so we will use **recall** as the evaluation metric. A detailed explanation of evaluation metrics was provided in *Chapter 5*.

The result is 95.6% in the overall project, which is a good number.

An imbalanced dataset

A similar dataset is also available on Kaggle and was initially analyzed by us in *Chapter 6*. This dataset is in an imbalanced form, as only 20% of the rows are fraudulent. It is common for fraud detection tasks to be associated with imbalanced data, as there are typically more regular transactions than fraudulent ones. Some models may overlook minority classes, which can sometimes include the specific class we are interested in detecting. To address imbalanced data, there is a traditional approach of resampling the dataset in both directions, either by oversampling the minority class or randomly deleting rows of the majority class in an undersampling exercise. More documentation on these procedures is provided in the *Further reading* section.

Presenting results

Data practitioners must possess strong communication skills to ensure that their findings are easily comprehensible for decision-making colleagues, clients, and in general, anyone who consumes these insights. It's crucial to tailor the presentation of findings based on the audience.

We can present the analysis with a **dashboard**, which we learned earlier in the book how to build with Dune analytics, Flipside, or Covalent. It's worth noting that not all visual analytics platforms offer the flexibility to query on-chain data; some are restricted to traditional databases. Platforms such as Tableau and Power BI are highly flexible, connecting with APIs and handling complex SQL queries from on-chain data.

We can also make use of corporate **slide** presentations, and informal **X (formerly Twitter) threads** can be employed to convey the results of data analysis. Regardless of the chosen medium, the goal is to capture and maintain the audience's interest. Starting with a compelling question and introductory sentence, keeping sentences concise, and delving into details only if the audience shows interest are key principles. A valuable resource on crafting engaging stories can be found in this X thread: `https://twitter.com/alexgarcia_atx/status/1381066483330117632`.

Regardless of the presentation platform, storytelling skills are paramount in delivering findings with a compelling narrative.

Summary

In conclusion, we have identified and discussed one of the key threats in the cryptocurrency space, highlighting the need for effective transaction monitoring and identification. To this end, we have undertaken a machine learning exercise at the Ethereum address level, where we have leveraged Etherscan to complete our dataset.

We have evaluated and compared various machine learning models, optimizing their performance through grid search hyperparameter tuning and cross-validation. By undertaking this project, we have dived into a subject matter where forensics professionals are active and remains a current news topic.

Blockchain forensics is one of the more innovative areas in data science applications, as models need to scale and keep evolving in order to adapt, to be able to spot new types of fraud and scams.

In the next chapter, we will dive into predicting prices.

Further reading

Following is a list of sources for your further reading purposes:

- PwC. (2022). PwC's Global Economic Crime and Fraud Survey 2022. https://www.pwc.com/gx/en/forensics/gecsm-2022/PwC-Global-Economic-Crime-and-Fraud-Survey-2022.pdf

- Furneaux, N. (2018). *Investigating cryptocurrencies: Understanding, extracting, and analyzing blockchain evidence*. John Wiley & Sons. Page 268.

- Sfarrugia15/Ethereum_Fraud_Detection. (n.d.). GitHub: https://github.com/sfarrugia15/Ethereum_Fraud_Detection

- Steven Farrugia, Joshua Ellul, George Azzopardi, *Detection of illicit accounts over the Ethereum blockchain, Expert Systems with Applications*, volume 150, 2020, 113318, ISSN 0957-4174: https://doi.org/10.1016/j.eswa.2020.113318.

- *Exploiting Blockchain data to detect Smart Contract Ponzi Schemes on Ethereum*. (2019, March 18). IEEE Xplore: https://ieeexplore.ieee.org/stamp/stamp.jsp?arnumber=8668768

- Ethereum security and scam prevention. (n.d.). ethereum.org. https://ethereum.org/en/security/

- Senilov, I. (2021, September 27). *Approaching anomaly detection in transactional data*. Medium: https://towardsdatascience.com/approaching-anomaly-detection-in-transactional-data-744d132d524e

- Janiobachmann. (2019, July 3). *Credit fraud || Dealing with Imbalanced datasets*. Kaggle: Your Machine Learning and Data Science Community: `https://www.kaggle.com/code/janiobachmann/credit-fraud-dealing-with-imbalanced-datasets`

- Jason Brownlee. (2020). *Random Oversampling and Undersampling for Imbalanced Classification*. Machine Learning Mastery: `https://machinelearningmastery.com/random-oversampling-and-undersampling-for-imbalanced-classification/`

- **Clustering**: Once we have clustered addresses, it is possible to build an anomaly detection identifier that takes as normality the parameters of the cluster to which each address belongs.

  Price, W. (2021, May 28). *Clustering Ethereum addresses*. Medium: `https://towardsdatascience.com/clustering-ethereum-addresses-18aeca61919d`

- Ethereum_clustering/main.ipynb at master · willprice221/ethereum_clustering. (n.d.). GitHub. `https://github.com/willprice221/ethereum_clustering/blob/master/main.ipynb`

- Storytelling resource: Insider. (2019, June 21). *Pixar's Secret Formula For Making Perfect Films | The Art Of Film* [Video]. YouTube: `https://www.youtube.com/watch?v=Y34eshkxE5o`

11

Price Prediction
with Time Series

A significant amount of time spent by analysts and researchers in the finance industry is devoted to predicting investment opportunities, including asset prices and asset returns. With the availability of large volumes of data and advancements in processing techniques, **machine learning** (**ML**) has gained momentum, expanding its application beyond asset pricing to areas such as insurance pricing, portfolio management, and risk management.

In addition to the well-known applications of ML in the financial industry, we can now consider the influence of Web3 and open data. As we have learned throughout this book, data in Web3 is accessible to anyone. Privileged information, such as bank balances or significant account movements, can be viewed by anyone who knows where to look, as explained in *Chapter 5*.

Many asset modeling and prediction problems in the financial industry involve a time component and the estimation of continuous outputs. This is why our focus in this chapter will be on time-series analysis, understanding what these outputs are, and how to model them. Our objective is to utilize historical data points, including the time component, to predict future outcomes, particularly in the context of predicting prices.

In summary, this chapter will cover the following topics:

- A primer on time series

- Database selection and feature engineering

- Modeling, training, and evaluation of results

We will employ both traditional statistical models and **deep learning** (**DL**) methodologies to capture the patterns and dynamics within the time series data.

Technical requirements

In this chapter, we will be utilizing the `statsmodels` library, specifically its time-series analysis packages (`tsa` and `statespace`). `statsmodels` is a comprehensive Python module that offers a wide range of classes and functions for estimating various statistical models, performing statistical tests, and conducting statistical data exploration. For time-series analysis, it provides essential models such as univariate **autoregressive (AR)** models, **vector AR (VAR)** models, and univariate **AR moving average (ARMA)** models. Furthermore, it offers descriptive statistics for time series, such as the **autocorrelation** and **partial autocorrelation** functions (**ACF** and **PACF**).

If you have not worked with `statsmodels` before, it can be installed using the following command:

```
pip install statsmodels
```

The documentation for `statsmodels` can be found at https://www.statsmodels.org/stable/index.html.

We will also be utilizing `pmdarima`, which allows us to interact with **automatic modeling AR integrated MA (Auto ARIMA)**. `pmdarima` serves as a Python wrapper for various statistical and ML libraries (including `statsmodels` and `scikit-learn`). If you have not worked with `pmdarima` before, it can be installed with the following command:

```
pip install pmdarima
```

The documentation for `pmdarima` can be found at http://alkaline-ml.com/pmdarima/.

We will also extract our working dataset from `yfinance`, which is an open source Python library that serves as an interface to the Yahoo Finance API, providing convenient access to a wide range of financial data, including stock market prices, historical data, dividend information, and more. To install the library, we have to run the following command:

```
pip install yfinance
```

The documentation for `yfinance` can be found at https://pypi.org/project/yfinance/.

All the data and code files related to this chapter can be accessed in the book's GitHub repository, available here:

https://github.com/PacktPublishing/Data-Science-for-Web3/tree/main/Chapter11

We recommend that you read through the code files in the `Chapter11` folder to follow along with the chapter effectively.

A primer on time series

Time Series is a collection of observations across time, spaced at equal intervals of time.

– Luis Alberiko Gil-Alaña

The collection of observations mentioned by Professor Gil-Alaña forms a sequence of events that unfold and evolve over time in chronological order.

These observations represent various data points that change or fluctuate over time, such as stock prices, temperature readings, sales figures, website traffic, number of blockchain transactions, and more. Each observation holds valuable knowledge about the past and provides information about future trends.

A 10-month time series representing the monthly closing price of **Bitcoin-US Dollar (BTC-USD)** looks like this:

Date	Close
10/1/2014	338.321014
11/1/2014	378.046997
12/1/2014	320.192993
1/1/2015	217.464005
2/1/2015	254.263
3/1/2015	244.223999
4/1/2015	236.145004
5/1/2015	230.190002
6/1/2015	263.071991
7/1/2015	284.649994

Table 11.1 – Segment of the BTC-USD time series (source: Yahoo Finance)

As we analyze time series data, we can identify patterns, trends, and fluctuations. These patterns may reveal recurring themes, follow a clear trajectory, or exhibit chaotic and unpredictable behavior. Here follows a visualization of the time series of the BTC price since 2015:

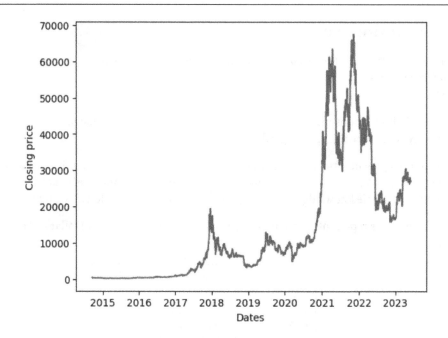

Figure 11.1 – Plot of the entire series

A time series comprises the following components:

Trend: This represents the overall directional movement of the series. A trend can be deterministic, driven by an underlying rationale, or stochastic, exhibiting random behavior.

In the next example, we observe a continuous upward trend since 2017, which has accelerated in the past 2 years:

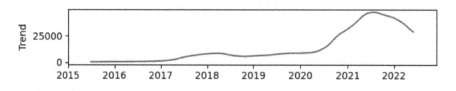

Figure 11.2: Graph of trend

Seasonal: This component refers to recurring cycles or patterns within the series that repeat over a specific timeframe.

In the given dataset, we can observe a drop mid-year and an increase toward the end of each year:

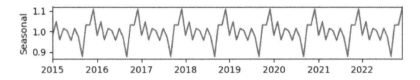

Figure 11.3 – Seasonal component

White noise: This represents the component of the series that is not captured by the trend or seasonal components.

In the given dataset, the component appears flat initially but exhibits peaks at specific points coinciding with peaks in the overall series, such as at the end of 2017-2018 and 2021:

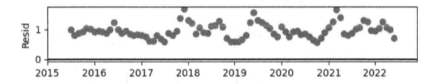

Figure 11.4 – White noise representation

To decompose a time series in order to analyze its components, we can use the following code:

```
decompose = seasonal_decompose(df, model= 'additive').
plot(observed=True, seasonal=True, trend=True, resid=True,
weights=False)
```

There are two additional concepts relevant to time series analysis: autocorrelation and stationarity.

Autocorrelation: This refers to the dependence between consecutive points in a series. It indicates that the value at a given time period is influenced by the measurements at previous time periods. The order of autoregression represents the number of previous values used to predict the present value, known as the *lag*. For instance, if we use the previous 2 months' prices to predict the monthly price of Bitcoin, it corresponds to an autocorrelation of order 2.

Stationary: A time series is said to be stationary if "*the mean and the variance do not depend on time, and the covariance between any two observations only depend on the distance between them, but not on a specific location in time*" (*Luis Alberiko Gil-Alaña*). Stationarity is an important assumption for many time series models and analyses. We can derive from the previous citation that a time series that has a trend or seasonality cannot be considered stationary.

For example, the following time series example has a clear upward trend, so it is not stationary:

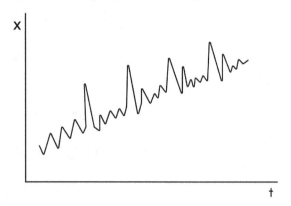

Figure 11.5 – Time series with trend

The following one has an increasing variance as it is progressing in time and trend, so it is not stationary:

Figure 11.6 – Time series with variance

The following has no trend or seasonality, so can be considered stationary:

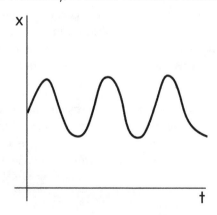

Figure 11.7 – Stationary time series

Now that we have the theory, let's introduce the dataset.

Exploring the dataset

For price prediction, we will utilize two datasets. The first dataset is the time series data of BTC prices, extracted from Yahoo Finance, with a daily granularity.

To extract it, we use the Yfinance library with the following code:

```
data=yf.Ticker('BTC-USD')
df= data.history (start='YEAR-MONTH-DAY', end='YEAR-MONTH-DAY')
```

The dataset contains multiple columns, but we will focus on the close column and the date. The `date` column needs to be used as an index with a frequency. The following code snippet can be useful if not sourcing from Yfinance, which already handles it:

```
df = df.set_index(pd.DatetimeIndex(df['Date'], freq='D'))
```

As a Web3 dataset, compared to traditional financial stock price datasets, it includes prices for weekends as well, reflecting the fact that the market operates continuously. When selecting a times series dataset, it is essential to ensure that there are no missing values or handle them using the appropriate techniques.

If it were necessary to work with business days only, the Pandas library has some additional functions such as `USFederalHolidayCalendar`, which imports holiday calendars and provides a list of holidays:

```
from pandas.tseries.holiday import USFederalHolidayCalendar
```

The `CustomBusinessDay` class provides a parametric `BusinessDay` class that can be used to create customized business-day calendars for local holidays and local weekend conventions:

```
from pandas.tseries.offsets import CustomBusinessDay
```

Additionally, we have prepared another dataset consisting of news articles and their corresponding **sentiment analysis (SA)**. For each day in the BTC price time series that we aim to model, we will match it with a set of news articles and their respective SA. We will test the hypothesis that incorporating external information from the real world will improve the prediction performance of the model. Other variables that can be considered include trading volume, the number of tweets containing the term *BTC*, days remaining until the next halving event (when the reward for Bitcoin mining is cut in half, and that takes place approximately every 4 years), and more.

During **exploratory data analysis (EDA)**, it's possible to discover missing values, outliers, or irregularities in the dataset. As discussed in *Chapter 1*, there have been instances where market prices were halted due to extreme volatility, such as the UST depeg. When faced with a dataset containing these issues, how should we address them? Non-time series-specific methods, such as mean or median imputation, are effective for stationary series. Time series-specific techniques include **Last Observation Carried**

Forward (LOCF), which replaces missing values with the immediately preceding observed value, and **Next Observation Carried Backward** (NOCB), which performs the same replacement with the subsequent observed value. Another method is interpolation, which can be linear, polynomial, or spline, depending on the assumed relationship between observations. Further resources on potential approaches to resolve this issue are provided in the *Further reading* section.

Before delving into the models, it is important to address the concept of train-test split for time series data. Unlike the traditional datasets we have analyzed so far, time series models inherently possess an endogenous temporality, which is precisely what we aim to capture. This means that the value's position in the time series order will have an impact on future points. In order to understand and capture this temporal relationship, we must maintain the chronological order of the time series and any exogenous variables. Randomly splitting the data is not suitable for time series analysis.

In this case, the test dataset will consist of the most recent portion of the series, while the training dataset will include all rows from the beginning of the series up to the selected test portion.

Sklearn provides a helpful class for performing this split, called `TimeSeriesSplit`:

```
from sklearn.model_selection import TimeSeriesSplit
```

The documentation can be found at the following link:

```
https://scikitlearn.org/stable/modules/generated/sklearn.model_selection.TimeSeriesSplit.html
```

The challenge we will try to solve consists of predicting the BTC price on dates that were not part of the training. Time series problems can be approached by using statistical modeling, which we will call the traditional method, and through ML, whereby we will train a **long short-term memory** (LSTM) model.

Discussing traditional pipelines

The initial approach involves statistical modeling, using models such as ARIMA, **ARIMA with exogenous variables** (**ARIMAX**), and Auto ARIMA. To work with them, we need to address two additional challenges: ensuring the stationarity of the time series and determining the appropriate model order.

Statistical models perform better when applied to stationary time series. Traditional statistical time series models such as ARIMA are more effective when dealing with stationary time series. Resolving this issue will be part of the preprocessing phase.

The second challenge lies in the modeling phase, which involves understanding the dataset, determining the appropriate lags, and defining time windows. We will approach the solution manually using the Auto ARIMA algorithm, which handles hyperparameters automatically.

Preprocessing

Various functions can be employed to transform non-stationary time series data into a format suitable for our models. Examples include differencing, logarithmic transformations, **moving averages (MAs)**, percent changes, lags, and cumulative sums.

Differencing calculates the differences between consecutive observations. This technique helps stabilize the mean of a time series by removing changes at a certain level, thereby reducing or eliminating trend and seasonality.

In the `Traditional time series models.ipynb` notebook, we start with a dataset that looks like this:

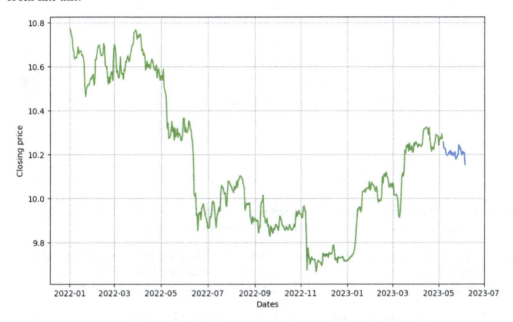

Figure 11.8 – Complete time series

To apply differencing, we use the following code:

```
df.diff().dropna()
```

After such a process, the dataset is transformed as follows:

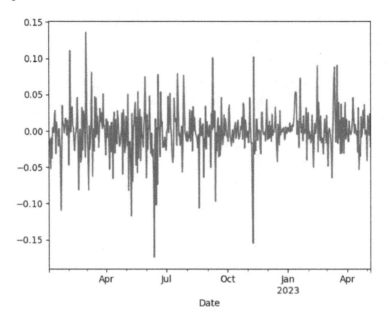

Figure 11.9 – Differenced time series

In some cases, differencing the data once may not result in a stationary series. In such instances, it may be necessary to apply differencing a second time to achieve stationarity.

Other functions such as percent change, log difference, and MA can also help reduce trend and seasonality, making the series resemble white noise. Log transformation is particularly useful when dealing with non-constant variance, while MA can be beneficial for series with high volatility.

To help determine if a series is stationary, we can employ statistical tests such as the Dickey-Fuller test. This test is a root-based test that focuses on the coefficient associated with the first lag of the time series variable. If the coefficient is equal to one (indicating a unit root), the time series behaves as non-stationary, which is the null hypothesis. We reject the null hypothesis if the test result is negative and statistically significant, indicating that the time series is stationary. There are other tests for similar purposes, such as the **Kwiatkowski-Phillips-Schmidt-Shin** (**KPSS**) test or the Phillips-Perron test. An explanation exceeds the scope of this book; however, all of them can be sourced from the same library we have been working on. Once we have a stationary dataset, we can proceed to modeling.

Modeling – ARIMA/SARIMAX and Auto ARIMA

Among statistical algorithms used for forecasting future values, we encounter ARIMA /SARIMAX and Auto ARIMA. ARIMA considers past values to predict future values, while SARIMAX incorporates seasonality patterns and exogenous variables. Auto ARIMA automates the modeling process based on training data.

The names of these models are derived from the concepts they comprise. **ARIMA** stands for **autoregressive (AR)-integrated (I)-moving average (MA)**. **SARIMAX** adds **S** for **seasonal** and **X** for **exogenous** as it can be fed with independent variables. **Auto ARIMA** adds **Auto** for **automatic modeling**. Let's delve into these concepts.

AR identifies the regression order of the time series onto itself. It assumes that the latest data point value depends on previous values with a lag that we determine; that is, *the number of lag observations*.

We can determine the regression order by using the PACF plot, which is part of the `statsmodels` library. The following code can be used to plot it:

```
pacf_td = plot_pacf(training_data)
```

The PACF measures the direct correlation between past values and current values and examines the spikes at each lag to determine their significance. A significant spike extends beyond significant limits, indicating that the correlation for that lag is not zero. The number of significant correlations determines the order of the AR term (p).

I identifies the number of differencing procedures required to make the series stationary.

MA models the error of the time series based on past forecast errors, assuming that the current error depends on the previous error with a lag that we determine. In essence, this corresponds to the size of the "window" function over our time series data and corresponds to the MA (q) part of the model. We can approach the order of q by examining the autocorrelation plot (ACF).

The ACF shows whether the elements of a time series are positively correlated, negatively correlated, or independent of each other. The horizontal axis shows the lags and the spikes show how relevantly correlated such lags are. We consider an ACF of order q based on statistically significant spikes that are far from zero.

To plot the ACF, we can use the following code, utilizing the `statsmodels` library:

```
acf_diff = plot_acf(df_train_diff)
```

Here is a rule of thumb to start testing models:

If the PACF has a significant spike at lag p, but not beyond, and the ACF plot decays more gradually, we will use the following order for the model: ARIMA (p,d,0):

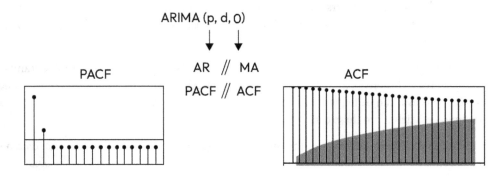

Figure 11.10 – Hypothesis 1

If the ACF plot has a significant spike at lag q but not beyond and the PACF plot decays more gradually, we will use the following order for the model: ARIMA (0,d,q):

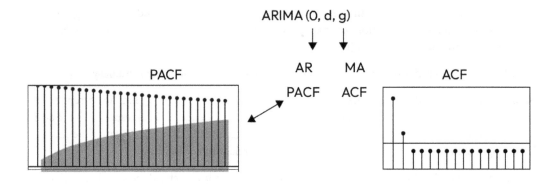

Figure 11.11 – Hypothesis 2

S feeds into the model the characteristic of regular and predictable changes that recur every m period of time. It will be modeled in a similar way as the time series. The specifics of the seasonal component of SARIMA are highlighted as follows:

SARIMA(p,d,q)(P,D,Q)[m]

The components are defined as follows:

- P: Seasonal AR order.
- D: Seasonal difference order.

- Q: Seasonal MA order.

- m: The number of time steps for a single seasonal period. To get this number, it is useful to decompose similar periods of time that we want to predict (always from the training dataset) to spot the seasonality. In the case under analysis, we see a seasonality of 8 days.

To evaluate the model, we utilize a traditional regression metric known as **root mean squared error** (**RMSE**). RMSE is a statistical measure employed to assess the accuracy of a model's predictions by calculating the square root of the **mean squared error** (**MSE**). MSE is the average of the squared differences between the original and predicted values. RMSE yields a single, easily interpretable value that represents the typical magnitude of errors made by a predictive model. A lower RMSE indicates a better fit between predicted and actual values, reflecting a more accurate predictive model. Another related metric is **mean absolute error** (**MAE**), which represents the average of the absolute differences between the actual and predicted values in the dataset.

RMSE is widely favored for comparing the performance of regression models, particularly because it is expressed in the same units as the dependent variable, facilitating a straightforward interpretation.

In the Jupyter notebook, we can observe that the model can be further improved. The result of the manual modeling is an RMSE value of 0.073.

Auto ARIMA

Auto ARIMA handles the task of tuning hyperparameters very well. It automatically generates the optimal values for the parameters (p,d, and q).

The metric named the **Akaike information criterion** (**AIC**), useful in selecting predictors for regression, is used to determine the order of an ARIMA model. Particularly, the Auto ARIMA model iterates during the fitting process to find the best combination of parameters that minimizes the AIC. According to the documentation, it functions *like a grid search*, trying different sets of p and q parameters. For the differencing terms, Auto ARIMA utilizes a test of stationarity, such as an augmented Dickey-Fuller test, and considers seasonality.

This approach significantly improves our model, saving time and reducing human errors. To implement it, we can use the following code:

```
pm.auto_arima(training_data, stepwise=False, seasonal=True, n_jobs=-1,
trace=True)
```

The parameters passed are as follows:

- `training_data`: This is the time series data we want to model.

- `stepwise`: A Boolean parameter that controls whether the function should perform a stepwise search for the best ARIMA model. If set to `True`, the function will perform a stepwise search (that is, it will iteratively consider adding or removing AR, MA, or I components). If set to

False, the function will search for the best ARIMA model using an exhaustive search over possible combinations, similar to a grid search. A stepwise search is faster but may not always find the best model.

- seasonal: A Boolean parameter that specifies whether the model should include seasonal components (for example, SARIMA). If set to True, the function will search for seasonal patterns in the data. If set to False, it will only consider non-seasonal ARIMA models.

- n_jobs: This parameter controls the number of CPU cores to use when performing the model search. Setting it to -1 means using all available CPU cores, which can speed up the search process, especially when we have a large dataset.

- trace: This is a debugging parameter. When set to True, it enables verbose output, which includes diagnostic information and intermediate results during the model search.

After implementing this model, the RMSE decreases substantially; however, it has room for improvement. Now, let's look at incorporating a specific domain or subject-matter knowledge.

Adding exogenous variables

Exogenous variables are additional pieces of information that can be included in our models. These variables can originate from the same time series, such as observing BTC price increases at specific hours or days, or they can be completely exogenous, such as SA of news or derived from X (formerly Twitter).

In our notebook, we incorporate the sentiment of the news of each day as an exogenous variable. The preprocessing of such a dataset includes the following:

1. Mapping the sentiment of the news according to the sentiment_mapping dictionary to the following criteria:

```
sentiment_mapping = {
    'Positive': 1,
    'Negative': -1,
    'Neutral': -1
}
```

2. We also identify dates where there has been an outlier in the number of news items related to BTC and reinforce its impact. To do that, we find the z-score value, which behaves as a threshold against which we will identify outliers. Those considered outliers are multiplied by 2. This is done with the following code in the traditional_time_series_models. ipynb file:

```
outliers = day_sentiment_df[z_scores > threshold]
outliers['sentiment_number'] = outliers['sentiment_number'] * 2
day_sentiment_df.update(outliers)
```

Both decisions in *steps 1* and *2* are arbitrary decisions of the data scientist and look to reflect in the data the fact that the crypto market tends to overreact to news, whether positive, negative, or neutral.

By applying the exogenous variable, ARIMAX and Auto ARIMA models show a decreased RMSE compared to their versions without exogenous variables, which is very positive:

- rmse - manual: 0.046

- rmse - auto: 0.062

We see that the manual tuning of the model outperforms the Auto ARIMA model when adding the exogenous variable.

To compare the performance of these models with the LSTM, we can compare RMSE metrics or reverse the results with the following code in order to compare USD prices. To reverse from logs, we can use this code snippet:

```
testing_data= np.exp(testing_data)
forecast_test=np.exp(forecast_test)
rmse_exog = np.sqrt(mean_squared_error(testing_data, forecast_test))
```

We have now reviewed the statistic model, so we proceed to build a DL model.

Using a neural network – LSTM

We explained in detail how LSTM works in *Chapter 8*. Briefly, LSTM serves as a specialized form of **recurrent neural network** (**RNN**) designed to detect patterns in data sequences. Its distinct feature lies in its capacity to preserve information over extended periods compared to conventional RNNs. LSTM overcomes this short-term memory problem by selectively retaining relevant information.

Preprocessing

We will treat the problem as a **supervised learning** (**SL**) task. For that purpose, we will modify the training set as follows:

1. Scale the dataset using the MinMaxScaler().

2. Iterate through the scaled dataset and retrieve the 60 days previous to the current price (y_train) and convert them into features for each price. The result will be a training dataset with 60 price columns as x_train features for each BTC price (y_train). In summary, for each data point that the model learns, it refers to the previous 60 days in x_train:

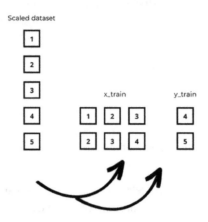

Figure 11.12 – Structure of the training dataset

We use the previous 60 days as input variables for each day considered as an output variable.

Model building

To build the model, we will leverage the Keras library. For that, we add to the model two LSTM layers with 50 neurons each, the first one with the input shape of our dataset.

We also add two dense layers with 25 and 1 neurons each. The structure of the model should be kept as simple as possible and is totally modifiable:

```
model= Sequential ()
model.add (LSTM(50, return_sequences=True, input_shape=(x_train.
shape[1],1)))
model.add (LSTM (50, return_sequences = False))
model.add (Dense(25))
model.add (Dense(1))
```

We will later compile with the Adam optimizer and choose mean_squared_error as the loss metric:

```
model.compile (optimizer='Adam', loss='mean_squared_error')
```

To save the callbacks, in order to analyze the results of our training, we set up the TensorBoard tool to read from a new folder that saves the logs:

```
tensorboard_callback = tf.keras.callbacks.TensorBoard(log_dir="./
logs")
```

Training and evaluation

We train our model with a batch size of 10 and 35 epochs:

```
model.fit (x_train, y_train, batch_size=10,
epochs=35,callbacks=[tensorboard_callback])
```

To evaluate how well the model predicts, we will build a new dataset with data from the last 30 days that has not been passed to the model. To do that, we need to follow the same steps that we executed for the training dataset in the *Preprocessing* section. We turn 60 rows into columns in x_test that become features of the 61st value that becomes y or the value to be predicted (y_test).

For the prediction, we will only consider the last 30 days and calculate the RMSE between the predicted values and the y_test values. To do that, we can use the following code:

```
np.sqrt(mean_squared_error(y_test, predictions))
```

If we plot the prediction and the ground truth data, the result is not bad. Please refer to the Chapter11/ LSTM.ipynb notebook for a colored version:

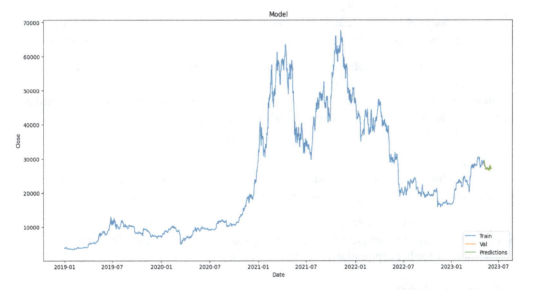

Figure 11.13 – Predicted and ground truth data

A comparison between the RMSE of the models shows that the LSTM approach performs better in this environment of high volatility of prices with a $457 error versus a $1,283 error of the best ARIMA model.

Some key differences to take into account are as follows:

- **Relationship between variables**: ARIMA models assume linear relationships between the input and output variables. They can capture some nonlinear patterns, but complex nonlinear dependencies present in the data will not be covered. LSTM models are better suited for capturing nonlinear relationships and long-term dependencies in time series data. This makes LSTM models more suitable for modeling nonlinear and sequential data with complex temporal patterns.

- **Training complexity**: ARIMA models involve estimating parameters such as AR, MA, and differencing terms. LSTM models, as with all **neural networks** (**NNs**), require more computational resources and training time. They involve training multiple layers of recurrent units with a large number of parameters. Training DL models typically requires more data and computational power compared to traditional statistical models.

With the libraries we analyzed, it is possible to examine both methods, compare the performance, and evaluate the accuracy of each model.

Summary

In this chapter, we explored the analysis of price time series for BTC in a market that operates continuously, exhibits high volatility, and can experience exaggerated reactions to news events.

We began by familiarizing ourselves with the fundamental concepts of time series analysis and introduced traditional models such as ARIMA and Auto ARIMA. For our use case, we transformed our price dataset into the stationary form and learned to apply the models to it. Lastly, we incorporated an exogenous variable such as the news into our model. This external information proved to be valuable, contributing to a reduction in the error metric we were tracking.

Furthermore, we delved into the LSTM model approach, which required us to restructure the dataset differently. This involved numerous modifications and adaptations to accommodate the specific requirements of the LSTM model, which ultimately performed better.

By employing a comprehensive range of techniques and incorporating external factors, we have gained valuable insights into analyzing and forecasting token price time series. These findings serve as a foundation for further exploration and refinement of our models.

Further reading

To complement this chapter, the following links may help:

- *Time Series Analysis in R Part 2: Time Series Transformations*. (n.d.). An online community for showcasing R & Python tutorials. *DataScience+*. https://datascienceplus.com/ time-series-analysis-in-r-part-2-time-series-transformations/

- *Computer Science. (2019, December 22). Stock Price Prediction Using Python & Machine Learning* [Video]. *YouTube.* https://www.youtube.com/watch?v=QIUxPv5PJOY

- *Luis Alberiko Gil-Alaña. (2021). Introduction to Time Series* [PDF document].

- *Cryptocurrencies and stock market indices. Are they related? LA Gil-Alaña, EJA Abakah, MFR Rojo. Research in International Business and Finance, 2020.* http://ddfv.ufv.es/bitstream/handle/10641/2229/cryptocurrencies%20and%20stock%20market%20indices.pdf?sequence=1&isAllowed=y

- *Modelling long memory volatility in the Bitcoin market: Evidence of persistence and structural breaks. E Bouri, LA Gil-Alaña, R Gupta, D Roubaud. International Journal of Finance & Economics, 2019.* https://onlinelibrary.wiley.com/doi/abs/10.1002/ijfe.1670

- *Abulkhair, A. (2023, June 13). Data imputation demystified | Time series data. Medium.* https://medium.com/@aaabulkhair/data-imputation-demystified-time-series-data-69bc9c798cb7

- *Jingjuewang. (2017, December 11). Handle Missing Values in Time Series For Beginners. Kaggle: Your Machine Learning and Data Science Community.* https://www.kaggle.com/code/juejuewang/handle-missing-values-in-time-series-for-beginners

- *Aldean, A. S. (2023, June 29). Time Series Data Interpolation. Medium.* https://medium.com/@aseafaldean/time-series-data-interpolation-e4296664b86

- *Holloway, N. (2019, March 16). Seasonality and SARIMAX. Kaggle: Your Machine Learning and Data Science Community.* https://www.kaggle.com/code/nholloway/seasonality-and-sarimax

- *Brownlee, J. (2020, December). Understand Time Series Forecast Uncertainty Using Prediction Intervals with Python. Machine Learning Mastery.* https://machinelearningmastery.com/time-series-forecast-uncertainty-using-confidence-intervals-python/

- *Chugh, A. (2022, March 16). MAE, MSE, RMSE, Coefficient of Determination, Adjusted R Squared — Which Metric is Better? Medium.* https://medium.com/analytics-vidhya/mae-mse-rmse-coefficient-of-determination-adjusted-r-squared-which-metric-is-better-cd0326a5697e

12

Marketing Discovery with Graphs

Data has played a pivotal role in marketing, empowering decision-making, and optimizing resource allocation for impactful campaigns. However, the inherent pseudonymity and complexities of blockchain data pose challenges for marketing teams where extracting maximum value is, in many cases, an ongoing opportunity.

One of the main applications that's used by marketing teams is clustering, which involves organizing groups with shared interests for customer segmentation. This technique was very successful primarily in social networks, facilitating recommendation systems for products and fostering new connections.

Similar to social networks, blockchain data, with its wealth of transactions, holds immense potential to deduce preferences from a few interactions. Label classification is another valuable use case, allowing marketing teams to identify and target communities within the blockchain effectively. By discerning communities, data scientists can help marketers overcome the limitations of pseudonymity and gain valuable insights.

In this chapter, we will delve into the following topics:

- A primer on graphs
- Database selection and feature engineering
- Modeling, training, and evaluating the results

By the end of this chapter, we will have had a comprehensive introduction to harnessing the power of networks and graphs for effective marketing strategies.

Technical requirements

In this chapter, we will utilize the `networkx` library, a Python library that's used for working with networks or graphs. It offers a range of tools and functions for creating, manipulating, and analyzing networks. This library facilitates node creation, adding information, and providing algorithms for analyzing and exploring networks, such as finding the shortest paths, calculating centrality measures, and detecting communities.

If you have not worked with `networkx` before, it can be installed using the following code snippet:

```
pip install networkx
```

The documentation for `networkx` can be found at `https://networkx.org/documentation/stable/index.html`.

We will also use **Gephi**, a free open source tool for graph plotting. Gephi is a user-friendly tool that's designed for visualizing and exploring graphs and networks. It assists users in gaining insights and analyzing complex relationships within graph data.

With Gephi, we can import data from various formats and select specific nodes to understand their positions in our dataset. The tool provides numerous statistical functionalities to support graph analysis. It allows us to filter, sort, and manipulate the graph based on specific criteria, enabling us to focus on relevant nodes and edges.

If you have not worked with Gephi before, it can be downloaded from their page at `https://gephi.org/`. A comprehensive guide to Gephi is available in the book *Gephi Cookbook*, accessible at `https://www.packtpub.com/product/gephi-cookbook/9781783987405`.

For our machine learning model, we will utilize the StellarGraph library. StellarGraph is designed for working with graph-structured data, specifically for tasks related to machine learning and data analysis. One of its key features is its integration with popular machine learning frameworks such as TensorFlow and Keras. StellarGraph provides methods to convert graphs into formats compatible with these frameworks, allowing us to apply machine learning models and algorithms to graph-structured data. The documentation for StellarGraph can be found at `https://stellargraph.readthedocs.io/en/stable/`.

If this is the first time you're using this library, you can install it with `pip`:

```
pip install stellargraph
```

All the data and code files related to this chapter, as well as the color images can be found in this book's GitHub repository at `https://github.com/PacktPublishing/Data-Science-for-Web3/tree/main/Chapter12`.

We recommend that you read through the code files in the `Chapter12` folder so that you can follow along with this chapter effectively.

A primer on graphs

According to Innar Liiv, "*Network science, sometimes considered a subfield of data science and sometimes an independent academic field, is a set of techniques, methods, and tools to study patterns in networked structures.*" An example of a network is the image of the London underground map:

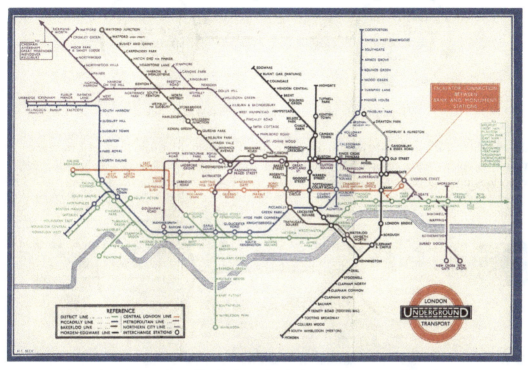

Figure 12.1 – An overview of Beck's design for the London underground map (source: https://en.wikipedia.org/wiki/File:Beck_Map_1933.jpg found under fair use)

In our exploration of networks and graphs, we will use these terms interchangeably.

The study of networks has gained significant interest in recent years due to their ability to explain relationships between entities simply. As explained by Professor Matías Avila, "*A network, also called a graph in the mathematical literature, is a collection of nodes where some pairs are connected by edges.*"

In this primer, we will explore fundamental concepts of graphs, including their definition and features.

A network consists of nodes (also referred to as vertices or V) that are linked together (by connections or edges or E). The graph or network is commonly denoted as G, with the notation G=(V,E).

In *Figure 12.2*, we can observe the components of the graph within the network formed between addresses `0xdac17f958d2ee523a2206206994597c13d831ec7` and `0x28C6c06298d514Db089934071355E5743bf21d60`:

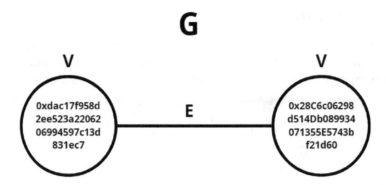

Figure 12.2 – The relationship between two addresses

The role of a data analyst is to derive meaning and actionable insights from data. Once we have found a meaningful connection, it is important to add context. For example, in the graph shown in *Figure 12.3*, we are looking at the relationship between a USDT smart contract and a Binance address:

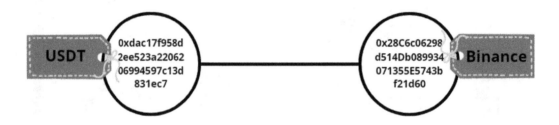

Figure 12.3 – The relationship between two labeled addresses

Types of graphs

Directed graphs (**digraphs**), as defined by Stamile, Marzullo, and Deusebio, are represented as "*A couple, G=(V,E), where V is a set of nodes and E is a set of ordered couples representing the connection between two nodes.*" The elements of E are ordered, indicating a direction from one node (usually referred to as the "source") to another node (usually referred to as the "target"):

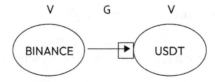

Figure 12.4 – An example of a digraph

In **digraphs**, nodes can be classified as indegree (the number of incoming edges to a node, representing the nodes in the graph that have directed edges pointing toward it) and outdegree (the number of outgoing edges from a node, representing the nodes in the graph that the given node has directed edges pointing toward). Indegree and outdegree provide insights into the connectivity and influence of nodes in a directed graph. Understanding this concept is valuable for various graph analysis tasks, such as identifying central nodes, studying information flow, detecting influential nodes, and assessing the structure and dynamics of directed networks.

An **ego graph**, also known as a neighborhood graph, focuses on a specific node called the "ego" node. It displays the ego node and all its neighboring nodes, along with the edges connecting them. Ego graphs are useful for analyzing the local structure and connections around a specific node of interest:

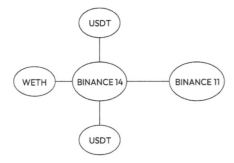

Figure 12.5 – An example of an ego graph

A **weighted graph** is a graph where each edge has an associated weight or value. The weights are numerical values that can represent various features of the relationship between the connected nodes, such as strength, distance, cost, frequency of connection, and so on. The weights provide additional information that can be used for analysis, training, and inference:

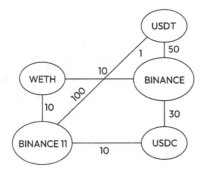

Figure 12.6 – An example of a weighted graph

There are many other graph patterns with their own characteristics and uses that are outside the scope of this introduction. But why are graph patterns important for our data analysis? Graph patterns help reveal the dynamics of relationships between addresses in the blockchain. In an article titled *Visualizing Dynamic Bitcoin Transaction Patterns*, the authors break down these patterns and provide corresponding explanations:

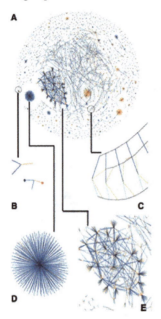

FIG. 4. **(A)** High-resolution (8k) visualization of a standard block; **(B)** detail of both a low (small node) and a high (large node) value transaction, **(C)** known and linked Bitcoin addresses, **(D)** a payout system, and **(E)** a highly associated disconnected component believed to be a coin-tumbling service to move amounts rapidly between addresses, obfuscating the source and destination of funds.

Figure 12.7 – Examples of graph patterns in a Bitcoin block

Attribution

Visualizing Dynamic Bitcoin Transaction Patterns, Dan McGinn et al. 2016; Published by Mary Ann Liebert, Inc.

This open access article is distributed under the terms of the Creative Commons license (`http://creativecommons.org/licenses/by/4.0`), which permits unrestricted use, distribution, and reproduction in any medium, provided the original work is properly credited.

In the subsequent sections, we will analyze a dataset of addresses belonging to two communities with different characteristics – one linked to the OpenSea NFT marketplace and the other to a centralized exchange named Binance. The characteristics of the relationship that each address has with its community can be seen in the pattern formed within the graph:

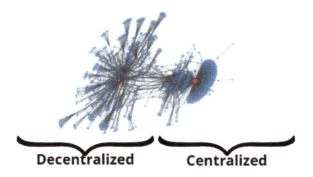

Decentralized   **Centralized**

Figure 12.8 – Relationships between target communities

Graph properties

Following the categorization proposed by Stamile, Marzullo, and Deusebio, we find it helpful to analyze integration metrics and segregation metrics.

Integration metrics show how nodes tend to be interconnected with each other. Among the metrics, we have the distance and the shortest path.

The distance is defined as *"The number of edges to traverse to reach a target node from a given source node."* The shortest path is the path with the lowest number of edges compared to all the possible paths between two nodes. If the graph is weighted, it is a path that holds the minimum sum of edge weights. We are interested in this concept because it will help us identify important nodes.

Another metric related to the shortest path is the **characteristic path length**. This is defined as the average of all the shortest path lengths between all possible pairs of nodes.

Another group of metrics is **segregation** metrics, which, as their name implies, look for patterns in which ties are more likely to exist between nodes similar to each other. They identify the presence of groups of interconnected nodes, known as **communities**. Among these metrics, we have the clustering coefficient and modularity.

The **clustering coefficient** is a measure of the degree to which nodes tend to group (or "cluster"). The rationale is that nodes tend to group with similar nodes to a higher degree than with random nodes. It is based on the division of triangles or triplets, which consist of three nodes and three edges. It studies the proportion in which a node's neighbors are also neighbors between each other. Local and global clustering coefficients exist here.

Modularity measures the strength of a network so that it can be divided into modules or communities. If the modularity of a network is high, it means that there are dense connections between nodes within a community and sparse connections between nodes that correspond to different modules. Both the Gephi tool and the Networkx library allow us to calculate modularity and identify communities.

Figure 12.9 shows the dataset that will be introduced in the following section painted in two colors, one for each community that's been detected:

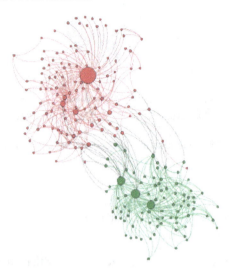

Figure 12.9 – Dataset communities with Gephi filters applied

This figure was created using Gephi with the following filters:

- **Topology filter**: Giant component

- **Degree range**: Above 3

- **Size of nodes**: Betweenness centrality

- **Color of nodes**: Modularity 2.0

Let's dive into the dataset!

The dataset

The dataset comprises a series of transactions with destinations set to Binance or OpenSea. These entities are served by multiple addresses, and for the sake of simplicity, we have selected one among the many associated with them.

The Binance 14 address (`0x28c6c06298d514db089934071355e5743bf21d60`) represents a Binance hot wallet that is used to facilitate the connection between the centralized exchange and Ethereum. The funds in this wallet serve deposits and withdrawals outside of Binance.

On the other hand, the address for OpenSea, specifically Wyvern Exchange v2 (`0x7f268357a8c 2552623316e2562d90e642bb538e5`), corresponds to the marketplace contract for OpenSea.

To replicate this dataset using Flipside, we can use the following query:

```
sql =SELECT from_address, to_address, tx_hash
FROM ethereum.core.fact_transactions
WHERE block_timestamp >= '2023-01-01T00:00:00.000Z'
   and   block_timestamp <= '2023-06-01T00:00:00.000Z'
   and to_address in ('0x28c6c06298d514db089934071355e5743bf21d60',
'0x7f268357a8c2552623316e2562d90e642bb538e5')
   limit [800]
```

For the visualizations, we can use the `draw_metric` function proposed in *Graph Machine Learning*, which highlights the nodes with the higher value of the metric under discussion. The analysis that we will carry out can be found in `Chapter12/features.ipynb` and the resulting DataFrame named `influencer_nodes.csv`.

Betweenness centrality is a measure that indicates the number of times a node serves as a bridge on the shortest path between other nodes. The larger the number of shortest paths between other pairs of objects passing through this specific node, the larger the betweenness centrality.

Interestingly, in `influencer_nodes.csv`, we can observe that USDT and **Wrapped Ethereum (WETH)** stablecoin nodes have high betweenness centrality, each connected with Binance and OpenSea, respectively. The following figure shows the nodes with higher betweenness centrality highlighted:

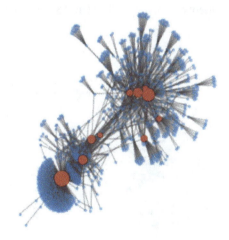

Figure 12.10 – Betweenness centrality on the dataset

The following information was taken from the CSV file, filtered by the `Betweenness Centrality` column:

Address or Node	Betweenness Centrality	Label
0x28c6c06298d514db089934071355e5743bf21d60	0.494010213	Binance 14
0x7f268357a8c2552623316e2562d90e642bb538e5	0.323956896	OpenSea: Wyvern Exchange v2
0xdac17f958d2ee523a2206206994597c13d831ec7	0.173128355	Tether-USDT stablecoin
0xc02aaa39b223fe8d0a0e5c4f27ead9083c756cc2	0.16215128	Wrapped Ether

Table 12.1 – Data filtered by the Betweenness Centrality column

Degree is the number of connections or nodes that are one link away from a specific node. More connected nodes tend to have more power and centrality.

In `influencer_nodes.csv`, we can see that, connected with Binance, we have USDT and USD Coin, and connected with OpenSea, we have WETH and Seaport 1.1 address (which is part of the OpenSea infrastructure):

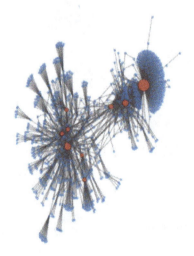

Figure 12.11 – Degree on the dataset

The following information was taken from the CSV file, filtered by the `Degree` column:

Address or Node	Degree	Label
0x28c6c06298d514db089934071355e5743bf21d60	0.370160529	Binance 14
0x7f268357a8c2552623316e2562d90e642bb538e5	0.101038716	OpenSea: Wyvern Exchange v2
0xdac17f958d2ee523a2206206994597c13d831ec7	0.094428706	Tether-USDT stablecoin
0xa0b86991c6218b36c1d19d4a2e9eb0ce3606eb48	0.046270066	Circle USD
0xc02aaa39b223fe8d0a0e5c4f27ead9083c756cc2	0.16215128	Wrapped Ether
0x00000000006c3852cbef3e08e8df289169ede581	0.029272899	Seaport 1.1 (OpenSea infrastructure)

Table 12.2 – Data filtered by the Degree column

Closeness centrality measures how close a node is to all the nodes in the graph. It is calculated by the average length of the shortest path from a specific node to all the other nodes and follows the rationale that the more central a node is, the closer it is to all other nodes. This metric can be correlated with centrality. In `influencer_nodes.csv`, we can see that the addresses with closer centrality are nodes connected between the two addresses with higher betweenness centrality (Binance 14 and OpenSea: Wyvern Exchange v2). They work as a bridge between the two communities:

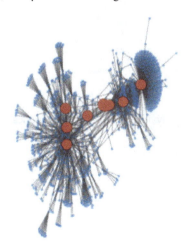

Figure 12.12 – Closeness centrality on the dataset

The following information was taken from the CSV file, filtered by the `Closeness Centrality` column:

Address or Node	Closeness Centrality	Label
0x411c104dcec01380ee86ea2d090ed3450850f1d6	0.33197098	No label available
0x28c6c06298d514db089934071355e5743bf21d60	0.33030801	Binance 14
0xc02aaa39b223fe8d0a0e5c4f27ead9083c756cc2	0.32937989	Wrapped Ether
0x6e785f2fdbdc899f8f08cc1517f82a585b44f9c5	0.32602094	renethecat.eth

Table 12.3 – Data filtered by the Closeness Centrality column

Eigenvalue centrality shows how influential a node is within a network, considering the scoring of the nodes it is connected with. The centrality will be higher if it is connected with high-scoring nodes. For this analysis, we need to respect communities because nodes will be important within a certain community.

If we calculate the Eigenvalue centrality within the Binance community, we can see that the USDT stablecoin smart contract and USD Coin have the highest eigenvector centrality. The drop in value in the subsequent addresses suggests that, generally, the addresses bridge to reach Binance through the stablecoin addresses:

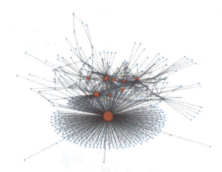

Figure 12.13 – Eigenvalue centrality on the Binance community

The following information was taken from the CSV file, filtered by the `Class1_ecentrality` column:

Address or Node	class1_ecentrality	Label
0x28c6c06298d514db089934071355e5743bf21d60	0.669654742	Binance 14
0xdac17f958d2ee523a2206206994597c13d831ec7	0.198603275	Tether-USDT stablecoin
0xa0b86991c6218b36c1d19d4a2e9eb0ce3606eb48	0.080423932	Circle USD

Table 12.4 – Data filtered by the Class1_ecentrality column

For the OpenSea community, the drop between the first two addresses and the rest of the addresses is less dramatic. As a decentralized structure, the scoring is dispersed. We can see Wrapped Eth, Uniswap, and the address of a collector named `renethecat.eth` (`https://opensea.io/ReneTheCat`) among the main nodes:

Figure 12.14 – Eigenvalue centrality on the OpenSea community

The following information was taken from the CSV file, filtered by the `Class0_ecentrality` column:

Address or Node	Class0_ecentrality	Label
0x7f268357a8c2552623316e2562d90e642bb538e5	0.553669353	OpenSea: Wyvern Exchange v2
0xc02aaa39b223fe8d0a0e5c4f27ead9083c756cc2	0.227218243	Wrapped Ether
0x00000000006c3852cbef3e08e8df289169ede581	0.208338034	Seaport 1.1 (OpenSea infrastructure)
0xef1c6e67703c7bd7107eed8303fbe6ec2554bf6b	0.17412939	Uniswap: Universal Router 2
0x6e785f2fdbdc899f8f08cc1517f82a585b44f9c5	0.133520629441651	renethecat.eth

Table 12.5 – Data filtered by the Class0_ecentrality column

Carrying out this type of analysis can help us determine the influencer nodes for a specific community. The concept of influencer depends on the context. For example, if we are analyzing a centralized exchange, we can learn which addresses they are using as reserves, which stablecoins are mostly used by their clients, and so on. For a decentralized NFT marketplace where individuals trade with their addresses, we can identify collectors, collection smart contracts, and more.

Derived from the analysis explained previously, we found an address labeled as "rene the cat" to be influential. If we merge off-chain information from OpenSea and X (formerly, Twitter) (both APIs were reviewed in *Chapters 3* and *4* of this book), we can retrieve the following actionable data, which is derived exclusively from blockchain data:

- **Address**: `0x6e785f2fDbdc899F8F08cc1517F82A585b44F9c5`

- **OpenSea collection**: `https://opensea.io/ReneTheCat`

- **Twitter handle**: `https://twitter.com/mmendiguchiia`

A note on presentation

Sometimes, presenting graph findings to an audience with no data background can be challenging. It is generally advisable to showcase the key nodes in a table, providing a user-friendly format that offers an overview of individuals listed based on selected criteria (such as highest closeness, betweenness centrality, and so on). This approach allows us to highlight individuals who appear on multiple top lists, as demonstrated in this section. This way, our audience can easily identify and understand the importance of these nodes.

With this analysis, we have identified influencer nodes. In the next section, we will shed light on the influenced nodes, those that belong to a community.

Node classification

As mentioned in the introduction to this chapter, when dealing with large graphs, such as the ever-growing blockchain transaction data, we may only have a subset of nodes labeled. These labels indicate certain protocols, user interests, and marketing segmentation groups. The challenge is to extend the labeling so that as all the nodes are added to the network, they belong to a segment or community. This exercise is performed in `Chapter12/Graphsage_node_classification.ipynb`.

In this particular case, we intend to build a marketing solution, but graph analysis is also used for discovering potential fraud detection or money laundering.

For this exercise, we will use GraphSAGE, which is a model built on top of a graph convolutional network. It is an inductive deep learning model for graphs that can handle the addition of new nodes without retraining. This feature is beneficial for transactional data that continuously grows as new addresses and transactions are added over time, eliminating the need to generate new training data to create a new model for the entire network. GraphSAGE is implemented within the StellarGraph library.

GraphSAGE is capable of predicting the embedding of a new node. To achieve this, the model learns aggregator functions that can generate the embedding of a new node based on its features and the characteristics of its neighborhood.

Figure 12.15 shows a simplified version of our dataset, where we can observe the two communities. GraphSAGE operates by sampling and aggregating information from a node's local neighborhood to generate node embeddings, which capture the structural properties and relationships within the graph. The algorithm iteratively updates the embeddings by considering the embeddings of neighboring nodes and aggregating their information. This allows GraphSAGE to capture the graph's global structure while leveraging local neighborhood information:

1. Takes a sample of each neighbohood   2. Aggregates feature information   3. Predicts labels based on
                                              from the neighbors   context aggregated information

Figure 12.15 – GraphSAGE learning steps

This process is called *inductive* learning as the model can infer that a general principle is derived from a body of observations, similar to how our brain functions. For additional technical explanations of this process, please refer to the *Further reading* section of this chapter.

Preparation

For this model, we will need to feed an **edges** dataset and a **features** dataset.

The **edges** dataset is the same one we analyzed in the previous section and is composed of transactions that interacted with the Binance 14 and OpenSea addresses.

The **features** dataset is built using the `influencers.csv` file, which is the output of the `Chapter12/features.ipynb` notebook. From this dataset, we will only use the 30 most important nodes based on the features criteria, such as betweenness centrality, node degree, and so on. For each node in the edges dataset, we will analyze whether they had any transactions with the 30 top influencer nodes.

Additionally, we'll provide a modularity dictionary to the Louvain community detection algorithm (included in the Networkx library) to determine the community assignment for each node in the edges dataset. We'll use the `best_partition` function, which computes the partition of the graph nodes and maximizes the modularity using the Louvain heuristics. The code snippet for this process is as follows:

```
partition = community.best_partition(G)
```

The result of this process is a well-balanced dataset where each node has 30 features, including the target column named community with values of 0 and 1. This is a binary classification task between two communities but it is possible to re-create this exercise with more categories.

Modeling

The first step in utilizing the model is to create a StellarGraph object from the datasets. This can be achieved by creating a graph from the two datasets using the following code snippet:

```
from stellargraph import StellarGraph
G = StellarGraph({"features": addresses_no_community},
{"transactions": edges})
```

Furthermore, we have two labels: {'community 0' and 'community 1'}. These labels have to be encoded. We'll use the binarize label from the scikit-learn library to perform that task.

As with all machine learning tasks, we must split the data into training and test sets using the traditional model_selection.train_test_split function from scikit-learn.

We will build a GraphSAGENodeGenerator object to feed the node features in sampled subgraphs to Keras:

```
graphsage_model = GraphSAGE(
    layer_sizes=[32, 32], generator=generator, bias=True,
dropout=0.5,)
```

The concepts of bias, dropout, and layers were introduced in *Chapter 6*.

The prediction layer will have an activation sigmoid because it is a binary problem. If there are more categories to predict, it is possible to change the activation to softmax:

```
prediction = layers.Dense(units=train_targets.shape[1],
activation="sigmoid")(x_out)
```

Training and evaluation

We'll train the model with 20 epochs. Here, we are interested in using accuracy as the evaluation metric. The loss metric is binary_crossentropy, which is consistent with the two-label task that we are addressing. We'll use shuffle to ensure that the data is shuffled before each epoch:

```
history = model.fit(
    train_gen, epochs=20, verbose=2, shuffle=True)
```

Given that the results are encoded, to interpret them, we must transform them back into their original format. For that purpose, we can use the following code snippet:

```
target_encoding.inverse_transform(all_predictions)
```

The accuracy on the test set is 99%. To see the results, we must create a new DataFrame with two columns – one containing the predicted community and the other containing the ground truth. This DataFrame and the confusion matrix are shown in the notebook.

Finally, a list of GraphSAGE demos can be found in the *Further reading* section.

Summary

In conclusion, this chapter delved into the fundamentals of graph networks, exploring various aspects such as node features, graph types, and their significance in data analysis. By understanding these foundational concepts, we laid the groundwork for further exploration and analysis of complex networks.

Expanding on this knowledge, we explored the characteristics of influential nodes within a graph formed by the interactions between two distinct communities --one centralized, such as Binance, and the other decentralized, such as OpenSea.

Marketing solutions are crucial in this stage of the Web3 economy. Companies such as Spindl are actively building tools to bridge the information and granularity gap between the Web2 and Web3 worlds. To achieve this, they are concentrating on attribution mechanisms that measure the actual impact of advertising on the protocols. Once attribution is achieved, it is needed to identify communities to target with campaigns. To aid this objective, we employed the GraphSAGE algorithm for the task of node classification. This methodology enables to expand limited labeling to the ever expanding Web 3 transaction data.

This is the final chapter of *Part 2* of this book. In the *Part 3*, we will analyze some practical advice so that you can start a career in Web3 data science while understanding the opinions of professionals working in leading companies.

Further reading

To learn more about the topics that were covered in this chapter, take a look at the following resources:

- Stamile, C., Marzullo, A., and Deusebio, E. (2021). *Graph Machine Learning: Take graph data to the next level by applying machine learning techniques and algorithms*. Packt Publishing.

- Liiv, I. (2021). *Data Science Techniques for Cryptocurrency Blockchains*. Springer.

- Spindl. (n.d.). *Introduction*: https://docs.spindl.xyz/spindl/overview/introduction.

- Regarding GraphSAGE:

  - Ruberts, A. (2021, May 4). *GraphSAGE for Classification in Python*. Well Enough: https://antonsruberts.github.io/graph/graphsage/.

  - Özçelik, R. (2019, October 25). *An Intuitive Explanation of GraphSAGE*. Medium: https://

`towardsdatascience.com/an-intuitive-explanation-of-graphsage-6df9437ee64f`.

- Demos:

  - *StellarGraph basics – StellarGraph 1.2.1 documentation.* (n.d.). Welcome to StellarGraph's documentation! – StellarGraph 1.2.1 documentation: `https://stellargraph.readthedocs.io/en/stable/demos/basics/index.html`.

  - *Attacker Traceablity on Ethereum through Graph Analysis.* (2022, January 27). Publishing open access research journals and papers | Hindawi: `https://www.hindawi.com/journals/scn/2022/3448950/`.

  - *Using Network Graphs to Visualize Potential Fraud on the Ethereum Blockchain.* (2022, September 29). NVIDIA Technical Blog: `https://developer.nvidia.com/blog/using-network-graphs-to-visualize-potential-fraud-on-ethereum-blockchain/`.

- NFT dataset:

  - *Blog_scripts/nft_network_analysis_blog_06042022/nft_analytics/nft_analytics_notebook.ipynb* at main · onthemarkdata/blog_scripts. (n.d.). GitHub: `https://github.com/onthemarkdata/blog_scripts/blob/main/nft_network_analysis_blog_06042022/nft_analytics/nft_analytics_notebook.ipynb?nvid=nv-int-txtad-930904-vt46#cid=an01_nv-int-txtad_en-us`.

- NNs (graph neural networks):

  - Prodramp. (n.d.). *Think Graph Neural Networks (GNN) are hard to understand? Try this two part series.* [Video]. YouTube: `https://www.youtube.com/watch?v=YdGN-J322y4`.

  - Avkash Chauhan. (n.d.). *Do you want to know Graph Neural Networks (GNN) implementation in Python?* [Video]. YouTube: `https://www.youtube.com/watch?v=VDzrvhgyxsU`.

  - *DeepWorks/GraphNeuralNetworks/Part2_Example2NodeClassification.ipynb* at main · prodramp/DeepWorks. (n.d.). GitHub: `https://github.com/prodramp/DeepWorks/blob/main/GraphNeuralNetworks/Part2_Example2NodeClassification.ipynb`.

Part 3
Appendix

In this part of the book, we will explore the next steps to use the knowledge we've gained. We'll delve into potential career paths and learn from leaders in the Web3 data space about their journeys – how they reached their current positions, their visions for the future, and the qualities they value in professionals within the field.

This part contains the following chapters:

- *Chapter 13, Building Experience with Crypto Data – BUIDL*
- *Chapter 14, Interviews with Web3 Data Leaders*
- *Appendix 1*
- *Appendix 2*
- *Appendix 3*

13

Building Experience with Crypto Data – BUIDL

If you fail to plan, you plan to fail. – Benjamin Franklin, 1790

Education empowers us to create value, whether by contributing to a company or establishing our ventures. If you've acquired this book, it is because you recognize the potential to unlock value from blockchain data—value that the market would pay for. In the Web3 landscape, there are a lot of **BUIDLing** opportunities to create solutions that contribute to the adoption of a more transparent system. According to Binance's website (https://academy.binance.com/en/glossary/buidl): *"BUIDL is a warping of the word "build" in the same fashion as "HODL." BUIDL is a call to arms for building and contributing to the blockchain and cryptocurrency ecosystem (…) The BUIDL movement believes that (…), people should start contributing proactively in order to help adoption and improve the ecosystem people invested."*

We have learned how to extract value; now, let's see what the market is willing to offer for that knowledge. Global brands such as Adidas and Nike and fashion icons such as Hermès have acknowledged this opportunity and established departments focused on Web3 analysis. Similarly, we can observe an ever-growing list of data-related roles on job search engines and company career websites, indicating the abundance of opportunities in this field. To grab those opportunities, we need to start *BUIDLing*.

In this chapter, we will learn the following:

- The importance of building a portfolio and where to showcase it

- Where to search for jobs on dedicated websites

- Where to study Web3 data skills

Showcasing your work – portfolio

Building a portfolio serves two primary purposes. Not only does it cater to potential job seekers but also to contractors, consultants, and business owners in search of prospective clients, and it also showcases our soft skills.

Firstly, a portfolio demonstrates what we have accomplished and the depth of our knowledge. It leaves a lasting impact on interviewers when we can show our work rather than merely describing it. For instance, if we have built a dashboard on Ethereum, it indicates our ability to replicate the process on other chains. Secondly, through the portfolio-building process, we gain valuable insights into the language, technical jargon, and current trends in the industry.

A portfolio also highlights soft skills that are highly valued by the market. We will delve into these soft skills later in this chapter, such as curiosity, passion, learning agility, and initiative.

There are many guides on how to build a portfolio for coding in general and data science in particular. Let's now explore where we can build our data analytics portfolio and where we can showcase our work.

Some of the following suggestions rely on collaborative building as analysts do not need to start from scratch when crafting a piece of analysis. They can use other analysts' work to fork their query, learn from it, modify it, and, in sum, build on top of it:

- **Create a Dune Analytics dashboard**: Dune Analytics is an excellent tool that grants open access to data for anyone to query. Building dashboards on Dune is open and free, and each public query can be read and reproduced. Noteworthy dashboards recognized by the community receive a "star," and featured analysts are designated as "wizards." These dashboards can be embedded into websites, and data generated by queries can be downloaded as `.csv` files. For assistance, Dune Analytics provides a series of informative videos on its Web3 data system: `https://www.youtube.com/@dunecom`.

- **Create an Increment dashboard**: Covalent, introduced in *Chapter 2*, offers the Increment tool, a set of no-code models that simplify analysis for those unfamiliar with SQL. These models combine dimensions and measures, tailored to cover **reach, retention, and revenue** analyses. For example, the retention area includes all necessary elements for building cohort analyses or analyzing multichain user bases, among other dimensions. All queries can be integrated into a dashboard and publicly embedded, such as on Notion.

- **Create a Flipside dashboard**: Flipside, also introduced in *Chapter 2*, allows analysts to build publicly available dashboards. With over 20 indexed blockchains and all log events adequately translated, analysts can query data with ease. Flipside also incentivizes analysts through a rewards system, where the creators of useful dashboards trending in the community and on social media are compensated. Further information can be found here: `https://docs.flipsidecrypto.com/our-app/analyst-rewards/top-8-dashboard-rewards`.

- **Create X (formerly Twitter) threads with Web3 data analytics**: As previously described, open blockchain data serves as the backend for many dApps open for monitoring. Traditionally, getting our hands on financial data was expensive and difficult, and access was limited to analysts at banks, hedge funds, and law firms that could turn it into analysis sold to clients for a lot of money. Now, it is possible to see first-class Web3 analysis backed up by real-time data where analysts can decipher trends, uncover root causes, and provide valuable insights based on concrete data, rather than mere speculation. Data is key, but if no data analyst can extract insights from it to convert it to information and knowledge, it loses a lot of its value.

Additionally, there are corporate initiatives funded by private companies that enable analysts to showcase their work. Companies occasionally run projects open to the community, which can serve as a recruitment process.

A recent example is Nansen, an analytics company that conducted a scout program, encouraging participants to complete a set of requests, particularly helping their attribution team to tag addresses. More information can be found here: `https://www.nansen.ai/post/introducing-the-nansen-scouts-program`.

Looking for a job

The primary platform to find jobs directly focused on Web3 is *Crypto Jobs List*, a website dedicated to Web3 opportunities. It has a specific tab for data-related roles, accessible through this link: `https://cryptojobslist.com/data`.

Another excellent website is *Web3.career*, which offers a better filter for data science jobs: `https://web3.career/data-science-jobs`. An alternative option is `https://www.web3creators.com/web3-jobs/data-analytics`. Traditional job engines such as AngelList and LinkedIn also post jobs, but their offerings are more diverse.

Larger companies typically have a **Careers** tab on their websites. For example, the Binance data department job search is posted at this link: `https://www.binance.com/en/careers/department?name=Data%20%26%20Research&job=`. You can view Dune Analytics' job page here: `https://dune.com/careers`.

Networking is another approach to exploring opportunities, though it might be a longer path. Posting on LinkedIn or Twitter, as previously described, can be effective. It is not unusual for a company you have researched to approach you and get in touch. Additionally, participating in learning sessions, which will be covered in the next section, can connect you with fellow data analysts who might recommend you for opportunities.

Preparing for a job interview

This is a brief section to reinforce the idea that thorough preparation using traditional data science resources, as outlined in the *Further reading* section, is highly advisable. The current Web3 ecosystem is predominantly composed of small and medium-sized companies seeking versatile data practitioners with a keen business sense and robust data science and analytical skills.

The nature of our data interview experience will vary based on the applied job position and the company's size. At a minimum, we can anticipate a technical (coding) challenge and a case study. The coding challenge assesses knowledge in areas such as data extraction, handling missing data, **machine learning** (**ML**) techniques, and Web3 database access. To prepare for the technical challenge, we can leverage online question lists, FAANG interview simulators, and Python and SQL skill challenges, among other resources.

The case study involves discussing a strategy for solving a presented problem or providing recommendations for a specific scenario. Preparing for business questions necessitates researching the interviewing company, understanding its business case and services, and having a grasp of business and financial concepts. This preparation enhances effective communication with the interviewer and facilitates collaborative problem-solving.

In the next chapter, where we showcase interviews with top Web3 data science experts, it becomes evident that they place significant importance on soft skills. Let's explore some of these skills that are particularly relevant in the Web3 landscape.

Importance of soft skills

Most blockchain companies embrace a remote-first culture, where teams from different locations work together toward common goals. In such environments, recruiters value specific soft skills in candidates:

- **Ability to work independently**: This skill means being able to work autonomously and accomplish tasks with minimal supervision and direction. The definition of a "job well done" is generally agreed upon with the manager and requires self-motivation, organization, planning, and problem-solving abilities. It also necessitates having a good working space and effective communication skills.

- **Strong written communication**: In a remote environment, most conversations occur in written form. Therefore, it is crucial to develop strong written communication skills.

- **Comfortable with acquiring new skills**: In remote work, managers often introduce new digital tools to streamline communication, work tracking, and other tasks. Being open to learning how to use these tools is important as they facilitate our daily work. Additionally, technology evolves continuously, impacting our work processes. With the advancement of models, it becomes feasible to execute simple queries through conversational chat (such as Dune, testing in Beta) or with drag-and-drop models (such as those Increment has built). However, our ability to learn new things and consistently search for value remains unchanged. By prioritizing value, we ensure that we always ask the right questions about the data.

- **Team player**: In a remote work environment, we tend to interact closely with those on our team, sometimes losing sight of other teams. It is essential to consciously connect with others and maintain a collaborative atmosphere. As team players, we must be accountable for our work, taking ownership of the consequences and rewards derived from the collective efforts of our team.

- **Emotional intelligence (EI)**: EI refers to our ability to understand and manage our emotions in the workplace. The blockchain landscape can be volatile and filled with stress and anxiety, but it also offers moments of real creation, where products that did not exist before are developed, and as analysts, we get the chance to measure their impact for the first time. That is a great feeling. Assessing our EI is an introspective exercise, but some of the traits we need to excel at include being active listeners to our colleagues, being open to feedback, and handling emotions within the team dynamic adeptly.

- **Agile methods**: The way of working in Web3 companies tends to be agile, which is based on flexibility, constant learning, and adaptability in self-organized teams. To achieve this, companies choose or test multiple methods to find the one that matches their culture. Methods such as Scrum, Kanban, and **objectives and key results** (**OKRs**) may be part of the way companies that we join work.

Where to study

Web3 data is experiencing rapid growth, and there are ample opportunities to explore this field. To accelerate your contributions, consider participating in training programs offered by various analytics companies. One highly recommended program is the *Data Alchemist* program, organized by the Covalent team. This program comprises four classes where a professor guides you through the dynamics and the latest market trends.

Moreover, they extend invitations to all alchemists to join a Discord server, where technical queries find prompt answers and additional resources for further study are readily available. The syllabus typically covers a range of topics, including chain and multichain analysis, **decentralized exchange** (**DEX**), NFTs, and loans.

In the last few years, there have been other training programs, such as internships that have trained data scientists, so stay tuned for those companies to start those programs again. One example was the Dune-Resident program.

A note on business impact

Working within a company, start-up, or any organization, we will encounter competing priorities, so it is crucial for the data practitioner to quantify the impact of any business data science project. In all roles within a company, including our own initiatives, we must be able to answer questions such as, "What is the estimated **return on investment** (**ROI**) for our project?" and "What is the business impact of our project?"

Firstly, to order priorities to have an impact, we can begin by analyzing business data science projects aligned with the company's objectives. If we cannot identify the business objective supported by our project, it may need to be deprioritized. Once we find the objective, we can identify a business sponsor who will assist us in gathering relevant data, making connections, and overcoming roadblocks.

Secondly, it is essential to consider the **key performance indicators** (**KPIs**) that will measure the impact of our project. Will our project increase the number of **active users** in the protocol we work on? Will the success of our project help our protocol increase our **market share**? Will the project enhance the **quality** of our service? Will the project improve the Web3 **experience** for our customers?

Thirdly, once we choose a metric, we need to estimate the percentage of impact we will have. Translating the impact of our projects into business language will help us lead successful endeavors.

There are many guidelines to learn how to quantify the impact of business data science projects, and we list some resources in the *Further reading* section.

Summary

In conclusion, this chapter delved into the significance of BUIDLing in the Web3 landscape to unlock value and generate opportunities. We reviewed the importance of building a portfolio, with a particular focus on data analysis. The chapter explored specialized job search engines where recruiters post relevant opportunities and where one can stay informed about Web3 data science trends to remain relevant in the market.

Additionally, we discussed what candidates can anticipate in a Web3 data science interview, covering both technical and business assessments. Furthermore, the chapter touched on the essential soft skills required to thrive in a remote-first industry.

Further reading

Following is a comprehensive list of resources that you can review to dive deeper into the topics covered:

- *Skiena, S. S. (2017). The Data Science Design Manual. Springer. (Chapter 13)*

  Chapter 13 of the Skiena book inspired the *Appendix* of this book. It is the answer to "Where to go now" once we finish our data science formation.

- *Dalton, S. (2012). The 2-Hour Job Search: Using Technology to Get the Right Job Faster. Random House Digital.*

  A methodological way to find a job we are passionate about. It is a step-by-step process that will help add order to the job search activity that in itself can be chaotic.

- *avcontentteam. (2023, May 10). How to Prepare for Data Science Interview in 2023? Analytics Vidhya.* `https://www.analyticsvidhya.com/blog/2023/04/how-to-prepare-for-data-science-interview/`

- *DataCamp. (2022, December). Data Science Interview Preparation. Learn Data Science and AI Online | DataCamp.* `https://www.datacamp.com/blog/data-science-interview-preparation`

- *Neeley, T. (2021). Remote Work Revolution: Succeeding from Anywhere. Harper Business.*

  A very good book about soft skills for managers who are leading and trying to thrive in a remote work environment.

- *Goleman, D. (1995). Emotional Intelligence. Bantam.*

  The golden rule of EI guidance: use our emotions correctly in favor of creating positive results and avoid suffering from our own emotions.

- *Data Alchemist Bootcamp Season Two. (2022, June 18). Covalent.* `https://www.covalenthq.com/data-alchemist/`

- Crypto podcasts list: `https://cryptojobslist.com/blog/top-crypto-podcasts-career-web3`

- *How do you measure the impact of your data analysis projects? (2023, June 26). LinkedIn.* `https://www.linkedin.com/advice/3/how-do-you-measure-impact-your-data-analysis-projects`

- *Quantify the Business Impact of Your Data Science Project. (2022, February). Towards Data Science, Medium.* `https://towardsdatascience.com/quantify-the-business-impact-of-your-data-science-project-b742e4b3208f`

14

Interviews with
Web3 Data Leaders

I knew exactly how that baby felt when he finally found his mother.

– Sheryl Sandberg (Lean in).

Jeff Olson, in his book *The Slight Edge*, dedicates a chapter to emphasizing the significance of learning from individuals who have already experienced success. The concept is illustrated in the following diagram:

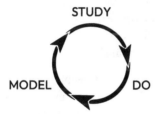

Figure 14.1 – Learning wheel (adapted from: "The Slight Edge," page 192, Chapter 13, Learn from Mentors)

The preceding diagram shows that learning extends beyond a combination of reading and hands-on practice; it also involves gaining insights from the experiences of professionals in the field.

While this book has consistently integrated theory with practical exercises, there exists a third avenue of learning known as *learning through modeling*, which we aim to explore in this chapter.

In the past, individuals pursuing a profession would apprentice under a master of that trade, someone who had the firsthand experience and could impart authentic knowledge. With this concept in mind, I have reached out to some of the leading minds in Web3 data science, seeking their perspectives on the past, present, and future of the industry.

Hildebert Moulié (aka hildobby)

Data accessibility created a new job for me.

Hildobby is a data scientist at Dragonfly. His X (formerly Twitter) account can be found at `https://twitter.com/hildobby_`.

Gabriela: Can you walk me through your career journey and highlight the most significant experience or role that has shaped your current expertise in the crypto space?

Hildebert: Currently, I work at a venture firm called **Dragonfly** (`https://www.dragonfly.xyz/`), which focuses on investing in crypto-related companies. I am a data scientist in the team, and I think I got there in a very unconventional way, which I'm pretty happy about. I'll start now from what got me here. After my bachelor's, I wanted to have some actionable experience in terms of what I want to do in the future, and so I had the occasion of joining a company called **Kaiko**, which is a central exchange data company in crypto run by a family member. I got the chance to be hired, and at the beginning I was that annoying intern that you hire because I was the little cousin, but it ended up going very well and I really liked it. I also got to know a lot about the crypto space, and what drew me to keep being interested is definitely the *ethos* and the ideology of the whole ecosystem, the fact that anyone can contribute in their own way.

When my parents convinced me to do a master's degree instead of working straight away, I went abroad to Amsterdam. I did my master's in computational science, which is basically modeling, and I got a job while studying in a dairy data company where the job was really interesting but the subject was not interesting to me, if that makes sense. The industry wasn't the most fascinating to me. It is an extremely slow-paced industry; there's not really anything happening, you know; it's not exciting to me, at least.

So, when the COVID lockdown hit, like a lot of people I got bored and I wanted to get back into crypto and I was like "how can I contribute in my own way or at least get to understand the whole thing better?" It was really about me understanding and *playing around first*. Then I found **Dune analytics** (`https://dune.com/home`), where I did not need to run my own infrastructure, just worry about getting insights out of the data. I played around with Dune for probably around 9 months, sharing anonymously on Twitter (now X). I wanted to prove to myself that it was more about what I shared rather than who I am that is interesting. Eventually, some people started to reach out offering freelance jobs, and the more that happened the more I considered quitting my studies to go through this project full-time. It was a very hard decision as my family was very against it. I knew that if I did it I would go full in the project, and I was at a point where I had so many freelancing gigs that my whole week was already filled. I was making money, yes. It was also cool that Dune also supported me being a *Resident Wizard*, which is a program that started two years ago and that helped me basically be able to publish data without necessarily worrying about getting funding and gave me the freedom to focus on topics that no one would pay you directly to study but everyone is a bit interested in. For example, how does the entire market look in a sector, and similar questions. I enjoyed that process.

I kept having some freelancing jobs, and then eventually I wanted to join a company to be able to do the same but without worrying about the organization, working with people on projects and worrying only about the data. A characteristic of the requests that I see in freelancing is that the company that pays for the analysis tends to be biased in what they want to see in the data, and I think that it's hard to be objective when the money is directly involved in that aspect. So, I'm happy I got the chance to eventually join Dragonfly as a data scientist in July 2022, almost a year and a half ago. It is possible that your hobby can turn into a full-time job.

Crypto is very powerful because it puts the individual in the spotlight rather than big companies that already have made a name for themselves; anyone, depending on their contribution, may have some impact in the space. *It doesn't matter who you are or where you come from.* It is very powerful because you can become your own creator thanks to the fact that crypto takes transparency in data to another level; data is public and everything works with a different dynamic. And Dune is one part of it; data now can be looked into by anyone, and Dune makes it easy so that anyone can focus on extracting value from the data itself rather than needing to focus on the backend matters. Also, it has become a good place to search for crypto analysis in the same fashion as when looking for videos we go to YouTube.

Gabriela: Do you consider data science for Web3 a niche? Will it remain that way or will crypto data expand to other use cases? What other parties do you see consuming our analysis in the future?

Hildebert: I think crypto is at a point where it has plans to expand and is already very useful, maybe not in the conventional use case that you would have thought about in the first place but consider, for example, stablecoins. Stablecoins are a big solution for countries where it is not easy for people to have bank accounts or to protect from inflation. It enables a way to transact where there is no third party and it removes potential fees that are in force in the current systems.

There is a lot of efficiency to be unlocked in the cryptocurrency industry versus the current systems, and I think we have reached a technology that has tons of potential but is currently in the same stage as the internet in the early 90s, where maybe we have no idea exactly what it is, but despite those first steps you notice the use. At that time, it was still possible to see people asking "why do I need email if I can send letters?" For some, it may feel that it is a fad and then eventually the industry will find its use cases, like today with social media, that is huge. I think it's a technology that takes a while to understand and that we will see how it can help and there's a lot of sectors that can be helped.

Take another example, **Spindl** (`https://www.spindl.xyz/`), which is one of the Dragonfly portfolio companies. I work with them quite closely, and I'm always excited about the new things they are developing. Today, blockchain advertising is very scammy, and that is because it is hard because there is no connection between Web2 and Web3, there is no service such as Google Ads that gives you a vision of how your ads performed, who you are targeting, what worked, and what did not. This information is very valuable to the industry.

We are now building blocks that are needed in order for the expansion. It takes a while to get all these building blocks working as the foundation to finish the whole thing. I have no idea what in 10 years will be the next thing, but I don't think anyone would have necessarily foreseen where we are now six years ago. I don't think anyone predicts those kinds of waves coming in; they just happen when the technology is mature.

Gabriela: What developments in the crypto ecosystem have piqued your interest, particularly in terms of their potential to onboard the next billion users?

Hildebert: In my opinion, it is not necessarily something specific but it's broader and is part of the new concept of the whole system. Compared to the established systems, I think crypto has the potential to replace all those structures where, currently, *third parties* are needed. They will be abstracted or removed, and it will impact in terms of fees and costs, which have a tendency to be a race to the bottom, which makes sense because it is all about efficiency. At the end of the day, the user is the real winner because you end up with fees that are not absurd and because it is totally possible that someone will appear and take over with a better product or a less expensive one. This way, we improve competition. I think I am pretty happy with this.

The other feature I want to highlight is the *cross-border* characteristic of crypto that really ties the world together. I guess international payments are a good example of what is a normal, frictionless service right now that may not be easy in some places, and this technology does help a lot in that regard. You know it is much cheaper to do international payments on crypto, and you don't need anyone to approve receiving funds, as long as there is internet and a wallet address.

The transparency of the data makes the competitive landscape much clearer because everything is done in a public manner and can be analyzed publicly, at least on public blockchains, and multiple competitors are coming in to see if there is some angle where previously someone could step in and be like "OK, well we think we can thrive with lower fees," and everyone wins in this place.

For this to really have an impact, education and regulation are necessary. I think well-regulated crypto would be awesome, and I think that we will get there eventually. In conclusion, I'm excited because of these two aspects, fees and cross-border payments.

Gabriela: Considering the ongoing advancements in AI, there is a general feeling that AI is advancing over intellectual work. In your opinion, how do you think we should adapt to this progression and pivot? Most importantly, where do you see the emerging opportunities in this changing landscape?

Hildebert: I think AI just brings in intellectual work to an equal footing. Each of us needs help in our own way, and that is what AI is doing. I think it makes you push whatever you're doing further. Take data as an example. Now, for basic data analysis, you don't necessarily need someone to look into it because AI is able to execute good models to comprehend it, and its output is reliable. Consequently, analysts can (now that this is tackled) go further and actually push research a step ahead. It is far from the place where I'm scared of it overtaking what I do because I think it just pushes us rather than replaces us.

Gabriela: If someone would like to work with you, what would you like to see on their profile? Soft skills (the ability to work independently, team player, emotional intelligence, agile methods) and hard skills (tools and techniques)?

Hildebert: I think it is very important, especially with all the companies working remotely, that you have *independence.* I want to work with an independent person, I don't want to need to constantly be behind someone because if it ends up taking away too much of my time we lose the discussion part. I want to discuss with you, I value when someone brings a challenge to what I know. I tend to really like people who don't necessarily agree with me. It is what generates really good conversations, and I think it's better than conversations where people agree with everything because you don't necessarily get value out of it. This industry is less about big companies having egregious amounts of meetings working like an echo chamber, rather more about focusing on what everyone is delivering and on what each person can bring to the table.

My advice is to focus on the work and the outputs rather than working hours or exactly monitoring everyone in a very standard Web 2.0 formal company way. I think what is cool is the individual and what this person brings to the table. I think we all have our skills and can bring something to the table, just like there's different forms of intelligence, you know, some people are very good at writing, some people are really good at coding, some people are really good at sports, and everyone working together create good products.

About hard skills, I value understanding what crypto is and the *industry.* You don't understand the data until you understand what is behind the data. One industry is very different from the other, and what matters in one industry may not work in another. This is also why, when you make dashboards, you want to show first and foremost the things that are interesting. Understanding the market is maybe more important than coding or anything else. It will let you know if you can articulate what is most important and showcase that first.

Storytelling is also important. When I look at dashboards, I expect to see what is most important. I should be able to assess how whatever I'm looking at is performing based on just one or two charts, and I can always dig further and further if I am interested in it. Good *presentation skills* are ideal for the data scientist because a lot of great work gets lost because it's really badly presented, and there are many things that get pushed forward because people are really good at marketing but actually don't have much substance in their work. So, in conclusion, for me, a good mixture of industry knowledge and presentation skills is really necessary.

Something actionable for me when I am recruiting is that I couldn't care less about your CV. What matters more to me is that you know what you bring to the table. And to create value, it is important to understand the technology and the blockchain space, and then you don't just get there without practice. I think the best way to get there is to get started. If you're interested, *you need to start*, and you will become an expert eventually. I think that if I look at the people I find successful in whichever industry, it's people who try things, and very rarely do they succeed on the first try, but they keep trying. I want to work with people who I can say "I've seen your work and I find it interesting," and it's something I haven't seen, or you bring something to the table clearly. This does not come from going to a really good school that not everyone has access to. Like I said, the whole crypto space puts us on an equal footing. Prove what value you create instead of showing me your academic credentials.

Gabriela: What recommendation do you have for someone who is learning more about data in Web3? And to someone that wants to migrate from another industry to Web3?

Hildebert: Like I said before, try things. Trying new things usually leads to unlocking what people you have access to and who you are able to reach because they also care about what you are doing. In this space, people will be happy to help you when you ask interesting questions. When in this trying phase, I recommend reaching out to people (who you don't necessarily have time to respond to), but if you are bringing something new to the table and have questions that are very insightful or interesting then they're more likely to get in contact.

Also, build a *reputation*, especially in crypto data; when I look at dashboards, I do not have the time to dig into everyone's code and distinguish signal from noise, and it takes a while to build trust up. But if Michael Silberling (`https://twitter.com/MSilb7`) or Chuxin (`https://twitter.com/chuxin_h`) publish something, I know they've won my trust because I've seen their work plenty of times and I know they follow best practices. In one of the chapters of this book, there is a recognition that there are still no solidified standards. This is true and the analyst has to be ready to iterate. Blockchain data is an iterative process, and we are currently at initial stages compared to what I imagine we can have in the next few years.

Also, this highlights the importance of the whole preprocessing part because it gives insights just by cleaning the data. One thing I worked on last year was NFT trading and what the wash trading criteria (note from editor: this analysis is mentioned in *Chapter 4*) is. If you look at it in its raw form in trading, it is very sporadic in terms of activity, but if you manage to clean the organic activity and filter out that inorganic activity it is possible to end up with much cleaner data that has a lot more insights to be taken out. In this sense, there's a lot of work to be done, probably a backlog of many years because there are so many avenues to investigate.

I think *consistency* and reputation go hand in hand. It is necessary to continuously deliver sharp analysis because if you ship misleading or inaccurate data, your reputation takes a hit and I won't trust you anymore. We all make mistakes. I have made many mistakes, but it is important to be transparent and say sorry and clarify when something was inaccurate and deliver a fixed version of it. No one has a perfect vision of everything; it's an iterative process, but as long as you value transparency, we are good. This is a transparent system, and I think people in the system should be transparent. Users do not have the time to verify everything; with time, they eventually learn to trust.

Our job is transforming what is *complex into simple* and, like I said before, a lot gets lost in too-high levels of complexity. To be able to simplify it, it is necessary to digest the data and really understand the complexity to be able to translate it. I will generally go from a high-level understanding and then scroll to go deeper and deeper. This is maybe the way because you can address everyone's needs rather than going straight away to detail, as that may get confusing.

For dashboards, the hook is very important, and that is composed of important data. The same thing happens with videos on YouTube. You are essentially stealing people's time when they approach one of your dashboards and you want to make sure that it's time well spent. If you do not work on your hook, they won't stick around and watch all the stuff you publish. The hook is very important, and then you can always go deeper, but the reality is that 90% of people only want to see the high-level analysis, and then there are 10% that will go deeper, like to the operational level. How do we craft the best hook? It is an iterative process where I try slightly differently every time, and now it comes down to something extremely simple, like one sentence and then the main chart of what I'm trying to publish. The idea is that if the analyst wants to read more, they can go to the thread, but the idea is already very simply presented.

Jackie Zhang

We are a very adaptive species.

Jackie Zhang's role is of Developer Relations at Dune Analytics. Her LinkedIn can be found at `https://www.linkedin.com/in/jackieyingzhuzhang/` and her X (formerly Twitter) account is `https://twitter.com/agaperste`. She is also a host of the *Journey of the Unordinary* channel available at `https://www.youtube.com/@JourneyofTheUnordinary`.

Gabriela: Can you walk me through your career journey and highlight the most significant experience or role that has shaped your current expertise in the crypto space?

Jackie: I will start where I am now and reverse back to see how I reached here. My title is Developer Relations for Dune Analytics (`https://dune.com/home`). Dune is a crypto data company, so that is where the crypto comes in. Also, the company is composed of a small team, so I have the opportunity to think a lot about the product and how we sell and grow. I think you can already see the pattern of my interests about bridging crypto and data and also product and community. If you ask me to define myself, I am like a bridge builder, and I am quite happy with this role.

Going back to what led me to where I am, at college I studied computer science and finance, and after college I worked as a software developer for Deutsche Bank. I quickly realized that I wanted to be a bridge, even in the software developer role. I was good at connecting the internal users and bridging the gap between the requirement and the code. There is another aspect in that it led me to think "This is what I want to do," and it is more personal because for a long time I did not think about that at all.

I came to the US from very traditional Chinese parents who give you guidance about what you should do, and even though I wanted to study international relations, they suggested computer science because it is much easier to get hired with computer science. I did it, but I still was having visa problems after almost 10 years of living in the US. So, I was facing this visa issue and I was either going to be sent by my company to London basically, or I had to do something else. So I decided to go back to grad school. I already knew that I wanted to transition more to something different from software development. I chose data science, which is closer to the business side, and then after graduation I took a regular data science job at Fidelity. Truth be told, I did a lot of web development stuff that one year and while I was there.

I was lucky to have met my husband, and I solved my visa issue through our marriage. Then I felt for the first time I had the freedom to think about what I really wanted to do. I don't really know how to question myself too much about what I want to do or what I am passionate about. So, I solved it by saying *"OK I'll just see where I end up spending the most time"*. This is where crypto interest started. It was already a theme, and I would spend a lot of time looking deeper into it, exploring. This is the place where all my free time went, and I realized that I have never really felt an attraction like this. At first, I just wanted to do it, and then eventually I had to be in crypto full-time. Something that really excited me was the promise of being able to distribute the resources in the world better. I have this drive inside of me about the crypto ideology, but at the same time I like using crypto data that is open and can generate benefits to make it fairer. Having the technical skills has enabled me to transition and have a role in the business to which I am attracted by its *ethos*. It is an ideology, and then I realized I was happy doing it.

I think the current way of finding a job is already slowly changing. It's no longer like "oh, I send a resume and go through the traditional pipeline." Rather, you start working for the protocol and eventually get hired.

Gabriela: Do you consider Web3 data science a niche? Will it remain that way, or will crypto data expand to other use cases? What other parties do you see consuming our analysis in the future?

Jackie: OK, the first question is super easy: we are currently working in a niche. The second question, the short answer is only time will tell. Frederick (Dune's CEO) actually mentioned this matter at the DuneCon, when he cited Steve Jobs' quote:

"...people ask me, "Why should I buy a computer in my home?"

...well, to learn about it, to run fun simulations.

...but other than that, there's no good reason to buy one for your house right now.

But there will be. There will be."

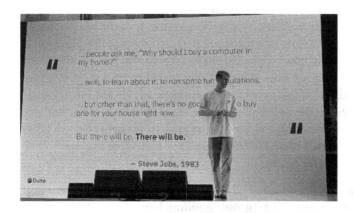

Figure 14.2 – Photo from the DuneCon 2023 in Lisbon, November 2

Time will tell, I hope it will. I think people in this industry like you have conviction, but your conviction is always a leap of faith. But I'm already seeing real data in that direction. I don't know the future, but if I zoom out in perspective, I think the Bitcoin ETF is a real thing. I don't think we have mentioned adoption, but more people are hearing about it, and last year, the perception was more negative; now, maybe it's more neutral. How it could be adopted in the future is through advertisement, performance marketing, and what Spindl (`https://www.spindl.xyz/`) is doing. I'm excited to see more of what they do.

Web2 is super closed doors, and even though there are many things that should be kept private, I think we could do so much more to come up with solutions in this landscape. If we can abstract from the underlying technology of what is complicated, like blockchain, and maybe move on towards what consumers want in an app where technology is transparent for them, I think it will expand.

Gabriela: What developments in the crypto ecosystem have piqued your interest, particularly in terms of their potential to onboard the next billion users?

Jackie: Basically, we don't know, and there are a lot of endeavors looking for that answer. I still think we are in an early stage because when you think about it, to adopt a product two factors come into play. You need to have the motivation to do it and then you need to have the ability to do it.

I think that, today, we are in a world where blockchain is being used as a store of value in highly inflationary countries or as a means of cross-border payment for sanctioned countries, but aside from that there is no other motivation for you to go through all the trouble that crypto is nowadays. I see smart people coming early into this space to try to arbitrage like money or traders. I also read about options traders and how crypto just enables them to do it so much easier than before. Even with open data, we are still not democratizing the opportunities that these very smart people wouldn't have had beforehand, so I'm really bullish on these ideas, but I'm not sure these extremely motivated and able people represent the next 1 billion users, many of whom struggle with their own lives, their next meal, and so on. In conclusion, I see the solution to onboard the next billion users related to everyday problems. It is not related to a new feature or something like that, rather the service has to solve everyday problems for people.

Gabriela: Considering the ongoing advancements in AI, there is a general feeling that AI is advancing over intellectual work. In your opinion, how do you think we should adapt to this progression and pivot? Most importantly, where do you see the emerging opportunities in this changing landscape?

Jackie: I think that until we have general artificial intelligence where robots are truly taking over the world, I don't think we have anything to worry about as we are a very *adaptive species*. If you think about it, at the beginning people couldn't write, right? So, scribes had a lot of work, but then everyone learned to read and write and scribes were not needed, but other jobs appeared. Another example is women, who would spend so much time washing clothes, and then the washing machine was invented and women started adding value to the market massively. I just think it's going to be fine. In the short-term vision, we still need a lot of analysts writing good SQL to train the AI. Take, for example, Dune AI, you need people to be able to write good queries and then to feed them into this model and evaluate if the result is correct. So yeah, I think in the short term there's plenty of need for people who write SQL, and then once we get to the point where we don't need people writing SQL, then people who have blockchain data knowledge are going to be fine because then everybody will need to extract the insights from the data, and so on so forth. Just like everybody can read nowadays, the same process will happen with SQL. And humanity will move to the next level. I think we will be completely fine, better and more efficient.

Gabriela: If someone would like to work with you, what would you like to see on their profile? Soft skills (the ability to work independently, team player, emotional intelligence, agile methods) and hard skills (tools and techniques)?

Jackie: On the soft skill part, I think the other side of independence is like *dependency*. This is that the person will show up and that you can trust. I will trust them if they do what they say they will do. Also, *inner drive* is important. You can't really assess passion or something, but the drive to get things done, because it is an indicator that they are interested in it. Another soft skill is *communication*, basic communication, but also the cross-functioning ability, like being able to talk to different people, to different departments, and trying to get everybody working together. You have to be able to make sure that everybody understands each other and then what needs to be delivered, the direction to go, and how to influence people so that they will come with you. It is like leadership anchored in communication. The *ability to learn*, the curiosity and ability to learn because you can always try new things.

In the hard skills, I would add *data savviness*, which means knowing what questions to ask, and I think that comes through experience. And then the regular skills, like SQL, Python, and industry knowledge, which is pretty standard. It is important to develop soft skills as you can always learn new things.

Gabriela: What recommendation do you have for someone who is learning about data in Web3? And to someone that wants to migrate from another industry to Web3?

Jackie: I feel like we've already mentioned this, but just do it, just go for it. Interest comes really as a natural flow, just one after another. Don't force yourself into it.

Also, you need to be consistent. The reason Andrew, Hildobby, and Coby are big and still continue to be big is because they always turn out valuable content. They don't just do one hit and then leave.

Also, specifically for people going to Web3 coming from Web2, I would recommend focusing on learning the crypto knowledge because the analytical skills will be enough to perform well on Web3. Data maturity in the space is still not there, so whatever they already have in terms of technical analytical skills is probably enough. I would like people from Web2 with more experience to come into Web3 to make the space more mature because I don't think we have enough people and there is so much to do. This is an invitation, please come over. This world is so open, there is so much that can be done, and it is very friendly. Imagine that in this space there are big, interconnected teams trying to solve this problem together with you, versus a lot of Web2 companies where there is a team of 5 data people, each one focused on their own thing. Also, in Web3, once you're done you start building on top of what others have built. This idea of composability is very present.

Simple and concise dashboards are very important. Most times, users look at 1 or 2 charts and they leave, right? It is the same reaction to a 30-minute PowerPoint presentation. How much can they really take away if it's not just about the data? Focus on making the takeaway super simple statistics. They have to be simple or the message will get lost.

Marina Ghosh

Whether you are curious and want to explore resources, or are embarking on a
full-on career change, you don't have to navigate this alone!

Marina is a Community Relations consultant at **Flipside Crypto** and a board member and contributor at **MetricsDAO**. Her X (formerly Twitter) account is `https://twitter.com/queriesdata`.

Gabriela: Can you walk me through your career journey and highlight the most significant experience or role that has shaped your current expertise in the crypto space? Please start with a short description of your current role.

Marina: In my work, I support data analysts in the blockchain analytics community as they grow their skills, produce open source insights that are valuable for Web3, and turn their skillset and passion into fulfilling careers. The fact that Web3 data, unlike data in Web2, is not proprietary or paywalled, creates a unique way for anyone to engage with it. The result is an ecosystem of enthusiasts and professionals that has emerged around on-chain data. That is exactly how I started down this path: by coming across this ecosystem, becoming one of this community's analytics enthusiasts myself, and making lots of dashboards!

Open source blockchain data analysis can lend itself to considerable upward (or lateral if you are switching industries) mobility. An individual who is curious about blockchains and is interested in picking up entry-level data analysis skills to start will find themselves with essentially unlimited topics to explore, while expertise gets progressively more sophisticated. Learning how to work with real-time data that describes real Web3 start-ups and communities can feel vastly more rewarding than downloading a mock or frequently used public dataset for practice. Early on, you start to create tangible value: find insights that can help a protocol in their business decisions, inform conversations around allocating capital, and help communities understand their favorite protocol better. Impact is helpful for someone to demonstrate in their job application when breaking into a Web3 data career, or a data-adjacent role in areas such as product, customer, or community success. But it also creates value transfers in the meantime, where Web3 projects compensate community analysts for created value – think freelance requests, retroactive grants, and analytics bounty and rewards programs.

I got deeper into the industry and more passionate about it by participating in things like these! (Except retroactive grants, which are on the bucket list as something I haven't yet received as an individual, only as part of a **Decentralized Autonomous Organization (DAO)** team). Now, I've ended up working with organizations like Flipside and MetricsDAO with which I first had a lot of touchpoints as a Web3 analyst community member.

Gabriela: Do you consider Web3 data science a niche? Will it remain that way or will crypto data expand to other use cases? What other parties do you see consuming our analysis in the future?

Marina: It is a large enough niche to feel all-consuming when you are a part of it! In all seriousness, I think an interesting crossover is **Real-World Assets** (**RWA**). Now that companies like Nike and Starbucks are adding a Web3 component to their business model, anyone can look at on-chain data at how successful that part of their business is (and these companies in turn need crypto data experts). Sports is another use case: a dedicated fan can go from trying to gauge the value of their physical trading card collection to looking at on-chain data for what their sports NFT collectible is worth. Gaming with in-game purchases is another industry that has embraced crypto, and by extension can gain many insights through blockchain data.

Gabriela: What developments in the crypto ecosystem have piqued your interest, particularly in terms of their potential to onboard the next billion users?

Marina: I shared my take on this topic recently on the Flipside blog (`https://data.flipsidecrypto.com/blog/new-kid-on-base-network-effects-could-onboard-the-next-billion-into-web3`)! To aid the crypto ecosystem's ambitious user onboarding goals, I think multipliers and network effects are what will create faster-than-linear growth. SocialFi helped Base onboard many users recently, not unlike the social networks of Web2, where you would join to follow your early-adopter friend, then more of your friends would sign up to follow you, and so on. Another multiplier is developers: protocols that focus on onboarding developers and a great developer experience will see some of those builders create apps that take off and bring on large groups of users. Projects that aim to become quotidian financial alternatives in less stable economic environments too have the potential of tapping into a network effect. For instance, a migrant worker who sends home a remittance in stablecoins will onboard their recipients onto Web3.

Gabriela: Considering the ongoing advancements in AI, there is a general feeling that AI is advancing over intellectual work. Do you agree? In your opinion, how do you think we should adapt to this progression and pivot? Most importantly, where do you see the emerging opportunities in this changing landscape?

Marina: For example, AI can help you fix your SQL query, but it can also help you learn a new coding language or library that you will then use. Programming aside, interpreting and drawing conclusions from blockchain data is one of the aspects that is very nuanced and therefore lends itself well to a human mind. Crypto data outputs are far from sufficiently standardized, and even after this aspect improves in the future, drawing data-driven meaning requires plenty of context (which typically needs people).

Gabriela: If someone would like to work with you, what would you like to see on their profile? Soft skills (the ability to work independently, team player, emotional intelligence, agile methods) and hard skills (tools and techniques)?

Marina: I will answer this for someone looking to break into blockchain data analysis. First, building one's base of technical skills for data analytics (and related fields such as data science or analytics engineering) is a well-resourced endeavor in this day and age. There exist resources (many of them free) in written, video, social media, and interactive formats, and they provide lists of skills as well as learning and practice materials that help gain them. A more elusive, but totally achievable, strength is to establish your voice and profile as someone who digs deep and produces quality Web3 insights, and foster your network and community (or even an audience) who find these insights interesting and useful, engage in conversations about them, bring requests, and offer feedback. Being actively embedded in communities and understanding data questions and needs is what sets apart an impactful Web3 analyst. This involves a mix of curiosity, being professional and friendly, and putting in the effort into being attuned to Web3 and its niches and projects, relationship-building, having conversations, and constantly thinking about what data-driven questions one can answer to bring value to the table.

Gabriela: And to someone who wants to migrate from another industry to Web3?

Marina: Whether you are curious and want to explore resources or are embarking on a full-on career change, you don't have to navigate this alone! Surround yourself with the community instead. This will help with many aspects of your journey, from finding resources to getting answers to your questions, meeting others in similar stages of familiarity with Web3 data, and building a network of peers and experienced blockchain data professionals. Luckily, there are already multiple specialized communities. You will find resources and a community around your crypto data tool or provider of choice (like Flipside); MetricsDAO is a tool-agnostic hub with many on-chain data professionals and enthusiasts and learning resources; Crypto Data Bytes on Substack offers a wealth of educational materials; and there also exist communities of crypto analysts who publish their work, like OurNetwork. Reading is a great way to find inspiration and meet data professionals. Bring your curiosity and friendliness, and you will find yourself in a community that supports your growth.

Professor One Digit

A blockchain is not a traditional database. Analysts don't write to it or correct it.

Professor One Digit is a data scientist at **Sovryn**. His X (formerly Twitter) account can be found at `https://twitter.com/onedigitmoney`.

Gabriela: Can you walk me through your career journey and highlight the most significant experience or role that has shaped your current expertise in the crypto space? Please start with a short description of your current role.

Professor One Digit: I am currently in the role of a data analyst as well as technical communicator for Sovryn. These two things go together, as each part of the role informs the other. I came into this role in an unusual way. I spent over 30 years in academia as an engineering professor before joining Sovryn, where I evolved into my current role from a purely technical communication role. I am very comfortable with high-level math, mathematical modeling, and programming. I'm also experienced as a technical communicator. The specifics of my current role are quite different from my previous career experience, but that general background gave me the foundation and confidence to evolve into this role.

Gabriela: Will it remain that way or will crypto data expand to other use cases? What other parties do you see consuming our analysis in the future?

Professor One Digit: I don't have a fully developed opinion on this. My general perspective is that crypto data analysis isn't fundamentally different from other data analysis. On-chain analysis has opened up a new area of application for data analysis and has stimulated a lot of creative metrics for analysis. However, the methods are similar to more traditional analysis. I can see crypto analysis taking on a larger role for on-chain forensics as well as analysis for trading and investing decisions.

Gabriela: What developments in the crypto ecosystem have piqued your interest, particularly in terms of their potential to onboard the next billion users?

Professor One Digit: I am very interested in rollups on Bitcoin that can use methods like BitVM, witness encryption, or proof-of-stake second layers to trustlessly peg Bitcoin into a more flexible layer on top of Bitcoin. This could well be a solution to the scaling problem.

Gabriela: Considering the ongoing advancements in AI, there is a general feeling that AI is advancing over intellectual work. Do you agree? In your opinion, how do you think we should adapt to this progression and pivot? Most importantly, where do you see the emerging opportunities in this changing landscape?

Professor One Digit: It makes it easier to figure out syntax or debug code, but that can sometimes free me to approach high-level issues without getting bogged down in the details. One area that could benefit from AI would be the ability to analyze a code base and describe the function of the system or to be able to answer questions about it. Another would be to identify vulnerabilities that are not evident on a first-order understanding of the code function.

Gabriela: If someone would like to work with you, what would you like to see on their profile? Soft skills (the ability to work independently, team player, emotional intelligence, agile methods) and hard skills (tools and techniques)?

Professor One Digit: Along with that would be the ability and willingness to tackle new problems and use new tools that aren't familiar to them.

Gabriela: And to someone who wants to migrate from another industry to Web3?

Professor One Digit: You have to know something about the motivation and culture of Web3. This means understanding why we are pursuing decentralization, permission-lessness, etc. Otherwise, it is hard to understand or appreciate the data and what it means. Understanding the basic idea and structure of a blockchain is a must. A blockchain is not a traditional database. Analysts don't write to it or correct it. Anyone who goes into this area should also learn about the subcultures and attitudes of Bitcoin versus Ethereum versus other altcoins. You need to work in an area that aligns with your philosophy about what is good for the world and where it is likely to go. Take your time and find a project you believe will change the world for the better, not just one that will pay your salary while you do cool things.

Appendix 1

Let's get started with the installation of the following environments.

Google Colaboratory

1. Go to your Google Drive and open a Google Colaboratory document.

2. Click on **Connect**:

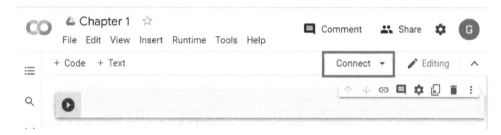

Figure A1.1 – Connecting Colab

3. It will show **Initializing**, **Allocating**, **Connecting**, and then **Connected**:

Figure A1.2 – Connected

4. If you click on **View resources**, it will show you the computer you are working with:

Figure A1.3 – View resources

Anaconda

1. Go to `https://www.anaconda.com/` and click **Download**. It will download Python and multiple popular libraries:

Figure A1.4 – Downloading Anaconda

An executable file will be downloaded. Launch it.

2. Click on the **Next** button and read and accept the license agreement:

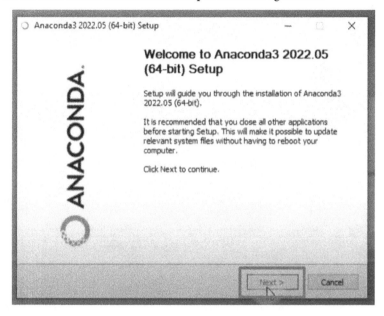

Figure A1.5 – Launching setup file

3. Some additional setup questions will appear.

   For the exercises in this book, you only need to do the following:

   - **Installation type**: Install for the **Just me** option.

   - **Install location**: Accept the defaults.

   - **Advanced installation options**: Register Anaconda 3 as the Python 3.9 system.

   Python 3.9 is the version as of the time of writing. It is expected to evolve, and that number may change.

4. Then, click on **Install**, wait for the installation to proceed, and click on **Finish**.

There will be two ways to work with Anaconda, depending on how comfortable you are working with the terminal. By clicking on the Windows **Start** button, you will see the Anaconda app or the Anaconda prompt. The Anaconda app looks like this:

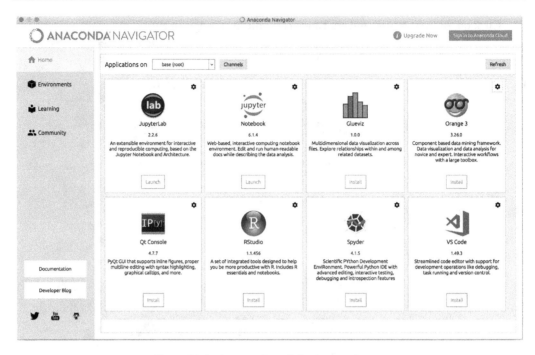

Figure A1.6 – An overview of the Anaconda app

The Anaconda prompt simply looks like a terminal. In order to be able to install the libraries that we will use and that are not pre-installed in Anaconda, you will need to add the pip distribution in the following way:

1. Go to the terminal and write this:

    ```
    conda install pip
    ```

    Then, press *Enter* and wait for it to download.

2. To create an environment, follow these steps (on the terminal):

    ```
    conda create --name web3data
    ```

    Click y and press *Enter*, and it will build the environment.

3. Every time you want to work in the same environment, go to the terminal and write this:

    ```
    conda activate web3data
    ```

4. To access the Jupyter notebooks where we will work, once the environment is activated, write this:

    ```
    jupyter lab
    ```

    A Jupyter notebook web page will launch on the localhost.

An alternative is to launch Jupyter Notebook from the app by simply clicking the **Launch** button. It will open a localhost website. There, go to the folder where you will save your work and click on the **New** button at the top left. It will offer a list to select an option; choose **Python3 (ipykernel)**, and it will open the notebook where we will work:

Figure A1.7 – An overview of Jupyter Notebook on the Anaconda App

Ganache

Ganache is a software designed to create a personal local blockchain network for testing and development purposes. It is a key component of the Truffle suite framework, which also includes Drizzle. Truffle serves as the development environment, testing framework, and asset pipeline, while Drizzle provides a collection of various frontend libraries. Let's see how to access Ganache:

1. Go to `https://trufflesuite.com/ganache/` and download the program according to your OS:

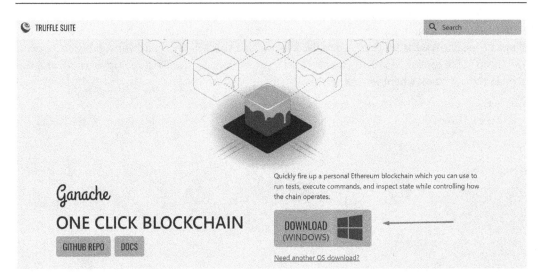

Figure A1.8 – Ganache download

2. Launch the downloaded executable file, read and accept the terms and conditions, and confirm if you wish to enable analytics or not.

3. Once the Ganache program is launched, navigate to **QUICKSTART**. This will be your Ethereum environment for testing. You will see a page similar to the one that follows:

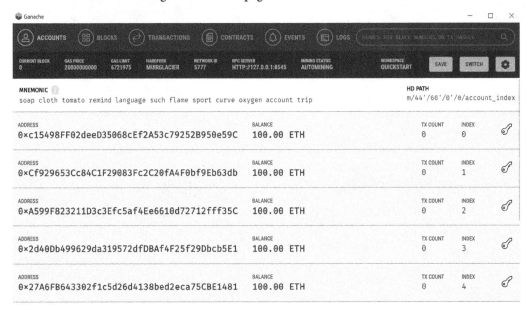

Figure A1.9 – Ganache QUICKSTART

Infura

1. To begin with, visit `https://infura.io/` and click on **SIGN UP**, then enter your email address and password:

INFURA
PRODUCTS
USE CASES
PRICING
DOCS
RESOURCES
EN
SIGN UP
LOGIN
EVERY BLOCKCHAIN JOURNEY BEGINS WITH A SINGLE STEP
BUILD

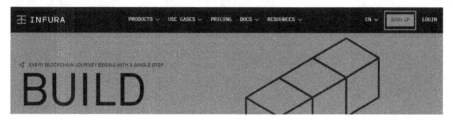

Figure A1.10 – Infura sign up

2. After reading and accepting the terms and conditions, click on **CREATE A FREE ACCOUNT**. Check your e-mail for a verification link. Click on it to confirm your account.
3. A set of demographic questions will appear. Choose the answer that applies to you.
4. Create your first project by giving it a name, such as `web3datascience`:

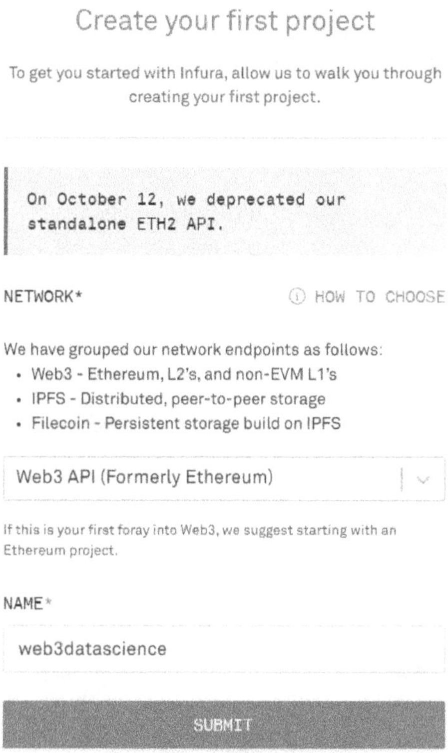

Create your first project
To get you started with Infura, allow us to walk you through creating your first project.
On October 12, we deprecated our standalone ETH2 API.
NETWORK*
HOW TO CHOOSE
We have grouped our network endpoints as follows:
• Web3 - Ethereum, L2's, and non-EVM L1's
• IPFS - Distributed, peer-to-peer storage
• Filecoin - Persistent storage build on IPFS
Web3 API (Formerly Ethereum)
If this is your first foray into Web3, we suggest starting with an Ethereum project.
NAME*
web3datascience
SUBMIT

Figure A1.11 – Project creation

5. Click on **SUBMIT**. This will take you to a page like the one shown next:

Figure A1.12 – User dashboard

6. Navigate to **MANAGE KEY** in the gray box to find your API key:

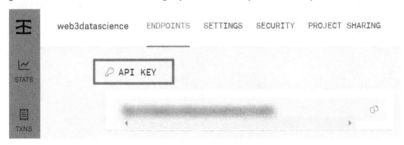

Figure A1.13 – API key information

Appendix 2

Following are the steps to create a **Developer** account on X (formerly Twitter) and get the API keys:

1. Go to `https://developer.twitter.com/` with your X account duly signed in. There are multiple subscription plans; to carry out the exercises on `Chapter03/Social.ipynb`, you will need at least a **Basic** subscription:

Find the right access for you

Free   ⟶   Basic   Pro   Enterprise

Figure A2.1 – Subscription options

Once access has been granted, we should create a project. Give the project a name:

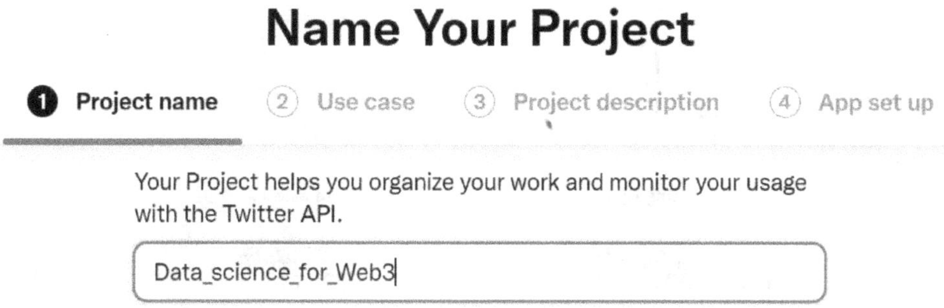

Name Your Project

① Project name   ② Use case   ③ Project description   ④ App set up

Your Project helps you organize your work and monitor your usage with the Twitter API.

> Data_science_for_Web3

Figure A2.2 – Project name

Select a use case from the options provided:

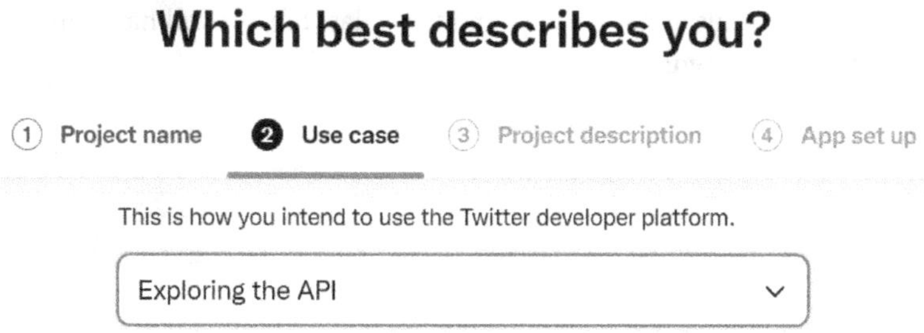

Which best describes you?

① Project name   **② Use case**   ③ Project description   ④ App set up

This is how you intend to use the Twitter developer platform.

> Exploring the API   ⌄

Figure A2.3 – Drop-down list of options

Describe the project in more detail:

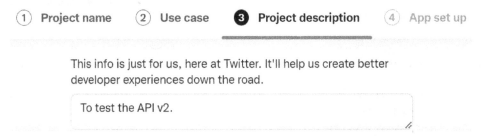

Figure A2.4 – Space to describe the use case

2. Once the project is created, we create an app that will be related to the project. Each subscription has a set number of apps that can be connected to a project:

Add an existing App or create a new App

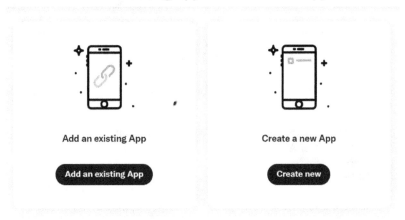

Figure A2.5 – Options for apps

3. We need to provide details about the app, and in the last tab, we will have our API keys; this is where the app will be used:

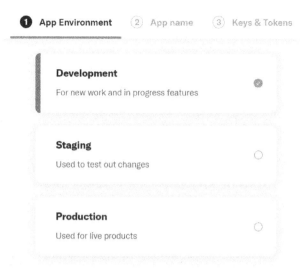

Figure A2.6 – App environment options

Provide a name for the app:

Name your App

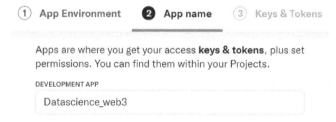

Figure A2.7 – Name of the app

In this tab, we will see the generated API keys – a set of three keys: API key, API key secret, and bearer token:

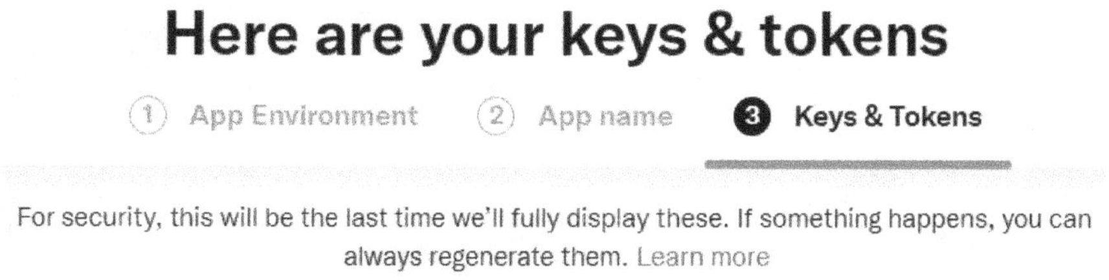

Here are your keys & tokens

Figure A2.8 – Keys & Tokens tab

Appendix 3

Here's an analysis column by column of the Dune Analytics `nft.trade` table with additional comments to those of the documentation connected with the sale of Bored Ape #6633 analyzed in *Chapter 4*. (source: `https://dune.com/docs/data-tables/spellbook/top-tables/nft.trades/#column-data` and `https://dune.com/queries/3268989`):

- `block_time`: The timestamp of the block where the transaction was added.

- `nft_token_id`: The ID of the token that is being transferred. In the case we analyzed in the notebook, the number would be `6633`.

- `erc_standard`: The standard followed by the smart contract, denoting how the project was structured. This can be **ERC 20**, **ERC 721**, or **ERC 1155**. The table also shows a **SuperRare** standard.

- `platform`: The column will show the marketplace where the trade was made.

- `platform_version`: Some marketplaces evolved with time and changed their smart contracts. The way to query information and the functions may vary depending on the version of the platform.

- `trade_type`: According to the documentation, this table indexes three types of trades:

  - **Single Item Trade**: Where a single transaction contains a single item.

  - **Bundle Trade**: Where a single transaction contains multiple items.

  - **Aggregator Trade**: Where in a single transaction there is a transfer of multiple items from various marketplaces at once.

  But when querying the data, we see that the column refers to the primary or secondary sales:

- `category`: The category of activity performed by the smart contract ranging from auctions to traditional sales.

- `nft_project_name`: The name of the NFT project in a human-readable style; for example, Bored Ape Yacht Club or CryptoPunks.

- `evt_type`: In the case of Bored Ape 6633, it will be `trade`. The options in this table are `trade`, `redeem`, `mint`, and `swap`.

- `usd_amount`: The price paid in the transaction. The price is the result of multiplying the quantity of the transferred currency (for example, ETH/USDT) by the market price at the moment of the transfer. According to the Dune documentation, the market price is sourced from third-party databases.

- `seller`: The seller of the piece of art on the marketplace. In the case of Bored Ape 6633, the seller had the `0xde2…06ef` address.

- `buyer`: The buyer of the piece of art on the marketplace. In the case of Bored Ape 6633, the buyer had the `0xb4…cb57` address.

- `original_amount`: The price paid expressed in the token/currency amount in which it was transacted. In the case we are following, it was ETH. This value is decoded, meaning that it is translated from the format that was originally reflected on-chain.

- `original_amount_raw`: The price paid but without decoding the decimals.

- `currency_symbol`: The currency or token used to generate the transaction.

- `original_currency_contract`: The contract of the currency or token used. This is very useful when searching for transfers of tokens on ERC-20 tokens. For example, if the payment for an NFT sale is done using USDT or DOC, we will need to search for a transfer in the USDT or DOC smart contracts logs. Within the logs, we will find movement between the two involved addresses.

- `currency_contract`: This is relevant when the currency is wrapped to be used in the exchange. For example, for Ethereum, the wrapped contract is WETH and the contract is `xc02…6cc2`.

- `project_contract_address`: This is the collection contract address that, in combination with the token ID, will provide uniqueness to a non-fungible item. In the case of the Bored Ape Yacht Club collection, it will be `0xbc…f13d`, as we saw at the beginning of *Chapter 4*.

- `aggregator_name` and `aggregator_address`: These columns are empty in the transfer under analysis. They include the addresses of the aggregators in case any of them participate in the trade.

- `exchange_contract_address`: The address of the marketplace where the transaction took place. In the case of the collectible that we are following on the notebook, the marketplace is OpenSea and the address is `0x7b…d12b`. These smart contracts handle the transfer and payment of collectibles listed on the platform.

- `tx_hash`: The transaction hash of the sale.

- `block_number`: The block number in which the transaction was included.

- `tx_from`: The initiator of the transaction. In the case of the sale of Bored Ape 6633, it is the buyer.

- `tx_to`: The recipient of the transaction. In the case of a sale within a marketplace, it is the exchange smart contract that receives the transaction and activates the relevant functions to execute the sale. In the case under analysis, it is the OpenSea exchange address.

- `royalty_fees_percent`: Royalty fees going to the creator (in %). In the case of the sale of Bored Ape 6633, it is 2%.

- `royalty_fees_amount`: Royalty fees in the currency used for this trade. In the case under analysis, it is 3.99975 WETH.

- `royalty_fee_amount_usd`: USD value of royalty fees at the time of execution. In this case, it is USD 12,929.991825.

- `platform_fees_percent`: Platform fees (in %). In this case, it is also 2%, the same as the royalties.

- `platform_fees_amount`: Platform fees in the currency used for this trade, so the amount is 3.99975 WETH.

- `platform_fees_usd`: USD value of platform fees at the time of execution. The amount is USD 12,929.991825.

Index

Symbols

1Inch team
  reference link 121

A

accuracy 162
activation functions 164
Agile methods 275
Akaike information criterion (AIC) 243
ambiguity 185
Annual Percentage Yield (APY) 122
anotherblock.io 92
Application Binary Interface
  (ABI) 18, 62, 142
application programming
  interfaces (APIs) 23
  REST API 24
  RPC APIs 24
arbitrage 124
ARIMA/SARIMAX 241
ARIMA with eXplanatory variables
  (ARIMAX) 238
art business, with blockchain
  anti-money laundering (AML) practices 102
  artist 92

business landscape 91, 92
clients 92
data extraction 93
floor price 97, 98
marketplace 92
redefining 91
wash trading 98-102
artificial intelligence
  venn diagram 153
Auto ARIMA 241
automated market maker (AMM)
  platforms 116

B

balanced dataset 162
batch size 164
bias 166
bias-variance trade-off 158
Binance 20, 57
  working 58-60
Bitcoin 10
  tokenomics 17
Bitcoin information page, on CoinGecko
  URL 55
BitcoinTalk.org forum 73
block 38

Packtpub.com

Subscribe to our online digital library for full access to over 7,000 books and videos, as well as industry leading tools to help you plan your personal development and advance your career. For more information, please visit our website.

Why subscribe?

- Spend less time learning and more time coding with practical eBooks and Videos from over 4,000 industry professionals

- Improve your learning with Skill Plans built especially for you

- Get a free eBook or video every month

- Fully searchable for easy access to vital information

- Copy and paste, print, and bookmark content

Did you know that Packt offers eBook versions of every book published, with PDF and ePub files available? You can upgrade to the eBook version at packtpub.com and as a print book customer, you are entitled to a discount on the eBook copy. Get in touch with us at customercare@packtpub.com for more details.

At www.packtpub.com, you can also read a collection of free technical articles, sign up for a range of free newsletters, and receive exclusive discounts and offers on Packt books and eBooks.

Other Books You May Enjoy

If you enjoyed this book, you may be interested in these other books by Packt:

The Essential Guide to Web3

Vijay Krishnan

ISBN: 9781801813471

- Get an in-depth understanding of Ethereum's ecosystem, its status, and key EIPs and ERCs
- Gain practical skills using non-custodial wallets such as MetaMask for blockchain transactions
- Write, debug, and deploy smart contracts on test networks
- Discover Web3 dev tools and set up a local environment
- Get to grips with tokenomics and create ERC20, ERC721, and ERC1155 tokens
- Explore decentralized storage with IPFS and integrate it into your Web3 projects
- Expand your NFT strategy with APIs and SDKs to lead in the NFT space

Mastering Blockchain - Fourth Edition

Imran Bashir

ISBN: 9781803241067

- Grasp the mechanisms behind Bitcoin, Ethereum, and other cryptocurrencies
- Understand cryptography and its usage in blockchain
- Become familiar with the theoretical foundations of smart contracts and blockchain consensus
- Develop DApps using Solidity, Remix, Truffle, and Ganache
- Solve issues relating to privacy, identity, scalability, and security in enterprise blockchains
- Dive into the architecture of Ethereum 2.0
- Delve into emerging trends like DeFi, NFTs, and Metaverse
- Explore various applications, research topics, and future directions of blockchain

Packt is searching for authors like you

If you're interested in becoming an author for Packt, please visit authors.packtpub.com and apply today. We have worked with thousands of developers and tech professionals, just like you, to help them share their insight with the global tech community. You can make a general application, apply for a specific hot topic that we are recruiting an author for, or submit your own idea.

Share Your Thoughts

Now you've finished *Data Science for Web3*, we'd love to hear your thoughts! Scan the QR code below to go straight to the Amazon review page for this book and share your feedback or leave a review on the site that you purchased it from.

https://packt.link/r/1-837-63754-7

Your review is important to us and the tech community and will help us make sure we're delivering excellent quality content.

Download a free PDF copy of this book

Thanks for purchasing this book!

Do you like to read on the go but are unable to carry your print books everywhere? Is your eBook purchase not compatible with the device of your choice?

Don't worry, now with every Packt book you get a DRM-free PDF version of that book at no cost.

Read anywhere, any place, on any device. Search, copy, and paste code from your favorite technical books directly into your application.

The perks don't stop there, you can get exclusive access to discounts, newsletters, and great free content in your inbox daily

Follow these simple steps to get the benefits:

1. Scan the QR code or visit the link below:

https://packt.link/free-ebook/9781837637546

2. Submit your proof of purchase.
3. That's it! We'll send your free PDF and other benefits to your email directly.